Rugged Waters

Dear Tamar,
Continue to WOW US.

Rugged Waters

Black Journalists
Swim the Mainstream

Wayne Dawkins

Wayne J. Dawkins

August Press
Newport News, Va.

RUGGED WATERS

For information, address August Press,
P.O. Box 6693, Newport News, VA 23606
www.augustpress.net

Cover photos: White House photo, upper left
corner. All other photos by Darrell T. Hazelwood

Cover design by Rob King

ISBN 0-9635720-7-5

Library of Congress
Control Number: 2003092892

First edition

10 9 8 7 6 5 4 3 2 1

In memory of Lisa Baird,
Andrea Ford, Joyce Ingram
and Toni Joseph.

Also by August Press

Black Journalists: The NABJ Story
Wayne Dawkins, ISBN 0-9635720-4-0

Welcome to Exit 4: Enter at Own Risk
Rosemary Parrillo, ISBN 0-9635720-1-6

Goodnight Sweetheart Goodnight:
The Story of the Spaniels
Richard G. Carter, ISBN 0-9635720-2-4

Sometimes You Get the Bear
Dan Holly, ISBN 0-9635720-5-9

Blackbird
Betty Winston Baye, ISBN 0-9635720-3-2

Out of My Mind
Elmer Smith, ISBN 0-9635720-6-7

To order any of these titles
write to P.O. Box 6693
Newport News, VA 23606

Or call (800) 268-4338
Internet: www.augustpress.net

Contents

Preface

Although the National Association of Black Journalists proved its value as a year-round, full-service association in the 1990s, much of this book will focus on 40 concentrated days during that decade, the four to five days that members would gather annually for conventions.

By simply paying the registration and showing up, the members raised half of the money NABJ needed to function year round.

During that week, scores of job switches or new hires were initiated or consummated.

In the summers of 1994 and 1999, summits of 6,000 then nearly 7,000 journalists of color – African-American, Hispanic, Asian American and Native American – were successfully staged. And a third summit is scheduled next summer (2004) in Washington, D.C.

NABJ ADVANCED from becoming well known in the journalism industry at the start of the 1990s to becoming a brand name in mainstream America during the 1990s. The association was named in a skit on the CBS-TV sitcom "Murphy Brown."

By the late 1990s, Ebony magazine began including the NABJ president among its 100 most influential black Americans.

In 1996, that convention had the most unlikely but significant trio of guests under the same big tent: a GOP Presidential nominee (U.S. Sen. Bob Dole); an incumbent Democrat Vice President (Al Gore), and the leader of the Nation of Islam (Minister Louis Farrakhan).

Indeed, NABJ raised its profile and peaked in membership numbers and exposure during the Chicago 1997 and Washington 1998 conventions.

NABJ and its journalist members were among the witnesses and recorders and gatekeepers of huge stories:
• The Rodney King beatdown and Los Angeles riots (1992);
• O.J. Simpson trial and Million Man March (1995);
• Bill Clinton, the first two-term Democratic president since FDR in the 1940s (1992-2000);
• The mainstream emergence of the Internet, circa 1995.

Since then, the association has become comfortable, complacent and, alarmingly, vulnerable to attack *because of* many things it did well. Dozens of members moved into top editing and broadcast executive ranks. Scores of members became middle managers, commentators or specialists.

Coverage changed dramatically compared to what 44 original NABJ founders struggled heroically to accomplish 15 to 20 years earlier: it was much more inclusive and nuanced. Overwhelmingly, NABJ members were committed to changing the mainstream media from within. There were many victories. These changes did not sit well with right-wing critics who claimed – out of willful ignorance or deceit – that we were radicals ruining journalism.

Nor did many of our stands sit well with left-wing activists, who insisted that black journalists must be outsiders instead of insiders. NABJ was battered by radicals because of its neutrality regarding Mumia Abu-Jamal, a death row inmate turned cause celebre.

MAINSTREAM WATERS were rugged waters. This book intends to define the great change – dizzying change – that occurred over a single decade.

This is also a reminder to reclaim and redefine the activities that made NABJ rise as a powerful association before declining at the start of the 21st century.

We need competitive elections again. Many members did not run for offices because of their distaste for politicking. Yet, it is the passion that comes with partisan combat that strengthens a group.

Trouble set in in 1995 when 13 of 17 board seats – including the presidency – were uncontested. The lone-candidate presidency was repeated in 1997, although until a few months before the election, there was the promise of a competitive race.

At this writing, there are several proposals to reduce the size of the board or institute a ladder system that grooms leaders. Whatever course is decided, members of NABJ must engage and reclaim their association in order to meet the new challenges of this century.

Wayne J. Dawkins
May 2003

Chapter 1
Westward

For six years, 1983 to 1989, Thomas Morgan III, as treasurer, guided the National Association of Black Journalists during its growth spurt. He began when NABJ had 334 members and less than $50,000 netted from several years of conventions, history that were stored in shoeboxes. At the end of his term, Morgan handed his successor a 1,600-member association and a $1 million stock portfolio. 1

Morgan vacated the treasurer's seat in order to ascend to the presidency of the 14-year-old association. He was elected in a three-way contest, defeating Ruth Allen Ollison and Robert Tutman.

Morgan was the first openly gay president of NABJ. His sexual orientation was an issue during the election. Many members ignored the whispers and innuendoes about the New York Times reporter with pretty black boy looks who spoke in a measured baritone, deliberately slow in order to hide his childhood stutter. But other members wondered aloud whether a homosexual president could be a pox on the face of what had become the largest organization of journalists of color. 2

Morgan's homosexuality was a potent election issue that could have been used to defeat him because many members seemed ready to elect NABJ's first woman president after six men at the top.

Ollison was a strong candidate; she served four years on the board as a regional director, then national secretary and in 1989 she was an assistant news director for WTTG-TV, the FOX TV news station in Washington, D.C.

Tutman, a Chicago-based CBS News cameraman, was a self-professed outsider and he ran a distant third to Morgan and Ollison, who battled for votes.

Morgan prevailed 325-244-47, winning 53 percent of all votes cast.

Questions about Morgan's homosexuality would shadow his presidency but he had to confront another daily dilemma during his first year as president. In 1989 he was selected as a Nieman Fellow at Harvard for the 1989-90 academic year.

The fellowship is a paid sabbatical that journalists pine for. Nieman fellows are discouraged from writing, books primarily, during their nine months of school and they are expected to take advantage of the free time to study and reflect so they can return to their newsroom as more cerebral journalists.

Morgan said the Nieman curator was willing to allow him to do whatever was needed as NABJ president. When Morgan was selected, it was known that he was running for NABJ president and that if elected, the Nieman program would share him with the association. "Any loss that I might experience would be my own," said Morgan, "not the Nieman program."

Morgan would test the limits of Harvard's Nieman expectations. And he could expect little sympathy from NABJ members, who wanted year-round services and an accessible leader.

Morgan juggled the responsibility of association president and school. He barnstormed on behalf of NABJ at least once a month. Sometimes, it was twice a month, although most of those trips were on weekends, free time for all fellows. The New York Times, Morgan's employer, supported his presidency and paid for travel and hotel expenses. 3

International Summit

In December 1989 Morgan and 60 other African-American journalists went to the Caribbean island of Jamaica to participate in a first-ever International Conference of Journalists. Journalists from South Africa, Zimbabwe and Colombia joined the American and Caribbean newsies and total attendance was 250. 4

Jamaican President Michael Manley called for debt relief from leading nations. Jamaica's $4.4 billion foreign debt was twice the size of its gross domestic product. The Jamaican dollar was inflated, worth $6.31 to a U.S. dollar. 5

Drug trafficking and coverage of it was a flashpoint at the conference. Attendees could not help but notice the visible police presence at the airports. Manley made no apologies for protecting his country. During the four-day conference, Caribbean journalists complained about police department "Jamaican files" on so-called drug posses. The island journalists complained that black and white foreign journalists carelessly repeated loose police language and Jamaicans in general were stereotyped.

The conference ended with the groups planning to hold the next conference in Senegal, West Africa, possibly at Goree Island, the notorious embarkation point from the slave trade to the Americas.

Nightmare in Boston

The February 1990 NABJ Journal examined a double homicide case in Boston. In fall 1989, Charles Stuart, white, said a black man robbed and seriously wounded him, and in the process killed his pregnant wife, Carol. In racially tense and media rich Boston, the incident ignited intense press coverage, especially by the competing dailies, The Boston Globe and Boston Herald.

A black male suspect was identified, then released. After additional investigation, police shifted their scrutiny from the purported black suspect to Charles Stuart. It turned out the husband wounded himself, killed his wife and unborn son, then invented the black assailant – a believable stereotype of an urban nightmare. When the hoax was revealed, black civic leaders expressed outrage and called for a boycott of the Globe and Herald.

What made the high-profile case especially intriguing was that a black journalist directed the leading daily's coverage, Globe assistant managing editor Gregory Moore. In the NABJ Journal, Moore discussed the coverage with interviewer Alexis Yancey George, a producer at WBZ-TV, Boston.

Did the media fail in reporting the Stuart murder case?

No. I don't think it achieved what the public hoped it would, and what media managers hoped it could achieve. Rumors and speculation don't belong in newspapers and on television. In the final analysis, the media really learned a hard lesson about the inability of people to tell the truth.

We now know that many people we had gone to in the course of trying to poke holes in Charles Stuart's story, knew the truth or some semblance of the truth and didn't tell. Despite the best efforts of good reporters, a lot of people knew the truth and couldn't be compelled to tell it.

Did racism play a role in the coverage?

I feel race played a part in reaction to the Stuart shooting on almost every front, from the lack of skepticism by some people to overreaction on the part of others. I don't think anyone could say race was not a factor in that.

Does that include the news decision making process?

In some ways, yes, but I also say there were other factors that influenced media coverage. In part, Stuart's story had some credibility because the media believed it could happen there, but there were other factors at play. It was a sensational crime, it played to our desire to believe victims and played to our sympathies for a dying, pregnant woman and the seemingly desperate attempt of her husband to get help.

During the Q & A there was a reminder to all journalists to be mindful not to overemphasize black crime suspects on the front pages and at the top of local news broadcasts while ignoring black communities in daily reports.

Said Moore: "The whole newspaper is what we have to be judged on, not just the front page. Clearly there is room for non-crime coverage, non-crisis coverage of communities of color on the front page of every newspaper in this country."

Phoenix Fallout

The NABJ board of directors intended to hold its quarterly winter meeting in Phoenix, Ariz. Jan. 12-14. Far West meetings were rare and this was to be only the third western trip for the association since 1975.

Meeting in Phoenix meant a show of support for a small but growing number of black journalists working in the Mountain states and the meeting, the first ever in the Rocky Mountain region, would remind people that in the summer the association would stage its first West Coast convention ever, in Los Angeles. 6

Unfortunately, the anticipated meeting was canceled. NABJ received word from Arizona Secretary of State Jim Schumway that the state-wide observance of the Martin Luther King Holiday was expected to be rescinded. The federal government established the King holiday in 1983 on the third Monday of January. In 1989, the Arizona legislature approved a Jan. 15 state holiday that was signed into law by Gov. Rose Mossford. Thousands of Arizonans responded by sending in petitions ordering a statewide referendum on whether to keep the holiday.

Morgan and the board canceled their meeting in protest. The president said, "We cannot in good conscience spend our money and do business in a state which has shown repeatedly that it will not commemorate the values of truth, freedom and justice that the Rev. Martin Luther King so courageously embodied."

Phoenix officials said that despite the state referendum, it would continue to recognize the King holiday as it had for six years, but the damage was done. NABJ moved its winter meeting to Los Angeles in March. 7

The March 1990 NABJ Journal announced that the association established a Hall of Fame and would induct seven black journalists.

The journalists were Dorothy Gilliam, Washington Post columnist and chairwoman of the Institute for Journalism Education; Malvin R. Goode, retired ABC News correspondent and consultant for the National Black Network; Mal Johnson, an NABJ founder and retired White House correspondent with Cox Broadcasting; photojournalist Gordon Parks; Cable News Network anchor Norma Quarles and syndicated columnist Carl T. Rowan, who began his daily newspaper career in 1948 at the Minneapolis Tribune.

Ted Poston, the New York Post journalist who served from 1937 to 1972 was inducted posthumously.

The seven men and women were cited for "outstanding achievements in journalism" and their "pioneering efforts in paving the way so that others may follow."

In addition to the seven, a dozen African-American Pulitzer Prize winners were recognized at the April 5 banquet in Washington, D.C., and four more African-American journalists who were members of Pulitzer Prize-winning newspaper teams were recognized. The gala raised $25,000 for the NABJ scholarship fund. 8

It is mystifying that the Hall of Fame has been frozen since 1990. Was the program too expensive or did the NABJ leadership lose interest?

DeWayne Wickham, who was immediate past president at that time, said that the Hall of Fame lacked selection criteria and a timetable for nominating inductees to institutionalize this event, so the program fell by the wayside. Morgan said the event could have been repeated and improved by future boards. Why it was not, he said, should be answered by other presidents. Sidmel Estes-Sumpter, Morgan's successor, said she had very little memory of the Hall of Fame. "This was under Tom's watch," she said in reply to an e-mail query, "so I don't know what started it and why it was not continued. I think that probably no one got on top of this and it died for lack of interest." 8a

At the rescheduled March board meeting in Los Angeles, the NABJ board voted 9-8 to no longer accept corporate underwriting from tobacco companies. The decision was influenced by R.J. Reynolds tobacco company's attempt to target a high-nicotine cigarette called "Uptown" to black consumers. Test marketing of Uptown ended in January after U.S. Health and Human Services Secretary Louis Sullivan (the lone African-American in the Bush cabinet) angrily criticized R.J. Reynolds for trying to sell the highly addictive cigarette to blacks. 9

After a raucous NABJ board debate, Morgan cast the deciding vote that nixed tobacco. At the previous meeting in

October the board agreed to accept tobacco and liquor underwriting on a case-by-case basis. In the association's early years, makers of liquor and spirits generously underwrote programs and convention events. That included the summer internship program and college scholarships.

By taking a public health stand and rejecting tobacco money, NABJ would have to plug a funding gap by tapping other sources.

In his May NABJ Journal president's column, Morgan announced that April member rolls swelled to a record 1,782 men and women, breaking the old record of 1,585 that month in 1989.

And speaking of numbers, the minority presence at daily newspapers had increased three tenths of one percent to 7.86 percent, reported the American Society of Newspaper Editors. Total newsroom employment grew by 700 men and women to 56,200. Nearly 20 percent of news hires were journalists of color and so were one out of three interns, reported ASNE.

Morgan wrote, "We are disappointed but not surprised ... Too many newsroom managers are comfortable with the status quo. They may not always say so but the small numbers of African-Americans, Hispanics, Asians and Native Americans in their newsrooms speak for them."

Morgan urged members to do three things:
• Get affiliate chapters to identify all black journalists working in print or broadcast and with the figures in hand, chapter officers should speak with news managers about hiring and promotion practices;
• Have regional directors begin discussions about hiring and promotion with state press and broadcast associations,
• And join other journalism associations such as the Society of Professional Journalists (SDX) and Investigative Reporters and Editors and make sure their leaders hear the diversity message.

The urgency of spreading the diversity message was dramatized in a most primal way at New York Newsday that May. Jimmy Breslin, the Pulitzer Prize-winning columnist, launched one of his patented tirades, shocking colleagues long accustomed to his outbursts. This time Breslin spewed invectives about Ji-Yeon Yuh, 25, a reporter and an American of Korean descent, for criticizing a column he wrote as sexist in a private, electronic message. Breslin read Yuh's criticism and fired off a computer message to editor Donald Forst: "I use the office to think and work," wrote the columnist with 40 years experience. "I absolutely will not tolerate being bothered. I have received a note from someone in Queens ... about my 'spewing sexism.'"

Breslin then stormed out of the office and yelled at staff: "The f------ bitch doesn't know her place. She's a little dog, just a little cur, a cur running along the street. She's a yellow cur. Let's make it racial." 10

The outburst drew criticism inside and outside of Newsday. Co-workers urged that Breslin be suspended without pay. The Portland Oregonian dropped Breslin's syndicated column because of the insults.

AAJA, NAHJ and NABJ sent telegrams to Newsday management urging that Breslin be suspended.

Breslin was suspended for two weeks without pay but not because of his racist outburst at the office. He was disciplined for appearing on Howard Stern's radio show four days later to joke about the potential fallout.

"(Breslin's) radio conversation with Howard Stern indicates a lack of sensitivity to what has been and continues to be a painful episode for all of us at Newsday and New York Newsday, and for the community," said his editor Forst, "And we told him so."

After 15 years, would the first-ever NABJ convention on the West Coast match the record-setting attendance of the 1989 New York, N.Y. convention that had 1,991 attendees?

America was in a recession and the slowing economy affected newsrooms employees. Would employees' companies pay their way or could members budget enough of their own money to go West? NABJ planners anticipated 1,600 people coming to Los Angeles, 20 percent less than New York, but a very optimistic number considering that the overwhelming share of members lived east of the Mississippi River and two to three time zones away.

Executive director Carl Morris was confident Los Angeles would boom, not bust. He said the best indicator of the effect of the tough times on big advertisers and on media revenues was the number of recruiters the media outlets sent. 11 One hundred twelve recruiters were coming to Los Angeles, about the same number of participants that came to New York, causing Morris to crow, "All the usual cast of characters will be there." 12

Morris also said that two factors had made NABJ conventions impervious to economic hard times:

• The growing job responsibilities (and salaries) of NABJ members as they grew older, allowing more of them to pay their way;

• And, the number of new faces at conventions. Morris said the latter trend became noticeable two years before in St. Louis. "Everybody said, 'Nobody's going to go to St. Louis,'" but a record-breaking crowd showed up and many of the people were first-time convention-goers. 13

The new faces meant that the location of conventions were having an increasingly smaller effect on attendance. "We could go to Alaska," Morris bragged, "and we'd still get a damn crowd."

Meanwhile, newsroom employees pressed their employers to loosen pursestrings and pay for more people to go to NABJ. 14

For years, the Miami Herald had a simple policy for underwriting employees who attended NABJ conventions. Individuals received $100, enough for one night's stay in the hotel or one-way air fare. African-American reporters and editors complained for years about the skimpy support compared to other papers of similar size. A minority caucus organized and pressed for changes. The Herald agreed to pick up the entire convention registration fee ($175) for employees.

At the Detroit Free Press, a corporate relative of the Herald (both papers were owned by Knight-Ridder Co.), the management paid for three recruiters and the full registration of any employee who wanted to go. Before 1990, the Free Press paid the full expenses of no more than two people each year. 15

Meanwhile, as Miami and Detroit expanded, The Boston Globe contracted. It picked up expenses for five people in 1989; the next year they covered two people. Boston's choice was a reminder that the recession made many companies tighten their belts.

Los Angeles Convention

The verdict on the first West Coast NABJ convention: Good speakers and panelists, well-organized for the most part, but definitely not cozy like the early conventions of several hundred participants.

The five-day event at the Century Plaza Hotel attracted more than 1,720 people, slightly exceeding the anticipated 1,600 attendees. Members were spread out among three hotels and connected by shuttle bus service.

The convention theme was "Words and Images: Challenges for the future."

L. Douglas Wilder of Virginia, seven months into his term as the first elected black governor in the United States, was the W.E.B. DuBois speaker. [16] He urged the delegates to strive for excellence and cover news from a balanced and global perspective:

"Yes, drugs, violence and teen pregnancy are issues which affect all too many individuals and families within black communities, and these stories need to be reported. But you sell the public short if you allow such stories to utterly dominate news coverage.

"The people throughout America, throughout all her communities, need to know the truth. And yet, some would prefer to keep the facts – and the people – in the dark."

Wilder also challenged members who worked in the black-owned media to include international and national topics in their news reports: "I fully understand and appreciate the abundant need to cover those issues of special interest and concern to the black community.

"But ... I know that you appreciate the importance of not covering these issues to the exclusion of those which affect all of society. In this age of growing international interdependence, too many of today's blacks know little beyond their own community." [17]

Wilder recognized DuBois' legacy of informing people of African descent in America and worldwide. He urged NABJ members to do the same.

U.S. Health and Human Services Secretary Dr. Louis Sullivan, the lone African-American in President Bush's cabinet, was the Aug. 3 banquet speaker. His opening words revealed he was still agitated because U.S. Rep. Pete Stark, D-Calif., a white liberal, recently called him a "disgrace to his profession and his race" for opposing a proposed national health insurance system.

Said Sullivan, "His (Stark's) incomprehensive comments of how to address the health needs of the poor and African-Americans are a disgrace to my race and profession." 18

Sullivan attacked Stark at least four times from the podium and forgot he was preaching to a sympathetic audience. People nodded in their chairs, others walked out of the ballroom eager to catch the "Tribute to Robin Harris," the late comedian. 19

The former head of Morehouse College School of Medicine urged the journalists to emphasize good health habits and prevention: "Prevention means Americans must have good health habits that include better dietary and prenatal awareness, immunizations, elimination of drug and tobacco abuse, use of seat belts, and curtailment of certain sexual practices.

"I'm asking for your pens and your prose. Your voices and your visibility will impart the message."

At the plenary session, "From Booker T. to Jesse (Jackson): Where does black political leadership go from here?" the effectiveness and vulnerability of leaders was questioned.

The panel included a journalist, an academic and politicians, notably, Jackson, the two-time presidential aspirant, who had never held elected office.

Poverty had not declined in communities represented by African-American elected officials, said Joseph Perkins, the journalist and columnist for the San Diego Union. Said Perkins, "I think it is incumbent upon black journalists to illuminate that point."

The academic, Harvard professor Linda F. Williams said, "Some of our black politicians really begin to seem as if they're in politics for their own political gain."

Jackson turned the spotlight around. Despite an increase in the number of black reporters and editors, he said, the media still fails to report on African-Americans fairly and thoroughly. 20

If you tell that to an African-American reporter, said Jackson, the response will be, "Yeah, but we've got white editors and white publishers."

African-American journalists and politicians "are in the same predicament," said Jackson. "Don't do black elected officials any special favors. Just write about us as you look in the mirror." 21

While the relevance of black politicians was examined, another big issue was the impact – or lack thereof – of blacks in Hollywood. A 10-member panel that included heads of Tri-Star Pictures and Disney Studios, actress Margaret Avery ("The Color Purple") and actor-producer Keenan Ivory Wayans participated in a two-hour plenary session. 22

Most of the panel agreed that while black people spent billions of dollars at the box office, they had virtually no key roles in the movie and TV industry, in front of or behind the camera. The session attracted an overflow crowd and occurred three weeks after the NAACP reported that there were fewer opportunities for blacks in Hollywood than 10 years ago.

Tri-Star chairman Mike Medavoy said when he told colleagues he was a panelist, "They responded, 'Are you crazy? You are going to face the firing squad.'

"If it was important enough for you to invite me here," Medavoy told the crowd, "then it was important enough for me to come."

Carl Morris served NABJ as its paid executive director since April 1987. Morris was appointed after the first salaried executive director, Dennis Schatzman, resigned after seven months in the job . 23

Morris managed the new national office (NABJ moved to Reston, Va. in fall 1986) during a sharp growing curve. Said President Morgan, "Carl Morris provided experienced leadership and organizational skills to the day-to-day management at a crucial period in our organization's development."

Consider these association facts:

• In 1989, NABJ topped $1 million in revenues for the first time. According to the annual report, revenues increased largely because of convention income, memberships and interest income from investments. The increase was up 52 percent from the previous year. 24

• Sixty eight percent of revenues were related to the national convention; 12 percent were from membership dues. The convention took 55 percent of association expenses, personnel was 19 percent of expenses and office operations took 9 percent.

• Thirty eight percent of members were full-time print journalists; 20 percent were broadcast journalists; 13 percent were associate members; 26 percent were student members and 3 percent were labeled "other."

• NABJ grew to 36 affiliate chapters.

"In large measure," said Morgan, upon Morris' departure, "He (Morris) contributed to NABJ's strong growth and reputation in the industry. As he prepares to meet his new challenges, we offer him heartfelt thanks for a job well done. We will miss his leadership." After more than three years, said Morgan, Morris' "Hair became a little grayer, his glasses of Boodles (gin) larger and his cigars longer." 25

Morris departed to become a media consultant. In Los Angeles, Linda A. Edwards was introduced as NABJ's third executive director and first woman executive director of the association, in which 64 percent of members were female.

Edwards, 33, was manager of broadcast services for the Chemical Manufacturers Association. She was a former Washington, D.C., TV journalist and member of NABJ and its Washington affiliate chapter. Of 45 applicants. Edwards was the winner among four finalists who came to Los Angeles and were grilled for 90 minutes each by 20 journalists sitting around a long table in a hot room. 26

page 14

Six months after South African freedom fighter Nelson Mandela was released from a 27-year prison stay, the Mandela effect was evident at the annual awards program in which 45 journalists were recognized. 27

"South Africa: the unfinished revolution," by Wil Haygood of the Boston Globe, and "Winds of change in South Africa," by Betty DeRamus of the Detroit News, were international reporting award winners. "Carole Simpson in South Africa" by Simpson, Herb O'Connor, Eric Wray and Artis Waters of ABC News Nightline, and "Mandela release," by Randall K. Blakey and John Davis of WBBM-TV Chicago, won awards in the television category.

A convention first was the launch of the daily NABJ Monitor and a daily 15-minute TV newscast, written and presented by 28 college internship and scholarship winners. Students gained hands-on experience, learning how to cover events under the guidance of professional journalists, who volunteered as editors. Convention attendees could read or watch activities they missed because of schedule conflicts.

Only five years prior, NABJ struggled to provide three scholarships and three internships; in Los Angeles the association was able to get nearly 30 students to produce daily convention reports. 28

Unity Preparations

On Oct. 6, the NABJ board of directors held its third meeting with the boards of other journalists of color organizations. The Atlanta meeting was the second convening four associations: NABJ, the National Association of Hispanic Journalists, Asian American Journalists Association and the Native American Journalists Association. 29

The groups continued planning a "Unity convention" of the general memberships of each group in Atlanta in 1994.

When the Unity partners did not meet, NABJ held its fall meeting. The board adopted a five-city media monitoring program and an adopt-a-prison newspaper program. Scholarship awards were hiked from $25,000 to $30,000. Portland and Central Florida (Orlando area) became the 37th and 38th affiliate chapters. The University of North Carolina at Chapel Hill was also approved as a student chapter. 30

That fall there was a strike against the New York Daily News. One union clashed with Tribune Co. management then other unions, including the Newspaper Guild that represented journalists, got involved by walking off the job. There were reports of advertisers bailing out and news dealers refusing to sell the newspaper because of threats of bodily harm. In Brooklyn, a newsstand was firebombed. 31

Daily News management sought replacement workers and turned to NABJ, the association that officially kept its distance when four black journalists sued the newspaper for racial discrimination in 1987 and won. The management asked NABJ for its membership list in order to recruit replacement journalists.

On Nov. 5, NABJ officers agreed to sell the Daily News a set of 2,000 mailing labels for $400. After striking black Newspaper Guild workers held three press conferences denouncing NABJ's decision, the officers reversed course and declined to assist the newspaper. Morgan said the officers would not take sides in the strike but wanted to make sure that members had information about available jobs. 32

"The idea of replacing striking workers is not an appetizing one for any of us," Daily News editor Jim Willse wrote in a draft of a letter intended for NABJ members. "But it is also a rare chance to build an editorial staff that truly mirrors the communities we serve, an evolution that otherwise would take years to complete."

Hispanic and Asian American groups rejected Willse's appeal. Morgan explained that "It became clear to us that despite our attempts to remain neutral, we were being drawn into the dispute between the union and management."

Chicago Sun-Times columnist and former NABJ president Vernon Jarrett said: "I was embarrassed by what happened here. How can we claim to be the voice and conscience of black journalism when we open our membership to employment as scabs in a labor dispute?" 33

The Daily News misstep was an unfortunate way for NABJ to close a successful year that was marked by an 11-percent increase in membership, a 52-percent increase in revenues and addition of services.

Chapter 2
Survival lessons

An ironic and amusing complaint was heard in the 1990s during convention week: "There's too much going on at once!"

This was true. From 8 a.m. until the evening on each convention day, about two dozen workshops and plenary sessions were conducted and, at times, a handful of these activities at the same time. 1

The simultaneous sessions were NABJ leadership's response to the concerns of veteran journalists that the conventions offered little that was relevant to them. With a vengeance, organizers scheduled workshops to satisfy not only beginning journalists but also mid-career and older professionals, as well as members with entrepreneurial or other interests. 2

By the early 1990s, it was unlikely that any African-American journalist could say with credibility that they did not know the National Association of Black Journalists existed. The association was visible enough for its name to be used as a set-up for a joke on the CBS sitcom "Murphy Brown."

Brown, a network television newswoman played by Candace Bergen, has a chat in the office of her new boss, played by Julius Carey, a black man.

Brown picks up an award on his desk.

"I got it from NABJ," says Carey's character.

Answers Brown, "I know, I have one too."

This pop culture example suggested that NABJ was established and expanding – initiating more ambitious projects and wrestling with thornier issues related to race and the craft of journalism itself. 3

Philadelphia fire

In December 1990 an intra-newsroom clash occurred at the Philadelphia Inquirer over the newspaper's Dec. 12

editorial, "Poverty and Norplant – Can contraception reduce the underclass," endorsing the notion that poor women be encouraged to use the new contraceptive implant Norplant.

"What if welfare mothers were offered an increased benefit for agreeing to use this new, safe, long-term contraceptive? wrote Donald Kimelman, the deputy editorial page editor. "All right, the subject makes us uncomfortable, too. But we're made even more uncomfortable by the impoverishment of black America and its effect on the nation's future. Think about it." 4 Gary Howard, 31, a black assistant sports editor and one of six children raised by a single mother on welfare, confronted Kimelman during an emotional staff meeting: "The summation of the editorial is ... that I shouldn't have been born."

Black and white journalists criticized the 13-member editorial board, which included three black members, for running the piece. Associate editor Acel Moore, one of the three, said he saw the editorial before publication and raised objections that resulted in minimal changes.

The internal dispute gained national exposure when reporter Vanessa Williams, president of the Philadelphia Association of Black Journalists, and editorial page editor David Boldt, debated the merits of publishing the editorial about the matchbook-like contraceptive on ABC News "Good Morning America." 5

The Philadelphia firestorm cooled after the Inquirer published an apology on the Sunday editorial page. And in the future, said Kimelman, the entire editorial board would be consulted on topics in order to reach consensus. If consensus was not possible, the paper might run two op-ed page pieces express the opposing points of view. 6

America at war

Iraq invaded Kuwait in August 1990 during NABJ convention week in Los Angeles. New York Times editor James Reston, a luncheon speaker, announced the news of war to the audience and excused himself to get to work. Hostilities continued through the end of the year. Then, on Jan. 16, 1991, the United States and allied forces launched an air assault against Iraq.

Cable News Network anchorman Bernard Shaw reported in prime time the bombing of Baghdad live from the ninth floor of a hotel room. Shaw, the 1989 NABJ Journalist of the Year, told viewers he could see "the sky light up red, yellow, orange. It's possible that planes are pounding targets 15 to 20 miles from here."

An allied ground invasion followed the air attacks and shadowing the military were hundreds of journalists, covering the biggest war since Vietnam about two decades previously. Ron Howell of Newsday was on the scene, but he criticized the paucity of fellow black journalists there. 7

Howell's colleagues included Larry Copeland of the Philadelphia Inquirer, Jonathan Wiggs of the Boston Globe and Charlayne Hunter-Gault of the McNeil-Lehrer Newshour and her producer Jackie Farmer. 8

The questions about black journalist participation were raised because unlike two decades before in Vietnam, a few thousand African-Americans now worked in the mainstream instead of a few hundred. Expectations were higher for more than a handful of black journalists to shadow a U.S. Army force that was about one-third black.

For Hunter-Gault, her gender affected the way she reported the story. While in Saudi Arabia in the fall, male crew members that she supervised had to drive her to assignments because Islamic laws barred women from driving. Some areas were off limits to women and she could not eat in restaurants alone.

The Gulf War lasted three months. Saddam Hussein accepted a cease-fire in April 1991. Cleveland reporter Willard Shephard of WJW-TV filed news reports while also serving as an Air Force Reserve fighter pilot. First Lt. Shephard told the Cleveland Plain Dealer that he flew roughly 30 combat missions. 9

At the winter NABJ board meeting in St. Petersburg, Fla. Jan. 11-12, it was recommended that student representative Roland Martin gain the right to vote and the board recommended that members decide whether to approve a student vote on the board when members voted on a new constitution at the summer convention.

The 10-7 vote was contentious. "Let experience count for something," said Sidmel Estes-Sumpter. "There's no way a student can know the real hell we go through in a newsroom."

But Martin of Texas A&M University countered that the association's 501 students deserve a vote on the board. His lobbying skill persuaded a three-member majority to side with him. 10

The board also recommended that full membership be granted to journalism professors who had at least five years newsroom experience before they left to teach full-time. As associate members, professors could not vote or hold office. These restrictions made some educators leave NABJ or educators who stayed complained that they were journalists with second-class status. Said Ohio State University professor Linda Callahan, who had extensive journalism experience, "I have students who were not born when I began studying the media who can start a job tomorrow and immediately be eligible for full NABJ membership."

Roots

In the February NABJ Journal, members got a first look at a reproduction of the list of original signers from the founding of the association in December 1975.

The article by Wayne Dawkins reported that 43 men and women founded NABJ. He soon discovered that there were 44 confirmed original members of the association.

Mal Johnson, the keeper of the list, forgot to sign it and although Vernon Jarrett's name was missing, he was a founder and member of steering committee that brought the journalists to Washington.

Before the article appeared, NABJ correspondence and publications estimated that there were 50 founders. 11

Embrace diversity

In February 1991, 8 percent of daily newspaper journalists were men and women of color and 54 percent of daily newspapers still did not employ minority journalists. 12

NABJ and several allies pressed an industry task force charged with integrating the press to take more aggressive action. The minority journalist association presidents met that February in Baltimore with about 60 representatives from the Task Force on Minorities in the Newspaper Business.

The 5-year-old group was supposed to provide American Newspaper Publishers Association members with information on how to diversify their work forces. NABJ was among the 60 partners, but its leaders were so unhappy with the Task Force's performance, the board the previous October threatened to withdraw.

Four months later, the boards of Hispanic, Asian American and Native American journalists echoed NABJ's complaints: the Task Force, funded by the American Newspaper Publishers Association Foundation, was not doing enough to embrace diversity.

"We wanted to force some action," explained Tom Morgan.

Task Force chairman Gerald Garcia, publisher of the Knoxville Journal, agreed to suspend the normal agenda of the annual meeting. He invited Terri Dickerson-Jones, an associate director of the American Press Institute (another partner organization) to lead the discussion. 13

Morgan and the other presidents pressed the representatives for results and better ways to measure performance. The Task Force set these short-term goals during the day-long meeting:

• Develop criteria that task force members would have to meet in order to participate in the group. This included evaluating the level of activity of the members' minority affairs committees or seminars on minorities offered at an association's convention.

• Create an annual award for newspaper companies that meet several criteria, including successfully hiring, promoting and retaining minorities and improving how the newspaper covers minorities.

• Compile a list of publishers who have successfully diversified their newspapers and use these individuals as resources for other newspapers that need advice on what to do.

(The lion's share of daily newspapers that remained all-white had circulations of 50,000 or less and were in small cities and towns. A frequent complaint from their managers was that they lacked the resources to recruit and that minorities were reluctant to come to their communities.)

Morgan held out the possibility that NABJ could still withdraw from the Task Force, but he seemed satisfied that the group was ready to melt an iceberg: "I'm encouraged by these actions, but I want results." 14

Another institution group that needed shaking up was college journalism schools. The Kerner Commission report of 1968 was not confident that campuses could reliably accept or train future journalists of color. (Kerner suggested an institute that did not develop on a mass scale).

Nevertheless, more minorities began majoring in journalism and communications in the post-civil rights, post-Watergate era. A concern was whether journalism programs were qualified to train a more diverse student population. Most journalism schools had no more than a token black faculty member. 15

Said Albert Fitzpatrick, a former NABJ president, "The schools lag behind the industry, which is bad enough." The Knight-Ridder executive spoke authoritatively because for six years he served on accreditation teams that certified campus journalism programs. In 1985, the Accreditation Council of the Association for Education in Journalism and Mass Communications (AEJMC) instructed schools to boost minority faculty, diversify the curriculum and expand minority enrollment. 16

The initiative was called Standard 12 and it said: "Organized efforts must be made to recruit, advise and retain minority students and minority and female faculty members and include in the curriculum information for all students about contributions to journalism and mass communications made by minority and female practitioners from early America to the present."

At the time 5 percent of journalism graduates were men and women of color but 75 percent of entry-level hires came from college programs. Also, minority faculty members on campus amounted to 2 percent. 17

Fitzpatrick and others urged black journalists to go over evaluation reports before the accrediting group. That year for example, 22 of 92 journalism schools were up for accreditation.

In 1991, Los Angeles Times media critic David Shaw wrote a series on newspaper bias and minority journalists. Over a four-month period 175 reporters, editors and publishers from more than 30 newspapers were interviewed. Here were highlights:
• Minority journalists said the overwhelming majority of press coverage still emphasizes the pathology of minority behavior, almost to the exclusion of normal everyday life. The press played a major role in perpetuating the ethnic stereotypes – and fueling the prejudices and ethnic conflicts – that polarize an increasingly multicultural society.
• No minority journalist interviewed suggested that these negative portrayals were the product of a conscious, racist decision by white editors and reporters. Even the most caustic critics of the press acknowledge that most white journalists mean well; it's not the intent but the results that trigger widespread criticism – and those results stem largely from ignorance, insensitivity, the absence of minority journalists from most newsrooms and, more important, the absence of minorities from most editors' offices.
• Despite vigorous efforts, even the Detroit Free Press – with several high-ranking black editors and a city population that's more than 70-percent black – doesn't do as good a job as "normal, everyday human beings," conceded publisher Neal Shine. While the paper's lifestyle section is offically called "The Way We Live," many blacks call it "The Way They Live." The Free Press had a much better reputation than most for covering black people, "When I'm out in the community covering something, and folks say, 'Well you work for a racist paper,' it's hard for me to defend" the paper, said reporter Constance Prater. 18
A study by the Center for Media and Public Affairs reported that for the second year in a row not a single black reporter ranked among the top 50 journalists with the most stories on the ABC, CBS and NBC network news shows.

John Cochran of NBC led the list. The study also reported that the number of stories aired by black journalists decreased from 5 percent in 1989 to 4 percent in 1990. 19

Two African-Americans, however, ranked among the 30 most prominent anchors – Carole Simpson of ABC ranked sixth as a presenter of stories on the air, and Ed Bradley of CBS ranked 14th. Peter Jennings of ABC was first.

At the time the study was released a coalition of writers led by activist novelist Ishmael Reed called for a "30-day tune-out" of prime time network news shows and "infotainment" programs that April. Reed has said often that the media sell products by investing heavily in negative images of people of color.

The study was "depressing and typical," said NABJ vice president/broadcast Callie Crossley, a producer at ABC-TV in Boston. "But these statistics are not as shameful as having the release of (Nelson) Mandela that year (1990) and really getting to see how many people of color were on the air. I think there was Carole Simpson (covering Mandela in South Africa) and that was it."

Skeptics said the CMPA study was misleading. The quantity of stories broadcast did not necessarily measure quality and others said the existing pool of black talent was still small and that a number of good black on-air reporters had moved off-air to producer jobs.

Still, George Strait, ABC medical correspondent and a black journalist, said that the number of African-American reporters at the networks – 15 – were at its lowest level since the initial push to get reporters in the 1960s and '70s. At one time the number was 21, said Strait. 20

Unlike local TV news, the networks were not required to report annually to the Federal Communications Commission on their minority hiring record. By March 31 local stations were required to show that a minority group's percentage of the workforce was at least 50 percent of the group's percentage of the overall marketplace. 21

African-American staff at local TV stations was fixed at about 10 percent since Vernon A. Stone began compiling statistics for the RTNDA, except for declines in 1984 and 1986 to 8 percent.

At the Philadelphia Inquirer, the newspaper announced a five-year plan to increase minority news staff from 13 to 18 percent. The objective was to make 50 percent of hires from 1991-95 racial minorities and white women in order to fulfill a "pluralism" directive issued by parent company Knight-Ridder in 1989. [22]

The Inquirer promised to steam ahead despite a recession – the newspaper lost $22 million in advertising revenue in 1990 – and a hiring freeze. Will Sutton, a former NABJ board member who was promoted to deputy city editor, was a founding member of the task force that urged Knight Ridder to "create a strong climate of diversity." [23]

About 40 percent of Philadelphia's population was black and only one-fourth of the Inquirer's 500,000 daily circulation was in the city, meaning that the newspaper was read mostly by predominantly white suburbanites.

Said editor Maxwell King, "As newsrooms go around the country, (the staff figures are) pretty good. But clearly, it's very different than the mix in the community we serve. We need to do more. I believe you get the balance and perspective in the newspaper itself from the balance and diversity of the staff."

Strike casualties

The five-month old New York Daily News strike ended in March and black journalists were casualties. Editorial writer and columnist Richard G. Carter was laid off and another black editorial writer, Pamela Moreland, left the newspaper to become editorial page editor of the Marin (Calif.) Independent Journal. The Carter and Moreland departures were noteworthy because they were hired as a result of the discrimination suit won by four black employees in 1987. Other journalists took buyouts, like Joyce White, a 19-year veteran who said she left involuntarily because of "restructuring" by new owner Robert Maxwell, a British publishing tycoon. [24]

According to estimates, 36 black journalists struck the newspaper, while 12 to 16 of them crossed the picket line.

NABJ, embarrassed the previous fall for agreeing to sell Daily News management the association mailing list in order to recruit strikebreakers, then cancelling the sale, issued additional sanctions against the newspaper in January: for the duration of the strike, the newspaper was not allowed to advertise in association publications or participate in the convention jobs fair. 25

Ethel Payne, pioneer

Ethel Lois Payne, the female dean of the black press and a 1982 NABJ Lifetime Achievement award winner, died May 28, 1991 at age 79. Payne of the Chicago Defender reported from 30 countries on six continents and covered U.S. Presidents from Dwight Eisenhower (whom she annoyed with a straightforward question about desegregating interstate travel at a 1954 news conference) through Ronald Reagan.

She was also credited with being the first black woman commentator on network TV. 26

Two years later NABJ awarded its first Ethel Payne Fellowships, honoring the late newswoman by allowing two journalists to report from Africa. 27

'Dig in our own pocket'

At the spring board of directors meeting May 31 to June 2 in Kansas City, Mo., also in two months to be the site of the annual convention, officers were anxious about money and whether there would be adequate convention attendance to raise enough. Because of the national recession, many media companies were not paying for members to attend the convention.

Dwight Lewis, the regional director representing Mid-South states and a journalist at the Nashville Tennessean, said it was time for members to raise their commitment to the association. "We have to dig in our own pocket," said Lewis, "and say, 'shit, this is important.'" Important indeed because convention registrations funded the majority of the $300,000 annual operating budget.

Said Sheila Stainback, region 2 director [Northeast] and convention program co-chair, "If members would like to see the national office funding the scholarships, sending out the (NABJ) Journal, sending out job listings, this is where the organization is funded from year to year."

Kansas City was shaping up as a hard-luck host city. The recession put a clamp on pocketbooks and wallets and the location in America's Heartland meant a flight for most members who lived along the Atlantic seaboard.

Kansas City was eager to get its chance to host since an earlier attempt in 1979 was canceled and moved to Washington, D.C. 28

Members heeded the leaders' challenge to support their association and come to Kansas City. They traveled creatively. Those who got financial assistance from their companies spread it around so co-workers could come. Members booked discount flights in advance, traveled as groups on Amtrak and packed into rented minivans. 29

In all, 1,259 journalists registered, less participation than Los Angeles, New York and St. Louis, but higher attendance than any convention before 1988. What mattered to Treasurer Jackie Greene of USA Today was the registration fees, that year paid mostly by personal instead of company checks, covered the $300,000 annual operating budget. 30

Convention goers lodging at the Hyatt and Westin hotels settled into the sensible Midwestern response to previous glitzy gatherings. 31

Kansas City, like New Orleans and Chicago, was famous for being among the greatest centers of jazz. The opening session, "From Bebop to Rap: The History of Jazz in America," paid tribute to that musical legacy.

Branford Marsalis talked about "the great CD (compact disc) scam." He said that CDs cost slightly more to produce than LP records ($5 vs. $4) but because CDs were marketed as "new technology," the retail price was $5 more than vinyl records. New technology meant little to a jazz artists because record companies dictated that musicians were not entitled to revised contracts or royalties even though their old recordings were being remastered as new technology. 32

Historically speaking, Marsalis told the journalists, the reason jazz was born in North, not South America, was because North American slaves were forbidden to use their African instruments and the European ones they adopted created the new music.

Workshops were much more structured than previous conventions. It was very appropriate in the old NABJ for conventions to be used as cathartic coping sessions in which black journalists vented their frustrations about being misunderstood, stymied or ignored in their overwhelmingly white newsrooms. This year however, the organizers heeded other members' wishes to place greater emphasis on career and professional development sessions.

"Many more of them are hands-on workshops," said Gregory Freeman of the St. Louis Post Dispatch, program co-chairman and Region 8 (Midwest) director. "You'll actually go away with something tangible. We've tried to avoid the panels where people tell war stories."

New Business Writers and Photojournalism task forces prepared workshops such as "Use of the Electronic Darkroom" and "Accounting for Non-Financial Folks."

And the board changed the focus of one workshop, originally called "The Art of Resume Writing," to "Fired, Laid Off and Looking for Work." 33

The polish that was added to specialty workshops and general sessions was surely influenced by another new task force: Women. Chaired by Barbara Reynolds, Inquiry editor with USA Today, 50 NABJ women held a June planning meeting in Washington, D.C. and seven weeks later in Kansas City the task force staged two major programs, a general session on empowering African-American women and a workshop on black women and management. 34

Madam President

Women were the majority of NABJ membership, however their emergence was most evident during the election of the new board of directors that week. Sidmel Estes-Sumpter was the second woman in the association's 15-year history to run for president. The Atlanta TV news producer and regional director (South) competed against Roy S. Johnson, a writer with Sports Illustrated who was a leader in the Sports Task Force that in three years lifted sports journalists from marginal to influential players in the association.

The other executive board races had women candidates for vice president/print (Dorothy Gilliam in a three-way contest); vice-president/broadcast (Sheila Stainback vs. incumbent Callie Crossley); secretary (Vanessa Williams) and parliamentarian (incumbent Jackie Jones). Only the treasurer's position was uncontested and it was held by a man, Jackie Greene.

Estes-Sumpter was elected president. She outpolled Johnson 348-317, winning 52 percent of member's votes. The presidential race was closer than many members expected. Geography played a key role. New York-based Roy Johnson won the populous regions that stretched from New York to Virginia, plus the West Coast, but Estes-Sumpter won overwhelmingly (3-1 ratio) in her home region and also won the Mideast, Midwest and Southwest regions.

Estes-Sumpter almost sounded as though she were in the pulpit as she accepted the presidency July 26: "I want to put the industry on notice that you now have to deal with a black woman!" There was enthusiastic applause and after it died down, she added, "And on top of that a black woman from the South! The times they are a-changing and the NABJ army is on the move and headed in your direction." 35

Of course, the NABJ president made policy with a board. But this time there would be plenty of sisterly allies. For the first time the majority of officers were women, including newcomer Gilliam, who won 45 percent of votes in a three-way contest. 36 Roy Johnson accepted Estes-Sumpter's offer to co-chair two committees, media monitoring and media ownership. Meanwhile, Washington-based TV news executive Ruth Allen-Ollison, the first woman to run for president of NABJ in 1989, bought an AM radio station in Dangerfield, Texas. 37

The menu of speakers, sessions and workshops were as appetizing (and most of the time as filling) as plates of Gates Barbecue Ribs, a Kansas City landmark that was explored by a busload of convention-goers who ventured out on a night pub crawl of clubs where Count Basie, Big Joe Turner and

Jay McShann once played.

At a luncheon, convention goers were introduced to Condoleezza Rice, a black woman and expert on the Soviet Union. From 1989 until spring 1991, Rice was first senior director for Soviet Affairs for the National Security Council, then special assistant to President George Bush for National Security Affairs. At the time of her speech she returned to her political science teaching post at Stanford University. 38

Rice told the crowd that it was important to become involved in covering foreign policy – it was necessary to show the world a multicultural face, like hers. Unfortunately, Rice did not accept questions after giving a pro-Bush administration speech that covered East (Soviet) vs. West (U.S.) relations but said nothing about North (industrialized nations, including the U.S.) vs. South (developing or underdeveloped nations of Africa, South America and Asia). 39

An attendee at the convention was Yelena Kanga, a black woman journalist and native of the Soviet Union. She was in the USA on a fellowship at a newspaper. Describing how many people initially react to her, Kanga said, "They look at me and say three things: 'She's black ... *she's black* ... SHE'S BLACK.'" 40

At the next day's luncheon, Emanuel Cleaver II, the first black mayor of Kansas City, warned the audience that U.S. cities were being neglected while the nation was focused on foreign policy that included the implosion of the Soviet Union and recent war in the Persian Gulf. Cleaver, an underdog candidate in that city of 435,000 that was 30 percent black, said local reporters often asked if he feared failure and the white power structure. Cleaver, a clergyman, said he answered, "You cannot fall off the floor." 41

Kansas City hosts had high hopes that convention goers would give a week-long boost to the local economy. Experts anticipated that NABJ visitors would pump in $2 million despite recessionary times. Inside the convention, organizers were determined to stage a glitzy, high-tech awards program that would match Los Angeles, but at half of the $100,000 cost in 1990. "We couldn't justify the spending," explained Estes-Sumpter. "We are doing all of the staging ourselves to give it a sleek look."

An added feature was video monitors provided by Dallas-based production company First Tuesday. NABJ leaders were also seeking ways to syndicate the program. A record 470 award entries were submitted. 42

While awards program organizers cut costs, other members tried new ways to raise money for the association. The Visual Task Force raised $6,000 for the scholarship fund by auctioning off photographers' prints. Impressed, the Sports Task Force promised to imitate the photographers and auction sports memorabilia next year in Detroit. 43

And chagrined, the leadership returned some revenue because of an on-site ethics dilemma. Inside the jobs fair pavilion, the Federal Bureau of Investigation worked from a recruiting booth, just like the majority of newspapers, broadcast companies and vendors. A number of journalists balked, then complained angrily to board members who stuttered explanations. Months earlier, the FBI sent a completed application and check to the national office and was accepted. No stealth or cunning on the FBI's part. NABJ leadership found itself in the same hot water that cooked them two years ago in New York when the Central Intelligence Agency was found recruiting at the job fair.

The Kansas City reaction was a replay of New York: The FBI was booted from the premises. Said Morgan, "We want to be careful that we are not associated with the intelligence-gathering agencies that are propaganda agents for the U.S. government."Many journalists had vivid memories of the negative role the CIA played in the African diaspora, plus memories of the destabilizing tactics of the FBI inside the civil rights movement. 44

Estes-Sumpter however wrote a letter of apology to the FBI "because they never should have been there in the first place. It wasn't their fault; they felt the brunt of hostilities."

Battle for Justice

President Ronald Reagan's two terms from 1980-88 were openly hostile to millions of blacks. Reagan's presidency was probably the most racially hostile since Woodrow Wilson's, the Virginian who occupied the White House from 1912-20, when Jim Crow was well established.

In post-civil rights era America, Reagan suggested that Martin Luther King was a communist, or at least a dupe, just before signing King's national holiday into law. While campaigning for president, Reagan gave a states-rights speech in Philadelphia, Miss., site of the murders of four civil rights activists by white segregationists. On Reagan's watch, Congress approved mandatory minimum federal drug sentences that doomed first-time or non-violent offenders to lifetimes in prison. Reagan railed against excess government regulation and waste and many people took his messages, rightly or wrongly, as code words for cutting jobs and services to many blacks and browns who depended on government.

Reagan served the maximum number of terms and his vice president, George Herbert Walker Bush, was elected in 1988. Bush, like Reagan, was a conservative, yet he promised a "kinder, gentler" style of governing, which suggested to many blacks that the brutal days of Reaganism might be easing. Bush was a supporter of the United Negro College Fund. Unlike Reagan, he recognized his black cabinet member Louis Sullivan. Reagan once mistakenly greeted his HUD secretary Samuel R. Pierce Jr. as "Mr. Mayor," and that cabinet member was notoriously invisible and ineffective. In Bush's administration, other blacks filled meaningful sub cabinet posts. Bush was manipulative and crafty with the hottest button buzzing African-Americans: Affirmative action. And much of the press were played like instruments by Bush's interpretation of that policy, and his opportunity to fill a U.S. Supreme Court seat just vacated by its first and only African-American justice, Thurgood Marshall.

In 1991, a civil rights bill promoting affirmative action was being debated in Congress. In the spring and through the summer, Bush scornfully called the legislation a "quota bill" and much of the national press parroted Bush's words in headlines and in the body of stories. 45 In fact, the bill forbid use of fixed numbers or percentages for hiring, which would be quotas, but instead recommended hiring goals that were not enforceable. Nevertheless, Bush framed goals and projections as quotas because as Newsweek noted in an April 29 article, "quota-bashing makes good politics."

Bush's control of language over the press extended to the steering of his candidate toward a Supreme Court justice's post. Clarence Thomas was a federal district judge and former head of the Equal Employment Opportunity Commission.

Thomas' record as a judge was ordinary, and his tenure at EEOC was odious. The agency neglected thousands of race and sex discrimination claims on his watch. Yet the image that the Bush administration emphasized to the press was that of a poor, black boy from rural Pinpoint, Ga., who overcame discrimination and poverty to excel in America. The inference was Thomas' humble past would make him sensitive to underdogs.

Thomas' confirmation appeared safe until he ran into rough traveling during Judiciary Committee hearings.

Anita Hill, a University of Oklahoma law school professor, worked with Thomas years ago at the U.S. Department of Education, then at the EEOC. That October, Hill told Senate committee members that Thomas sexually harassed her. Hill called Thomas' fitness as a probable U.S. Supreme Court justice into question.

The televised hearings were eerie: A cadre of black legal professionals that a previous generation of African-Americans might be shocked to see on TV in a chamber of power, were being interrogated by a committee of old white men – U.S. Senators – about their sexual behavior, imagined or real. The black professionals included Thomas, Hill and Hill's counsel, Harvard University Law Professor Charles Ogletree.

In addition two black journalists, Juan Williams of the Washington Post and Angela Wright of the Charlotte Observer, were pulled into the fight.

Four years earlier in April 1987, Williams charitably profiled Thomas' poor, humble upbringing in The Atlantic Monthly magazine. During the Senate hearings Williams dismissed Hill's harassment claims in a Washington Post op-ed piece. 46

Williams' written assault drew return fire; he was now a target. Several women employees at the Post came forward –

anonymously – and claimed that Williams had verbally harassed them by making explicit references to their anatomies, repeatedly asking them for dates and making inquiries about their sex lives. 47 The Post published a "note to readers," acknowledging that Williams, who defended Thomas in print against harassment charges, was now accused of harassment too by female co-workers. The husband and father of three children was instructed to write a letter of apology that was posted in the newsroom. 48

Angela Wright, the other journalist dragged into the fight about Thomas, became involved because she worked for him in 1984-85 at EEOC. Her parting with Thomas was stormy. She was fired, allegedly for not moving quickly enough to get rid of employees that Thomas believed were deadwood. Wright left to pursue a journalism career and despite differences of opinion with her supervisor, Thomas wrote a positive recommendation letter. 49

Wright's stormy dealings with Thomas included unwanted sexual advances, she said. Thomas vowed that she would be dating him and he asked Wright about her breast size. 50 Years later, Wright came forward during the Thomas hearings to point out that Hill's allegations were plausible because Hill's description of her experiences with Thomas resembled her own. 51

The Senate committee was leaked an unpublished column Wright wrote for the Observer that described Thomas' advances toward her. Wright prepared but was not called to testify. Her no-show was a combination of investigators' concerns that Thomas' advocates would brutally attack Wright's character, plus Wright's cold feet: "I'd just like to get back to my job as editor and cover the news – not make it." Thomas claimed that the questions about his alleged bawdy behavior made him the victim of "a hi-tech lynching for uppity blacks," in which the symbolic noose was nationally televised hearings. Yet Thomas' nomination did not die. The Senate OKed the president's choice and the conservative became the second black to sit on the high court.

And while Thomas was "lynched," two black journalists were mugged. 52

Ethics debate

In fall 1991, Disney World celebrated its 20th anniversary in Orlando, Fla. The entertainment giant sent party invitations to media industry leaders, including the 16 directors of NABJ. Two members, Regional Director Carolyn Sawyer (New England) and President Sidmel Estes-Sumpter, accepted the all-expense-paid trips for them plus a guest each. Sawyer's and Estes-Sumpter's choices set off a fierce argument among board members and past presidents about ethics and the integrity of the association.

Estes-Sumpter insisted her motives were pure: She went to Orlando to persuade Walt Disney Co. to host the 1995 NABJ convention. Said the president, "I have no regrets because I went as a person for our organization trying to plan for the future and I went only in that capacity. It just so happens that it coincided with the 20th anniversary. I did not participate in any of the 20th anniversary programs." 53

Estes-Sumpter added that she conserved some of the association's annual $30,000 board travel budget by letting Disney pay for the trip. Secretary Vanessa Williams, who received an invite, was adamantly against her colleagues' choices. Said Williams, "They (Disney) called me about three times and I told them 'no.' To me, it's a big and obvious conflict and I made it clear to Sidmel and Carolyn that I thought it was. "I think when we go to look at sites, we should pay for it ourselves or our companies should pay for it," said the Philadelphia Inquirer reporter. In addition to two board members accepting free trips, the NABJ logo was on Disney promotional literature for the Sept. 28 to Oct. 1 gala, suggesting that NABJ leaders endorsed the event.

They did not. Use of the NABJ name was approved by Executive Director Linda Edwards without board approval. On Oct. 19 an article appeared in trade journal Editor & Publisher that focused on the ethical discomfort of media organizations, including NABJ, accepting the Disney perks. Such publicity rankled former presidents like Merv Aubespin, who said: "I was uncomfortable with all the negative press and I would hope that our board would come up with a reasonable set of guidelines for us to operate under that won't put us under this situation again."

Also, Les Payne, who said: "At a time when the NAACP and concerned African-Americans are very critical and rightfully so of Hollywood, it would certainly be to the benefit of Disney World to reach an organization like the NABJ to put a better face on its policies. I see the full-blown possibility of a conflict of interest." 55

The board later resolved the issue in January 1992 this way: It voted that members will "keep in mind the ethical standards of the industry" in considering offers of free trips. Whether to take the trips will be considered "on a case-by-case basis," and the entire board is to be in on the decision.

In having an internal fight about ethics and the importance of avoiding conflicts of interest, NABJ did not struggle alone. NBC accepted freebies for 30 staffers and broadcast the "Today" show live from the theme park. After intense criticism, NBC announced that it would reimburse Disney and Delta airlines to avoid appearance of a conflict of interest.

Saluting excellence

Ten years after NABJ staged its first annual awards competition, categories and specialties expanded, entries mushroomed, and a nagging philosophical issue returned: Should NABJ limit its awards to black journalists? 54

Some members grumbled that too many journalists who were not black were now taking too many "Salute to Excellence" awards. The phenomenon was maddening to some leaders because they suggested that some news organizations denied black journalists chances at writing or presenting special projects or big breaking stories, or, were taking ideas from black staff members.

"Don't be ashamed to have a black organization promoting black excellence," argued Vernon Jarrett. He had heard that a newspaper won an NABJ award without having any blacks in decision-making positions. When the black employees pressed their newspaper, the editors pointed to their NABJ award. "It made the protesters look like damn fools, didn't it?" said the association's second president.

Another complaint from members was that because of progress and/or demographic realities, they were covering specialties or a wide range of topics that no longer met the awards criteria recognizing "Outstanding coverage of the *black* condition." 56

Estes-Sumpter lamented that as a TV news producer "I very rarely have anything to enter just on the craft of being a producer because my work is not about 'the black condition.'"

And some founding members were embittered because of rough treatment they said they received from the Pulitzer Prize board. Former president Payne had written a column noting that a Pulitzer editor's panel nominated him for a 1978 prize for coverage of the Soweto, South Africa uprising, then the prize was withdrawn by the advisory board. Selecting journalism award winners was political, said Payne, and he suggested that maybe NABJ needed its own advisory board system to screen nominations.

Jackie Greene, NABJ treasurer and a visual and technology editor at USA Today, was one of the few leaders strongly discouraging a blacks-only awards policy. Rumors and anecdotes of whites and other non-blacks winning too many awards were exaggerated, he said: "Out of the 40 first- or second-place awards, I bet there'd be eight whites."

Someone suggested a compromise solution: Limit the awards competition to NABJ members, technically a race neutral move because the membership included whites and other minorities.

Some white award winners emphasized the value of open competition. The NABJ award honors "the kind of reporting that isn't always recognized," said Susan Eaton of the Stamford, Conn. Advocate, which had no black reporters at the time. She was recognized with a "hard features" award for small circulation newspapers. Eaton wrote about the segregation of children under the guise of "ability grouping," a topic she said "was a battle to get into the newspaper," but relevant to her community because 50 percent of Stamford schoolchildren were black.

Perry Lang, a past awards committee co-chairman and a San Francisco Chronicle reporter, argued that NABJ could not solve the problem of black journalists missing out on plum assignments and the awards they reaped by denying whites and other journalists of color awards when they did award-worthy work. Said Lang, "We need to deal with why blacks are not getting those assignments." Meanwhile, he asked, "Are we here to uplift the greater black community, or are we here to uplift ourselves? By uplifting the greater black community, we also uplift ourselves." 57 The board agreed not to choose winners based on race or membership.

Survival lessons

The national recession of late 1990 through 1991 battered the press. A December New York Times report stated that in the previous 18 months newspaper employment fell on a scale comparable to the worst days of the Great Depression of the 1930s. From June 1990 to September 1991, reported The Times, newspaper employment declined by 20,000 jobs. Prestigious metropolitan dailies reduced staffs through buyouts, early retirements, unpaid sabbaticals and layoffs. 58

The recession appeared partially responsible for the deaths of two metropolitian newspapers, the Dallas Times Herald and Arkansas Gazette of Little Rock.

There were two near newspaper deaths: The Oakland, (Calif.) Tribune was rescued financially by the Freedom Forum (the former Gannett Foundation) and the New York Daily News, wobbly from a five-month strike, was purchased by British publishing tycoon Robert Maxwell. The Daily News' fate became perilous again when Maxwell died in a boating accident, then $1 billion was missing from his publishing empire. On the broadcast news side, local TV stations laid off news staff in a fashion similar to the purge of network news in the mid- to late-1980s. 59

During these hard times NABJ and its members learned lessons in survival. Many members answered the challenge to pay for their association's services when their employers declined to underwrite their professional development. And NABJ increased its emphasis on professional development programming to assist members looking for new work or new careers. Meanwhile, some members raised the national profile of black journalists, whether it was from covering the Gulf War in winter 1991 or by becoming players in a bruising confirmation that fall of a Supreme Court Justice.

Chapter 3
Crusading
for diversity

Mergers and downsizing of media companies continued though 1991 and into 1992. In January, National Black Network (established in 1973) and Sheridan Broadcasting Network (established 1972) announced they were merging into American Urban Radio Networks.

Fred Mattingly, vice president of marketing and communications for the new company, said consolidation meant that, "Now there's one-stop shopping for advertisers trying to reach the urban market."

Six hundred stations in the USA, Virgin Islands and Tokyo could reach 93 percent of African-Americans.[1]

Other observers said the merger was bad for radio news. Ken Smikle, who monitored black media as publisher of Target Market News, noted the plusses and minuses of the merger: "It will allow both companies to have a better opportunity for survival. The unfortunate part about it, however, is the loss of jobs that will result from such actions."

Jack Bryant, a co-president of the new company, said the news department was disbanded because "radio stations don't want news" he said. Listeners demanded more music, and managements catered to listener demands. But in a form letter, employees were told that the network news department was dissolved for "economic" reasons. [2]

Black and Overpaid?

While long-time radio journalists found themselves unemployed, a black journalist in Boston was under attack for being courted by rival media suitors. In November 1991, Boston Herald columnist Howie Carr quoted from an anonymous fax sent from the Boston Globe about Renee Graham, a black reporter at the Globe who was given a raise after being wooed by the New York Times. Carr erroneously reported that the Globe matched the Times' salary offer to Graham, then the columnist quoted "one ink-stained wretch" who complained that Graham's byline appeared "about as often as Halley's Comet.

"But Renee is black," wrote Carr, "And some on Morrissey Boulevard (the Globe's address) say that's what counted."3 A raise for Graham made her a lightning rod for resentment because other staff members had not received raises since the union contract expired more than a year before. Still, dozens of black, Hispanic, Asian and white Globe staff members were incensed that an anonymous attack on one of their co-workers was leaked to the competing newspaper.

A statement – initially signed by journalists of color, then whites signed on too – urged Globe management to "counsel all employees that we will not stand for such petty, racist backlashes."

After a second Herald column from Carr that quoted a "fax man" saying, "If she (Graham) were white would they have made this effort to keep her? ... That's the question here," Carr was challenged in his newspaper by Leonard Greene, a black Herald columnist: "Perhaps the question that should have been asked is: 'How many white reporters have gotten offers from better papers?' It sounds from this end like someone's a little jealous."

Greene also wrote that "Newspapers are also a business. I doubt that the Globe would open its safe just for the sake of keeping a black reporter on the payroll, especially when there are so many others out there that can be bought at a cheaper price."4 Greene chastised the Herald for contributing "to the general attitude that advances by people of color have worked to hold white people back."

Globe management pored over fax records and traced the leaked messages to the Globe State House bureau. Ten days after the firestorm erupted, Peter J. Howe, 26, a reporter who came to the paper straight from Harvard, posted a three-page letter of apology on the bulletin board and said he stepped forward to remove suspicion from his co-workers.

Howe apologized yet he blasted management for tracing the leak, calling it an act "straight out of the Nixon White House" and regarding his criticism of Graham said, "My hope was that by delivering an admittedly even inflammatory message, I could help push the Globe into discussing some matters of widespread but largely unspoken concern."

"A provocation" was what Graham called Howe's alleged apology. "I am angered by the arrogance and lack of contrition in his letter. He is sorry for being caught; nothing else. He still doesn't understand why his comments were so hurtful or divisive."

Howe was suspended without pay for two weeks.

Philadelphia Freedom

Tampa Bay region – St. Petersburg and Tampa, Fla. – was the venue for the NABJ winter board meetings in late January. Picking future convention sites was the top order of business.

Eight hotel companies and cities came calling and spent five hours trying to persuade the board to choose them as convention sites in 1995 and 1996. 5 These suitors recognized that the 2,200-member association pumped an estimated $1.5 million into a city's economy during convention week and membership was projected to grow at nearly 60 percent in three years. 6

Presenters included Disney, which promised an awards ceremony where recipients would ride down Disney World's "Hollywood Boulevard" in antique cars and leave to a fireworks and laser show accompanied by strains of Disney's classic movie "Fantasia." 7

Despite the offer of star treatment, the board passed on choosing Orlando, Fla. and Disney World as a convention site.

President Estes-Sumpter abstained from voting on the Orlando pitch. At the meetings, she and regional director Carolyn Sawyer were subjects of ethics questions for accepting trips the previous fall that were paid for by Disney. Estes-Sumpter acknowledged an "error in timing" in making the trip just when Disney was celebrating its 20th anniversary.

The board voted that members will "keep in mind the ethical standards of the industry" in considering offers of free trips. Whether to take the trips will be considered "on a case-by-case basis," and the entire board was to be in on the decision. 8

Disney's pitch was not accepted by a number of board members because they were wary of the company's treatment of blacks, and convention sites were selected based on potential hosts' hiring record and attentiveness to blacks and black culture.

During her fall visit to Disney World, Sawyer said "it was disturbing to see the lack of blacks in even the simplest jobs, like taking the bags."

Several board members said Disney had made strides in black employment, even at the top levels, but a majority of officers were not swayed. 9

What won board members over were cities that promoted their ties to Black America. The winners were Philadelphia for 1995 and Nashville for 1996.

The two Philadelphia presenters included Dwight Evans, a Pennsylvania legislator who chaired the state House Appropriations Committee. Philadelphia's tourism bureau had a black (or multicultural,) tourism committee and made a presentation tailored to African-American visitors. The city's other built-in advantage was it was the ancestral home of NABJ, which made Philadelphia a sentimental favorite for the milestone 20th anniversary convention.

Five original founders – Chuck Stone, Acel Moore, Claude Lewis, Joe Davidson and Reginald Bryant – worked for the Philadelphia media. 10 Stone of the Philadelphia Daily News was NABJ's first president. The constitution and bylaws of the Association of Black Journalists (ABJ) of Philadelphia was the model that built NABJ.

Moore of the Philadelphia Inquirer told the board that 50 black journalists at the two dailies plus the radio stations and the nation's oldest continuously published black newspaper, the Philadelphia Tribune (1884), supported hosting the convention.

The three African-American woman team from Nashville included Karen Coffee of the Opryland Hotel. Yes, Nashville was synonymous with country music, but the team reminded board members that their mid-south city was a center of black culture and achievement: Home to gospel music, Fisk University, (where W.E.B. DuBois was a student and newspaper editor) Meharry Medical College, Tennessee State University and the oldest black-owned bank in the USA.

Coffee and her teammates' pitch won over the board.

Orlando, Charlotte and Seattle were listed as contenders for the 1997 convention. Detroit, which was already hosting that summer's convention, and Toronto, were the other city presenters.

NABJ was in the third year of a five-year hotel contract with Westin hotels that would end in 1994 and the board had to decide how to house members at future conventions.

Board members decided against signing future multi-year contracts after it turned out that NABJ was growing faster than Westin could accommodate convention goers.

Even Westin representative John Lockwood told the board, "you shouldn't have entered into the five-year arrangement with Westin – or anybody. It instantly limits your ability to negotiate with other hotel companies."

Westin, Hyatt, Marriott and Sheraton made pitches to lodge members in the prospective convention cities. 11

At the board meeting the Pittsburgh Black Media Federation was approved as an affiliate chapter but there was troubling news that existing chapters in Syracuse, N.Y., Minneapolis-St. Paul and Baltimore risked losing affiliate status because its local leaders failed to send membership data to the national office. 12

Pierre Summit
The four leading journalist associations of color, led by NABJ, threatened to withdraw its memberships from a larger coalition of newspaper organizations unless there was

constructive action about diversity rather than idle talk and hand wringing. The Task Force on Minorities in the Newspaper Business allowed NABJ and Hispanic, Asian and Native American representatives to voice their concerns at a February 1991 meeting in Baltimore. Eleven months later on Jan. 10-11, 1992, a group of 38 newspaper CEOs, publishers and other leaders met at the Hotel Pierre. The meeting became known as the Pierre Summit. 13

The meeting was closed to press coverage. Arthur Ochs Sulzberger Jr., deputy chairman of the task force, played a key role in organizing the summit that occurred a week before Sulzberger, 40, was promoted from deputy publisher to publisher of The New York Times.

Meanwhile, the American Newspaper Publishers Association was about to merge with the Newspaper Advertising Bureau and become NAA – Newspaper Association of America. ANPA President Cathleen Black, publisher of USA Today, said that with the merger, one of its four standing committees would be diversity. 14

R. Roosevelt Thomas Jr. from the American Institute for Managing Diversity at Morehouse College was brought in to facilitate the sessions. "Never before have I seen a gathering of such heavy hitters to deal with a subject that is the very foundation of our organization," wrote Estes-Sumpter in her February NABJ Journal president's column.

"Dr. Thomas' approach to diversity was refreshingly unique, but it also offered some tough consequences for both the proponents and opponents of the whole diversity question. Much of what Thomas laid out for the CEOs was not new. It was just phrased differently or given from another perspective." Thomas, author of an often quoted Harvard Business Review article about the new concept "diversity," advocated for radical change in the corporate mindset at newspapers. White men were the fuel that powered daily newspapers for much of the 20th century, however the current and future workforce was another kind of fuel, a mix of white women, men and women of color and white men in a minority position. Newspaper leaders needed to recognize that hiring, mentoring and promoting people of color was much more than a moral choice; it was an economic necessity because of the demographics of the labor force.

Radical change in mindset meant a re-examination of affirmative action, long a strategy to get racial minorities through the doors of many workplaces. But once the people were in the door, what was done with them? Thomas urged that after nearly 25 years of affirmative action it was time for upgrades. CEOs and publishers needed to "manage diversity" by mentoring, promoting and retaining workers of color in addition to recruiting workers, whether by affirmative action or conventional hiring. 15

Wrote Estes-Sumpter, "While most of us bristle at the thought of abolishing affirmative action, we recognize that it does have its shortcomings. The issue for African-Americans in the newsroom is not confined to whether we can get in the door of the nation's newsrooms. Half of America's newspapers still don't have any people of color in their newsrooms. But beyond the numbers in other newsrooms is the issue of empowerment. That is the step beyond affirmative action." 16

Pierre Summit participants broke up into smaller groups and devised action plans for advancing diversity. The recommendations were to be refined at a spring meeting.

Dorothy Gilliam, NABJ vice president/print, said, "This is the first time that you had so many CEOs of major companies coming together to talk about the issue of diversity. We have set some very important things in motion." 17

White, Male Network News

A year ago in 1991, The Center for Media and Public Affairs reported that the presentation of network TV news was overwhelmingly white and male. In 1992 there was virtually no change. No black reporter made the top 50 for stories filed (George Strait of ABC ranked 57th).

Among anchors who read the news, Carole Simpson of ABC and Ed Bradley, a "60 Minutes" correspondent and occasional CBS anchor, again ranked No. 6 and 14 respectively in face time. Combined, racial minorities accounted for 9 percent of all stories filed – black journalists 5 percent, Hispanics 3 percent and Asian Americans less than 1 percent. Fourteen percent of news reports and 18 percent of anchor "tell" stories were presented by women.

Basing racial integration of the national news report on stories filed may have been superficial, yet appearances mattered too. If FCC rules enforced racial and gender integration of broadcasting, why were the national reports so white and male in an America where minorities and women were no longer invisible in the professional ranks?

Kenneth R. Walker suggested that black journalists remained outsiders in network TV news: they persuaded white news managers to get important stories on the air, but their lobbying earned them reputations as troublemakers. Walker wrote that such a reputation followed him from ABC News to the short lived "USA Today, The Television Show," that he co-anchored with a white male and two white females. 18

Walker stood alone in opposing on-air promotion of a multimillion-dollar diamond scheme with a South African company while economic sanctions were in effect. "This I refused to do," wrote Walker, "for reasons of ethics as well as justice.

"So this reputation follows me – much to my enormous regret. The only single thing I ever wanted was just to be the best reporter I knew how. But for an African-American broadcaster to do that, inevitably means that he will follow the maxim that first Frederick Douglass and later Mal Goode laid down for their progeny. Agitate! Agitate! Agitate!"

Black on Black Skirmish

While black journalists pressed daily newspapers and broadcast news outlets to integrate, expand and retain journalists of color, black journalists working in the mainstream dodged grenades lobbed by publishers of black-owned newspapers.

In September 1991, Robert Bogle, head of the National Newspaper Publishers Association (AKA Black Press of America) and publisher of the Philadelphia Tribune told NABJ:

"You are a bunch of black folks working for white people. And, who have walked away and divorced yourselves from the black press. You ain't the black press, you are people working for somebody's press.

"Come back home and join the brothers and sisters. If what we are doing isn't the best that we should be doing, then damn it, show me how.

"I think we should work together for the common good of our community. And if you can bring something to the NNPA that is going to help us, you're not just helping me, you are helping those 11 million black folks we serve every day."

Bogle's remarks disturbed Garland L. Thompson, an editorial writer at the Baltimore Sun, and previously executive editor of Bogle's newspaper. In a March NABJ commentary, "Black publishers should can the insults," Thompson wrote: "I cannot keep silent when Bob does a routine National Newspaper Publishers Association hatchet job on our group's sensibilities.

"I read his comments in the NABJ Journal and I have several reasons for saying they're a crock:
• NNPA's members couldn't find jobs for all of us who now work for the "white press" even if we all did decide to bring our talents home to the black community;
• NNPA member papers have great difficulty coming up with livable wages for talent they do employ ... what the NNPA has to understand is that $12,000 to $14,000 a year with minimal benefits is not a reasonable offer to a college graduate, much less people with real experience.
• Many of the African-Americans who work for major outlets have offered good advice to the historically black press. Include in that advice and concern our brothers and sisters in television have offered their compatriots in black radio. Many more times than not, the net result is that at best we get ignored. Worse, but as often, we meet vituperous repudiation. Who do we think we are, trying to tell them anything?"

The black press vs. blacks in white press skirmishes were fights between owners trying to save their eroding enterprises and workers trying to convince their bosses to integrate and diversify their enterprises. Six years later, Alexis Scott Reeves said African-Americans needed "a mainstream voice and caucus voice" in journalism, so the warring sides needed to co-exist. 19

Wrote Thompson, "Somebody has to develop the credibility to argue the African-American case in forums reaching white Americans, too. And somebody has to sit in the editorial board meetings, daily news meetings and newsrooms of the most powerful reporting agencies in the world, both to watchdog African-American issues and to fight for better attention to our needs." [20]

Sports Icons Scrutinized

Good examples of black journalists serving as eyewitnesses from mainstream platforms were the dozen journalists out of at least 250 newspeople who covered the trial of boxing icon Mike Tyson. [21]

Tyson was convicted in an Indianapolis court (Marion County Superior) of raping a Miss Black America contestant in his hotel room during the Black Expo festival in Indianapolis the previous summer.

Tyson, 25, was also convicted on criminal deviate conduct charges for attacking an 18-year-old college student from Rhode Island.

Some members of the black community screamed that racism influenced the Feb. 10 guilty verdict. A group of black ministers held a rally for "fairness and justice" for Tyson and sought a lenient sentence for Tyson when he returned to court March 26. Tyson faced up to 60 years in prison.

What the journalists saw, including the minority who were African-American, was a black sports icon convicted based on compelling evidence.

"He got the fairest trial money could buy," said E.R. Shipp, one of two New York Times reporters covering the trial. Shipp, who covered legal matters for most of her 12 years at the Times, said many critics of the verdict, "didn't read the stories ... They are going with their gut feeling that blacks didn't get a fair shake in this country and they don't care about anything else." [22]

Said Derrick Blakley, who covered the trial for WMAQ-TV (NBC) in Chicago, "I think our women deserve to be protected and respected just as well as our men deserve to be treated with justice."

Added Shipp "A lot of our more outspoken leaders, especially preachers, are rushing to Tyson's side and depicting him as the latest martyr in our history. In doing that they seem to be showing great disrespect for black women, not only the woman who was raped by Tyson, but all those women that form the backbone of their churches." 23

Credible criticism was about where most of the Tyson trial stories were placed. The Indianapolis newspapers kept the story in its news sections, but many papers, including the New York Times, USA Today, Philadelphia Inquirer and Boston Globe ran the stories in the sports sections.

The Globe wrote about the more than 100 complaints it received on the story's placement.

"This was definitely a news story," said Jane Harrington of WTHR (NBC), the only black Indianapolis-based TV reporter who covered the trial. "I didn't see this as boxing on trial. This was a man accused of rape who happened to be a boxer." 24

Another iconic black sports figure who drew the sharp scrutiny of at least one mainstream black journalist was tennis star Arthur Ashe.

Like the Tyson case, sports was not the news, yet unlike the Tyson case, the ethical and judgment issues for journalists were stickier.

Doug Smith was lead tennis writer for USA Today. The Virginian, like Ashe, was a childhood friend and high school tennis rival. Smith picked up a tip on his beat that Ashe had AIDS (Acquired Immune Deficiency Syndrome). After trying to verify the rumors for five days, Smith's editors asked him to contact Ashe and ask him directly if he were ill.

"It was not easy for Doug Smith to ask this question," wrote USA Today editor Peter Prichard. "He had known Ashe for more than 30 years."

The writer visited Ashe at a medical center in White Plains, N.Y. 25

Wrote Prichard, "Smith told Ashe he'd heard a report that Ashe was HIV-positive (the disease that can lead to AIDS).

"Ashe replied, 'can you prove it?'"

"We then suspected that the tip was true. Ashe asked if we could delay any story."

Ashe asked Smith to call his editor, Gene Policinski. Policinski talked to Ashe and asked again if he were HIV-positive.

"Could be," said Ashe, but he declined to confirm or deny the story. 26

Ashe said other journalists know about his condition and asked USA Today to delay the story. The national newspaper's editors said if they could get on-the-record confirmation that Ashe had the infectious disease, they would very likely print the story. Smith worked the phones but was unable to get anyone to confirm that Ashe was seriously ill.

Ashe, apparently thinking that a story was imminent, announced the news himself at an April 8 press conference. Ashe, 48, explained that he became infected with the HIV virus through a blood transfusion during heart surgery. He had known of his infection since September 1988, but kept the information among doctors, family members and a few friends. 27

USA Today, said Ashe, "put me in the unenviable position of having to lie if I wanted to protect our privacy (wife Jeanne and daughter Camera). No one should have to make that choice."

Doug Smith said he felt pain not because of fallout from a story he wrote, but from causing a newsmaker and friend to reveal private details in order to pre-empt a news story.

"I felt extremely bad about being part of a process that forced him (Ashe) to do something that he wasn't prepared to do," Smith told the NABJ Journal.

"We've talked since then, and we're OK. Philosophically, we feel we're obligated to do these things, but I've had two extremely anxious periods in my life. One was when I was in Vietnam, commanding troops. Another was the pain of having to leave my sons at a very young age because of separation and eventually divorce.

"The pain of those few days I had with Arthur equaled that. It stunned me that he had been this way for so long and I didn't know about it."

However, other journalists did know.

NBC "Today" show host Bryant Gumbel said Ashe told him confidentially in 1988. Gumbel told USA Today that he could make the distinction between "being told something as a friend or as a journalist."

And Sports Illustrated journalist Roy Johnson wrote that the previous September and December, he received telephone calls from "credible members of the tennis community," stating Ashe had AIDS.

Johnson said his "journalistic instincts were overcome by compassion and concern ... so that's why I said nothing," not even to Ashe.

Isaiah Poole, a former Washington Times reporter who was HIV-positive, said the press invaded Ashe's privacy: "It made his life needlessly difficult. HIV-positive people want for us to have the same ability to choose the terms for life and death like everybody else. USA Today essentially took that away from Arthur Ashe," said Poole, who at the time was executive director of LifeLink, an organization that provided AIDS counseling and support.

Ashe, revered as a courtly but determined humanitarian and activist, accepted Roy Johnson's invitation to speak at the Aug. 20 NABJ Detroit convention panel on AIDS and the African-American community.

Ashe died of pneumonia on Feb. 6, 1993, 10 months after rumors of his grave illness caused journalists to question the boundaries of privacy, ethics and newsmakers. 28

Black Women and Pulitzers
The NABJ Women's Task Force that organized symposiums and workshops in 1991 continued initiatives in 1992 aimed at empowering women journalists. At the request of Pulitzer Prize officials the task force submitted the names of two dozen African-American women who were good candidates to serve as Pulitzer jurors or as members of the governing board. The request came after Pulitzer Prize Board Chairman Michael Gartner read "Black Women Journalists and the Pulitzer Prize," a 1991 report by Linda Waller of the Dow Jones Newspaper Fund that documented the limited participation of black women in the Pulitzers at all levels – submissions, judging and oversight. 29

That spring, one black woman, University of North Carolina law professor Marilyn Yarbrough, sat on the 19-member Pulitzer Prize board and Rhonda Chriss Lokeman, a Kansas City Star editorial writer, was the only African-American woman among 65 jurors, who nominated candidates. 30 An African-American woman, Itabari Njeri, was among three finalists in the Criticism category for her June 23, 1991 Los Angeles Times essay, "Doing the wrong thing: In perpetuating the myth that blacks and whites who marry are misfits, Spike Lee shows in 'Jungle Fever' that he remains enslaved by a racist mindset."

Itabari Njeri's essay began this way: "Once, I was an infantile black nationalist like Spike Lee."

The essayist told Richard Prince of the NABJ Journal: "I knew from the reception of my work that this was Pulitzer caliber. I know the status of writing in our profession. [The piece] got one of the largest outpourings of mail the paper's ever received. It was 2-1 against me."

Njeri nominated the essay herself because she said the Los Angeles Times declined to do so. Editor Shelby Coffey III called Njeri's submission "a fine piece," but "we generally nominate people who are full-time writers who had a body of work." Njeri was on leave from the newspaper to write a book about inter-ethnic relations.

She agreed the Pulitzer Prizes for criticism are awarded for bodies of work, about 10 stories. For that reason, Njeri expected Leslie Savan of the Village Voice in New York City to win the award for her columns on advertising and the media. However, the Pulitzer Board gave no award and declined to say why. Estes-Sumpter called the decision "highly suspect." 31 Gartner told the Los Angeles Times that "It was the general belief of the board that while all three of the finalists in criticism this year were interesting, none of them were of Pulitzer Prize caliber."

Allan Temko, chairman of the Criticism jury, said he was baffled by the board's decision. Savan, said Temko of the San Francisco Chronicle, was the jury's first choice, and Njeri, 38, fell short because she submitted one entry. "If she had done 10 articles like that, she would have gotten the Pulitzer Prize. She's certainly a woman with a big future."

Robert C. Maynard, publisher of the Oakland Tribune and one of three blacks on the 19-member Pulitzer board, said that despite black journalists' miniscule showing overall (they played supporting roles in team projects but won no individual awards), he was optimistic that the picture would change: "As more and more journalists of color get in the position where they can write major takeouts, they will get more Pulitzer Prizes." 32

Chapter 4
L.A. Uprising

On March 3, 1991 in Los Angeles, drunk driver Rodney King tried to elude police but was caught. The moving violation would have been marginally newsworthy or unknown to the public had there not been a citizen's 86-second home video shot with a handheld camera that showed the end of the chase. King, a linebacker size black man, was shown lying on the ground, writhing from 56 baton blows from four white police officers. 1

The tape was broadcast on network news. Nationally, most viewers were shocked that police abused an unarmed defendant, but for many blacks and browns, the tape was confirmation of police brutality that occurred routinely in their communities but was dismissed by the white majority as fiction or even appropriate behavior.

The four police officers were charged with criminal conduct and because of extensive pre-trial press coverage, their cases were moved out of Los Angeles and 45 miles northwest to Simi Valley, a city of about 100,000 people in Ventura County. 2

Nearly 14 months after the beating, on April 29, 1992 an all-white jury declared that the four cops were innocent. The insane conclusion was the match that ignited rage in Los Angeles streets east of Simi Valley. Many black and Latino men began looting and burning property. Reginald Denny, a white truck driver, was pulled from his vehicle and beaten. Asian storekeepers were targeted for looting.

The press were confronted with a story that essentially was a replay of the Watts neighborhood riots of 1965, the result of a badly executed police stop on a humid August night that unleashed neighbors' pent up frustrations. How would the press perform this time?

Unlike a quarter century ago when people of color were virtually not in mainstream newsrooms, some like Paula Walker (Madison) of WNBC-TV in New York, were now news managers. Walker watched the mayhem via Los Angeles sister station KNBC's satellite signal. Walker instructed her control room staff not to linger on the images of violence any longer than necessary. She explained, "I told them you've got to show what's going on but you don't have to show 30 seconds unedited of someone getting hit in the head with a brick 25 times." 3 Walker was concerned that the images could inflame passions in sections of racially tense New York. Then, the acting news director called Los Angeles and advised reporters not to publicize the locations where looting was taking place without a police presence: "What I said to reporters is if you live in a neighborhood, are you going to tell people they can loot and there are no police around? They don't do it in Harlem (where she lived) and don't do it in South Central L.A." 4

Other broadcast journalists differed on how to cover the street violence. Immediately after the April 29 verdict, TV networks, and especially local stations, showed continuous coverage of the unrest, offering little context for the violent scenes bombarding viewers.

Some local anchors clumsily groped for words to describe the events they saw as residents poured into the streets and violence erupted.

Some referred to looters as "animals." 5

KNBC-TV Los Angeles news director Nancy Valenta defended her station's decision to broadcast some of the violence live: "Most people got their news of this from television. This is something they wanted to see. They didn't want to read it. In the initial stages, you needed to cover it live.

"I think it would have been irresponsible not to be on the air telling people these kinds of things are happening.

"Did we spawn or incite violence by showing pictures of looting? I think that's a very hard assumption to make." 6

Byron Miranda, black and an assignment editor for CNN in Los Angeles, believed his presence added a different dimension to his network's coverage. Miranda helped decide which material was sent to Atlanta for the national broadcast, where television crews would be sent, and what they would cover. Miranda worked to make sure that pieces, like one on residents fleeing the violence, contained the views of blacks and whites.

And he said CNN took this step to avoid appearing inflammatory: "They were very circumspect about showing the Rodney King (beating) video after the verdict."

CBS newsman Harold Dow made a point widely held by blacks, but proved difficult for many whites to accept: that in view of the horror aroused by the videotaped beating, in waiting for a verdict, Angelenos showed great restraint.

"They waited 14 months looking for justice," said Dow. "When they came out with a verdict, it was certain something was going to explode."

While television news struggled over appropriate ways to present the civil unrest, newspapers had internal clashes over how it went about covering the L.A. story, and other newspapers did soul-searching over how to deploy their staffs in central cities.

At the Los Angeles Times, wrote Sharon R. King in the June/July NABJ Journal, there was talk of bringing home a Pulitzer Prize for coverage of one of the worst urban riots of the 20th century. 7

But a number of African-American staff members and other staff members of color believed that their newspaper's coverage did not showcase journalism excellence, but instead revealed shortcomings in hiring, staffing and promotion.

There were so few African-American journalists at the Los Angeles Times, staff members complained that:

• No black editor was in early planning meetings where riot coverage decisions were made.

• The only black editor who handled riot-related copy was Linda D. Williams, who as an assistant business editor assigned and moved business-related copy only.

• Black staff members in the early days of the disturbances were used exclusively on the streets and fed their reports by phone to white reporters, who wrote the stories.

• When black reporters finally were assigned to write major stories, those tended to be about "black" issues rather than of an analytical nature.

• A team assembled to put together special, multi-day post-riot coverage initially was to be led by two white male editors. Sandy Banks, a black education reporter and former assistant metro editor, was added to the team only after general dissatisfaction of the black staffers became known.

Wrote King: "Debate over all aspects of coverage was heated in the newsroom and many Times loyalists were hypersensitive to criticism of the newspaper's efforts."

Linda Williams incurred the wrath of these loyalists. Some white reporters and editors said the editor betrayed the paper because she criticized the Times' approach at an NABJ spring regional conference in San Francisco. Williams said that the Times "bused" black reporters from its suburban bureaus into the central city and used the journalists as riot "cannon fodder" and would likely send them back to the bureaus as soon as the need for so many black faces downtown was over.

Williams comments were published in the Oakland Tribune and the clipping was posted in the Times newsroom.

"We don't need someone like that on the paper," was the overheard response of a white Metro staff member who read the clipping.

Williams' immediate supervisor, Bob Magnuson, who is white, called her into his office and roundly criticized her for (allegedly) spreading a false perception. Williams received nasty messages from another white editor. 8

Among journalists of color at the Times however, Williams' words drew a collective "amen," and some even thought her remarks were temperate.

"The thing about black people being 'bused in' is sort of a minor thing," said Andrea Ford, a Metro desk reporter. "When we need a chance to be in on the big stories, the glory stories, where there are chances to get experience, we are not involved."

The attitude of the paper, said Ford is, "We don't know what we're seeing."

Yet Ford suggested that her newspaper was wearing blinders because the Times' problems were deeper than one journalist's public criticism of riot coverage: "The paper has in many cases, ignored and devalued people of color before, during and after the riot. So I don't know that simply having had greater numbers would have helped."

Ford gave this example: A year before the Rodney King beating and two years before the riot, black staffers suggested that the Times look into an increasing number of reports of abusive behavior by police against black men. When the story list compiled by those reporters was presented to Metro editors, it was summarily rejected. Not the kind of project the paper was interested in pursuing, said the editors.

Could Riots Happen Elsewhere?

At other major newspapers, journalists wondered if their predominantly black and brown central cities were being covered adequately. Were they susceptible to a post-Rodney King verdict-inspired uprising?

This was a relevant question because as a business strategy, many big newspapers poured their newsgathering resources into the suburbs where predominantly white, middle class readers were still migrating from cities. Many black reporters were sent out to the suburbs because:

A) That's where the paper's prime readership was, and

B) The suburbs were for young reporters and often, senior white reporters, who covered a declining number of central city beats, and

C) covering poverty and crime in predominantly black and brown central cities did not rank high on many newspapers' priority lists.

Editors struggled with conflicting demands of chasing the most attractive demographic – suburban readers – yet live up to the ideal of the newspapers as public trusts that crusaded for the downtrodden, even when they were not seen as economically attractive.

Because of the Simi Valley verdict, the Chicago Tribune began putting more emphasis on problems in its black city neighborhoods, where about 1 million people lived, deputy metro editor Reginald Davis told Jerry Thomas of the NABJ Journal. 9 "We have spent a lot more time looking at the black male reaction, not only to the Rodney King verdict but to the way black men are treated by police in all economic levels. "We did a five-part series on race in America. We looked into our own city and areas of expertise – the community, sports and Washington – to look at how both blacks and whites perceive racism and how wide a gap there is. These are the types of things we did not start looking at until Los Angeles."

While the Tribune was adjusting its focus, the newspaper had plans that August to open a large bureau in affluent, predominantly white Lake County, Ill. Most of the Tribune's black journalists worked in the Chicagoland suburbs.

In Atlanta, black college students took to the streets in protest of the Simi Valley verdict and seemed to catch the Journal and Constitution newspapers off guard. Assistant managing editor Chet Fuller said the papers were forced to refocus coverage on inner-city problems: "We have known for a long time these problems were there, but they had a little less priority. We have decided to delve into the community to see what the students, who were the main source of the disturbance in the community, want.

"What kind of change are they looking for? And we will look at the people in the impoverished communities. Those are the Rodney Kings." 10 Atlanta's image was that of a black professional and middle class mecca with leaders like Andrew Young, Maynard Jackson and Bill Campbell. Yet the city still had a large mass of black, urban poor. Meanwhile, predominantly white suburbs – with prime readers and advertising consumers – continued to expand outside of the city boundary.

At the Washington Post, the newspaper was examining race relations and the mood of its central city before the Los Angeles eruption, explained assistant managing editor Milton Coleman: "We were not asleep at the switch," he said. 11

Coleman explained that the previous year, racial tension pulsed in Washington, D.C., Latino neighborhoods, and it was then that the Post focused on that mood. Reporter Lynne Duke was assigned to a race relations beat. "She's not just covering the NAACP," said Coleman. "She has done a number of stories on the views blacks have about whites and whites have about blacks."

Furthermore, The Post was all over race relations stories, according to Coleman, because his newspaper was covering a District of Columbia that was predominantly black (and at the start of the '90s, the Hispanic tensions signaled that the city demographics was becoming black and brown, the latter Latino) and many of the city staff journalists were African-American. 12

"I think we have more African-Americans in prestigious and decision-making positions, especially on our metropolitan staff, than any other paper," said Coleman, adding that of the eight top metro editors, only two were white men. "That was unheard of in 1968," the year D.C. was torn by rioting immediately after the murder of Martin Luther King Jr.

And in Cleveland at the Plain Dealer, the newspaper did not initially absorb the jolting message from Los Angeles, according to David Squires, an assistant city editor. He said that after the riot, his newspaper called an "impromptu meeting" of about 30 reporters and editors. Only one black editor, deputy suburban editor Clara Roberts, was present. Most of the black reporters were in the suburbs.

Said Squires, a former NABJ regional director, "I didn't even know they were having a meeting until it was started. Most of our decisions about coverage were not made by blacks, because we don't have many blacks in hard news decision-making positions."

The Plain Dealer had a new editor who arrived around the time of the L.A. uprising. Soon under David Hall, said Squires, "We've done a 360. We have formed a team of 20 reporters and three editors, including myself, to take an in-depth look at racism in the Cleveland area like we've never done before." The team was headed by Roberts. 13

TV news was generally faulted by black journalists on the scene for showing lots of graphic, live images of lawlessness and destruction, but little or no sober analysis of what was causing the chaos. What the live images failed to convey was that although the riot apparently was provoked by the brutal beating of a black man, then failed justice with the police acquittals, most rioters were not black. The majority of lawbreakers arrested were Latino. Their participation suggested involvement for other grievances or simply, criminal opportunity. Also, the images of battered white truck driver Reginald Denny could suggest that black Angelenos declared open season on whites, but in reality black on white attacks were not widespread, and in cases like Denny's, blacks and browns bravely rushed in to protect him and other whites from marauders.

Some TV news managers unapologetically said their medium was driven by images and it would have been irresponsible not to show the chaos.

For a number of metropolitan newspapers, the Los Angeles uprising pricked news managers to look at staffing and coverage. Even as papers made strides in hiring journalists of color and often to the paper's credit, integrating them into different newsroom departments, like suburban bureaus, the LA uprising exposed the neglect of central city coverage in many places.

At the Los Angeles Times, a weekly community news section that focused on South Central and other black and brown inner cities neighborhoods, was launched.

Also, Andrea Ford, one of the four black reporters on the 74-member Times metro staff, was assigned to cover the Christopher Commission, the panel investigating the city police department. When the panel released its findings of racism and brutality and recommended that Police Chief

Daryl Gates resign, Ford said the editors started adding reporters – white reporters – and she was eased out.

"I just stopped getting assignments," said Ford. "I had covered that story myself for three months. I had done all the grunt work, gone to all the night meetings. But soon as the story got sexy..." 14

After the Rage

In preparing for its late August convention, NABJ shifted gears in response to the Los Angeles uprising.

Since the convention would be in Detroit on the 25th anniversary of the devastating riot in that city and other cities in 1967, reflection on conditions then compared to the present was anticipated. But the breaking story in Los Angeles compelled organizers to adjust the theme of the opening session to "After the rage: A look at African-American leadership," and the urban crisis in numerous U.S. communities. 15

Organizers and leaders also offered members more incentives to register and get to the convention. For the first time, NABJ agreed to accept credit card payments – Mastercard and VISA – for registration at the convention in August. Pre-registered attendees continued to pay by check or money order.

And travelers who were promised discounts if they flew to Detroit on official convention airlines American or Southwest became the beneficiaries of deeper discounts. Airline industry competitors were slashing prices as much as 50 percent during the outbreak of a price war, and NABJ members were able to take advantage of the discounts.

By summer 1992 it was too soon for most news media people to recognize that the early 1990s recession had ended. People were reeling from the damage – layoffs, buyouts and downsizings.

The previous summer when the recession impact was unmistakable, many NABJ members were not deterred by cuts in sponsorship and underwriting by their companies. Individuals reached into their pockets if necessary and paid their registration and travel expenses to the convention.

In Detroit, President Sidmel Estes-Sumpter rallied members to again make a strong showing: "We are being closely watched by the news media. Similar groups have suffered a great deal because of the recession and other factors. Due to the fact that NABJ members rallied, used their own resources and volunteered their services to our programs, we have prospered and held our own.

"The issues facing our profession have become more defined. The unrest in the streets and the apparent voter dissatisfaction with the political system shows that there are thousands of untold stories out there that affect the African-American community.

"The absolute necessity for a diversified newsroom is evident. The news media are going through a revolution and we must lead the discussion on the priorities and remedies." [16]

By the July 24 early bird deadline, 1,302 people pre-registered for the convention, a number that surpassed the 1,259 total registration for the 1991 Kansas City convention. Certainly, Detroit convention registration would grow larger from several hundred last-minute attendees.

However, association leaders cautioned that NABJ finances were fragile. Weeks before the convention, some customary events were still not underwritten, like a $45,000 Friday night banquet that previously was paid for by The New York Times.

"If members want the organization to be self-sufficient," said Treasurer Jackie Greene, "It takes membership dues and convention registration fees."

The Contender

A few weeks before Aug. 19, NABJ received confirmation that Arkansas Gov. Bill Clinton, the Democratic nominee for U.S. President, accepted an invitation to address the association.

For the first time, an authentic presidential contender agreed to speak to NABJ before the election. In 1984, candidate Jesse Jackson addressed the association, but it was after he withdrew from the race.

In 1980, third party independent candidate John Anderson, an Illinois congressman, addressed NABJ. The first candidate to address a convention was U.S. Sen. Edward Kennedy of Massachusetts. Kennedy challenged fellow Democrat and incumbent Jimmy Carter for the nomination and lost, then Kennedy addressed NABJ the same week as Anderson. 17

Clinton agreed to make a 30-minute morning appearance on Friday, Aug. 21. Incumbent George Bush was also invited to Detroit. There was a possibility that he would address members via satellite. 18

Wearing Two Hats

At the "Black America 1992" forum that opened the convention Aug. 19, U.S. Rep. John Conyers, D-Mich., attacked mainstream black journalists. The 13-term congressman said the men and women were not confronting their white bosses and they should force change and quit their jobs if necessary.

Moderator Carole Simpson of ABC News challenged Conyers. Show evidence, she said, that black journalists were not struggling vigorously to produce, fair, accurate news reports.

Conyers backed down, yet his attack resembled the feedback Estes-Sumpter said NABJ and its members received after its NABJ Journal June/July special report on the LA uprising. "We were wearing two hats," said Estes-Sumpter. "We had a stake in interpreting the frustration on the streets. We were still part of an industry that has been historically distrusted by the (black) community. but for us journalists, the choices are still complex. We're told to chose sides, but we're not supposed to. Some people don't understand the ethical responsibilities we have."

For example, during the business meeting that week, members voted 27 yes, 25 no, with eight abstentions, to let the association continue to accept underwriting money from subsidiaries of tobacco companies, like Kraft, maker of Velveeta cheese but part of RJ Reynolds Tobacco Co.

Scores of members were no-shows because they got in line early to catch the sneak preview of Spike Lee's "Malcolm X" movie. Those who persevered and waited to vote ended up with access to the screening through a side door and their choice of the best seats. 19

Filmmaker Lee electrified an overflow auditorium crowd with 12 minutes of clips from his upcoming film, starring Denzel Washington. Five rough cut scenes included a spine-tingling recreation of one of Malcolm X's speeches at a Harlem Square rally, prompting spontaneous applause. 20

Lee pitched his epic with the eagerness of a political candidate, exhorting the audience to forgo work and school to see "Malcolm X" the day of the scheduled Nov. 20 opening. "We have to come out in force," he said, to show distributor Warner Brothers that the movie was worth its projected $34 million budget. During Lee's Q & A with the audience, music and chatter seeped in from a reception next door and occasionally interrupted the filmmaker and audience and forced all participants to speak up.

Later, student journalists would teach a local newspaper a lesson in accuracy and reporting.

Bill Clinton

Several hundred members showed up by 8 a.m. to get up-close seats and also clear the security gantlet in order to hear Gov. Clinton.

When Estes-Sumpter introduced the governor, jokingly she said that the Clinton most recognizable to her members was George, the funk musician. The crowd laughed uproariously and the governor, smiling but looking stunned, reached into his jacket pocket for a pen and pad to make a note about George.

Clinton offered a rote rundown of his positions on the economy, health care, education and welfare reform to a polite and attentive audience that was smaller than the crowd at the "Malcolm X" preview the previous night.

Clinton specifically addressed African-American concerns only when asked during a brief Q & A with a panel of NABJ members. In response to Chicago Tribune columnist Clarence Page's query about the Sister Souljah controversy, the candidate replied, "If you'll forgive me, I have to be president of all the people ... broadening the base is how you win." 21

Clinton pledged his commitment to diversity, saying that if elected, he'll ensure that his Cabinet and other appointees would "look more like this country." But some in the NABJ audience still wondered why the Democrat saved his thunder – including a response to a just concluded Republican Party convention – for an appearance later that day at the Economic Club of Detroit. 22

Clinton's visit did allow NABJ students at the daily convention newspaper, the Monitor, to critique a Detroit News story that morning. The News' Susan Stark reported that Spike Lee gave a raucous party. In fact the loud music and crowd noise came from the Clinton party reception next door to Lee in the hotel. The students challenged other facts in the story and soon the reporter and her editor were backpedaling from the flurry of questions. 23

At the convention:

• Speaker William Gray III eloquently defended the United Negro College fund he now led. "No one ever got anywhere by getting rid of their own institutions," said the former Pennsylvania Congressman, explaining that he was tired of having to justify the existence of historically black colleges. "If Notre Dame (founded for Catholics) is relevant, Morehouse is relevant." 24

• Marian Wright Edelman of the Children's Defense Fund and often called the 51st Senator, pleaded, "Let's hear about the children who are *not* killing somebody. Most black kids are making it. We need to change the perception of the outside community of who we are." Then she spent $800 at the "Dolls of Color" booth.

• At a forum on presidential coverage, Kevin Merida of the Dallas Morning News demonstrated the difference African-American managers can make. Merida described how he suggested that a reporter ask Clinton why he hadn't been as fervent in discussing bloodshed in Somalia as he had been about Bosnia in Eastern Europe. Clinton replied that he hadn't really thought about Somalia, but he added the African nation to his litany the next day. 25

• NABJ members raised money – $4,640 with its photo auction, and Carole Simpson, on winning the Journalist of the Year award, announced that she was donating $5,000 to begin a scholarship fund for two students in broadcasting. Simpson challenged all of her peers "who hold the big jobs" to join the association and lend their support. 26

• Chuck Stone, NABJ's founding president, accepted the Lifetime Achievement Award and said, "United we stand, divided we fall, but brothers and sisters, together we kick ass."

• In addition to the vote on accepting underwriting from tobacco subsidiaries, members voted 135-80 for public relations practitioners who had been journalists for five years or more to be upgraded to full membership. And by a 148-66 vote, the student representative on the NABJ board was given a vote.

In all 1,826 people attended the convention, a 31 percent increase over Kansas City in 1991. During the four days, members haunted the job fair and reggaed half the night, groused at the slow elevators at the Renaissance Center, and gawked at the gilt and red marble opulence of the Fox Theater, where the awards program was held.

And it seemed each and every member took from the convention a moment or two that was absent from the printed schedule. National Public Radio correspondent Cheryl Devall held a quiet toast of water glasses with two good girlfriends from a couple of jobs back and they pledged to meet every year from then on. They skipped the Friday banquet to make time for each other. This was because as one participant in a panel on fellowships commented, for some of us, "this four days a year is a fellowship, a chance to step out of your job and renew your life."

Yes, NABJ was riding high from a well-attended convention that drew a presidential contender and leading black newsmakers in politics, education and health. Walt

Harrington, a white Washington Post writer who won a print features award, said he wished his white colleagues could be present "to breathe in the optimism in the air" he found at the convention. 27

Andrew's Fury

For a segment of NABJ convention goers, going home would be devastating. Partying in Detroit, Miami-area journalists were blithely unaware of Hurricane Andrew approaching South Florida, said Dan Holly of the Miami Herald, adding, "It didn't occur to our editors to warn us to catch earlier flights until it was too late for most of us. 28

"So we stayed in Detroit a couple of extra days. It was hurry up and wait for the airports to reopen. It's not like we could have fun, missing such a great story. Besides, many of us had no idea if we had homes left.

"When I got back, I wasn't going to complain; I figured everybody had other things to worry about. But then a white reporter joked about how all the black reporters had been 'conveniently away.'

"I said: 'If we were considered essential to this operation, somebody would have made sure we were all on a plane Saturday night.'

"She looked shocked when she realized I would not join her in the joke. Another white reporter jumped to her defense: 'It's not like anybody intentionally didn't call the reporters. We had so much to worry about, we just weren't thinking about you at all.

I said: 'That's my point.'" 29

Seeing Andrew's fury up close made Holly wonder how anything in its path remained standing:

• Tall, stately trees were ripped clean from the ground;

• Thick telephone poles snapped in half;

• An office building had gaping holes where the wind had ripped off concrete, like skin that was peeled away. Stop signs and lampposts were twisted into grotesque shapes;

• Airplanes, boats and large mobile homes were flipped upside down. A mobile home parked looked like Godzilla had trampled it, Holly thought as he flew over it in a helicopter while on assignment.

Amazingly, his home was untouched, even a glass vase that had been sitting outside his balcony survived. Holly had running water and electricity the day after the hurricane, so he was able to shave and wear a tie and neatly ironed shirt to the office.

At work he encountered blue jeans, T-shirts and stubble. Almost no one had electricity or running water. People spoke in hushed tones about others who had lost everything.

At least nine people in the Herald newsroom – including Leonard Pitts Jr., music critic, husband and father of five children – lost their homes. 30

Holly quietly slipped off his tie. For the next week he wore jeans and T-shirts to work.

Hurricane Andrew rearranged South Florida with devastating unpredictability. In late summer NABJ rearranged its office dramatically in order to manage growth and change. Executive director Linda Edwards' 2-year contract was not renewed. She would leave at the end of September. "Linda and the board mutually agreed it was time to make a change in leadership in the office," said Estes-Sumpter. 31

Edwards was the association's third director in six years. Dennis Schatzman served less than a year, Carl Morris served a little more than three years and Edwards completed two. A search began for a fourth director and under the new configuration the hire would have increased responsibility for fund raising and convention planning. An office manager was to report to the executive director and be in charge of day-to-day operations. The staff in Reston, Va. would also include a publications director, program director and administrative assistant. Said Edwards, "We had plenty of big accomplishments. We met our goals." Edwards wanted to increase membership to 3,000 and it rose 65 percent to 2,736. NABJ's fund-raising base expanded to 17 organizations from five, said Edwards, and the association was on the verge of launching a fully funded 24-hour telephone job line. "It was a great and wonderful experience. I wouldn't trade it," said Edwards. "But we move on." 32

In October, Walterene Swanston, director of diversity programs for the American Newspaper Publishers Association, was hired as an interim executive director. Swanston was named director of the NABJ Children's Project, 25 writers, editors and photographers documenting self-help and advocacy for African-American children. This project was funded with a $100,000 Freedom Forum grant.

In the meantime the board was narrowing the list of finalists from 44 applicants. Swanston said she would not be a candidate. The board was prepared to select a permanent director at the January 1993 meeting. 33

The Oakland Tribune survived a devastating earthquake in 1989, won a Pulitzer Prize a year later for photography and got a loan from the Freedom Forum in 1991 in order to continue publishing. On Oct. 12, 1992, the Tribune ended its distinction as the only African-American owned mainstream daily when it sold to Texas publishing tycoon William Dean Singleton. About 600 employees waited anxiously for Nov. 30 to see if they would have jobs.

Publisher Robert C. Maynard, 55, was undergoing treatment for prostate cancer and his health was a probable reason he was stepping away from newspapering. Pearl Stewart, a former Tribune editor who was working in San Francisco, was named editor of the paper by the new owners. 34

Chapter 5
Bruised in Big Apple

Richard Prince joined the editorial page of the Democrat and Chronicle in Rochester, N.Y. in 1985 as a columnist, later adding editorial writing. He wanted to see what other writers were doing, so Prince assembled pieces by other black columnists along with his own and began a column exchange by mail. Prince also distributed some of these collections in the Democrat and Chronicle newsroom. Some dubbed the collection the "Black Pack" or "Prince Pack."

Patricia Gaston, who had worked with Prince on the copy desk in Rochester and left in 1986 for the foreign desk of the Dallas Morning News, was a big help. She would send him clippings from the Morning News and some other places as grist for Prince's column. Some of those pieces were columns by African-Americans and Hispanics.

Prince put them in the package. His father back home in Long Island would send Les Payne's column from Newsday. In addition, Prince would clip columns from the New York Daily News, New York Times, Boston Globe, Washington Post and other papers that came into his office, and include them in the package.

Tom Morgan ran for president of NABJ in 1989. Morgan and Prince had worked together at the Washington Post in the 1970s before Morgan left for the New York Times. Morgan asked Prince to support him and he did. When Morgan won at the New York convention, Prince asked him on the night of the awards ceremony whether NABJ would assume the responsibility of mailing out the columns Prince had been packaging. Morgan agreed. 1

Prince was ecstatic and told the other columnists. By then, word had spread among more columnists, and additional people were added to the list. Tim Giago's "Notes from Indian Country" became a staple, adding a different perspective. Likewise, William Wong of the Oakland Tribune supplied an Asian American view. However, NABJ's taking over the task did not come to pass.

Some of this bonding among columnists was enhanced by meetings at the NABJ convention. Prince conducted a workshop on column writing at the 1992 convention in Detroit, and before that, columnists would see each other at workshops on editorial writing, or just at the convention as people hung out. 2

Trotter Group

NABJ founders and op-ed columnists DeWayne Wickham and Les Payne for several years talked about assembling a group of black columnists in order to share common experiences. Said Wickham, given the daily pressures of the journalists, it was easy to see the grand plan fall by the wayside because organizing the group seemed to lack a compelling event.

Two 1992 events sprung a trio – Wickham of USA Today/Gannett News Service, Payne of Newsday and Derrick Jackson of the Boston Globe – into action. In January, Wickham and Jackson went to the U.S. Naval Base at Guantanamo Bay, Cuba, to see how thousands of Haitian refugees being held against their will were being treated. The so-called refugee camp was actually a prison camp, said Wickham, encircled by barbed wire and guard towers and full of people held hostage to a foreign power.

"Exposing this charade," said Wickham, he and Jackson wrote several columns, dispatches unlike anything that were sent to U.S. newspapers. 3 Later that year, U.S. Presidential candidate Bill Clinton promised to end mistreatment of those fleeing Haiti's despotic government and give them "refuge and consideration for political asylum until democracy is restored" to Haiti. Clinton's promise raised the hope that Haiti and other issues of importance to African-Americans might be lifted out of the political bog if the Democrat from Arkansas were elected. 4

Recognizing that a change in administrations might focus more attention on black America, Wickham, Jackson and Payne put out a call for the first meeting of the Trotter Group, named in honor of William Monroe Trotter (1872-1934), editor of the Guardian newspaper of Boston. 5

In a letter of invitation to 40 black columnists, Wickham invoked these words of columnist H.L. Mencken:

"The Negro leader of today is not free. He must look to white men for his very existence, and in consequence he has to waste a lot of his energy trying to think white.

"What the Negroes need is leaders who can and will think black."

Of the 40 journalists invited, 18 answered the call and were founding members of the Trotter Group. They met Dec. 8 and 9 at Harvard University in Cambridge, Mass., where Trotter and W.E.B. DuBois were classmates.

Trotter was notorious for a 45-minute argument he'd had inside the White House with President Woodrow Wilson about race relations. In 1914, with lynching increasing and Jim Crow tightening its grip on blacks, Trotter asked Wilson where he stood on racism. The president and Virginian told Trotter, "Segregation is not humiliating but a benefit ... your manner offends me." 6

During the argument Trotter said, "Two years ago, you were regarded as a second Abraham Lincoln ... Now we colored leaders (who supported Wilson) are denounced in the colored churches as traitors to our race."

The argument made the front page of the New York Times. The mainstream press called Trotter everything from a poor representative of his race to possessing "superabundant untactful belligerency" to nigger. Many African-Americans publicly criticized Trotter's judgment. W.E.B. DuBois, however, praised Trotter for his fearlessness and unselfish devotion to the higher interests of the Negro race. And Oswald Garrison Villard, a grandson of abolitionist editor William Lloyd Garrison, said that perhaps "one has to be rude to get into the press and do good for a just cause."

Trotter's legacy of lone wolf protest, which included upsetting a U.S. President, wrote Jackson, cannot be forgotten, and was commemorated with the founding of the Trotter Group. Each fall thereafter several dozen columnists gathered to discuss their craft or meet with experts in what essentially were national editorial board meetings.

After the inaugural Trotter meeting at Harvard in 1992, Nieman curator Bill Kovach was added to Richard Prince's column distribution list, which in September 1993 had 34 people.

Prince's column writing ended in 1993, when the Democrat and Chronicle made him the op-ed editor in order to fill a vacancy. That's about the time when his U.S. mail packages ended as well. Prince left the Democrat and Chronicle and Rochester in 1994 to return to Washington.

By the late 1990s, because of the Internet, people did not have to go through all the cutting-and-pasting that Prince did for seven years.

In 2002 Prince resumed doing a column exchange from time to time in his online "Journal-isms" column on the Maynard Institute's web site. Unlike the pre-Internet days in the late '80s and early '90s it's now all electronic and a lot easier.

Images Mattered, Too

While the Trotter Group focused on bringing stronger black viewpoints to opinion pages, other people began to pay attention to African-American images in editorial cartoons. The stock and trade of editorial cartooning was exaggeration and satire. However, when did artistic license cross the line into gratuitous racial stereotyping?

Gary Fields' January 1993 NABJ Journal article, "Drawing on stereotypes," examined the state of daily newspaper editorial cartooning. With more African-Americans in the news, whether they were newsmakers or ordinary people, this phenomenon exposed deficiencies in many cartoonists, a field almost exclusive to white men.

Seattle Times cartoonist Brian Bassett could not win. He drew Jesse Jackson and shaded his face, and readers complained that Jackson was too dark. Bassett drew Jackson the next time without shading and other readers complained that he was not dark enough.

Boston Globe cartoonist Dan Wasserman used zebra-like stripes to show color in black people's faces and that technique drew reader complaints.

The few black cartoonists who drew for mainstream newspaper audiences felt comfortable drawing black caricatures using facial features and without shading. Rob King of the Camden, N.J. Courier-Post explained, "There's a way to draw noses and lips without overdoing it. You can use hairstyles. I always thought shading was an invention of the white cartoonist who used it because they don't want to offend anybody."

Bruised in the Big Apple

In November 1991 British publishing tycoon Robert Maxwell, 68, who purchased the New York Daily News' earlier that year, died in a boating accident off the Canary Islands, then $1 billion was missing from Maxwell's publishing empire. The Daily News was declared bankrupt and its odds of survival were deemed questionable.

Another publishing tycoon, Mortimer B. Zuckerman, owner of U.S. News & World Report and The Atlantic Monthly magazines, stepped in and bought the newspaper (its assets) in January 1993.

Zuckerman immediately broke the Newspaper Guild, the union representing editorial, circulation and advertising employees, by eliminating 34 percent of those jobs, according to the Guild. Of those cuts, 21 black men out of 39 Guild members were dismissed, including every black male reporter who was working at the paper. Ten of the 36 black women in the Guild were fired. Among Hispanics, 29 percent of the men and two of the five women were terminated.

Also, 38 percent of all workers over age 40 were let go. 7

Among the dismissed was reporter David Hardy, one of the four plaintiffs who successfully sued the Daily News for racial discrimination in 1987.

The firings seriously wounded black journalists and horrified local activists in New York City. The Daily News was the sixth largest daily U.S. newspaper at 759,068 circulation and 44 percent of the tabloid's readers were people of color. 8 "I'm not sure Mr. Zuckerman realizes what he has done to the racial demographics of this paper," said Hap Hairston, African-American and the former metro editor, who was demoted to running the business desk and editing the columnists.

Said Tony Moor, an African-American copy editor who was retained, "every black man who was writing is gone. The company is saying they needed to tighten up the staff and get rid of the dead wood, the people who couldn't cut the mustard. Not a single black man can cut the mustard?"

On Jan. 22 a small contingent of black leaders, including the Revs. Al Sharpton and Herbert Daughtry and state NAACP leader Hazel Dukes, met with Zuckerman for two hours. On Jan. 29 an NABJ contingent led by Estes-Sumpter met with Zuckerman. According to the board members, the publisher agreed to:

• Personally review the records of all African-American employees who were released and reconsider re-employment of some of these workers.

• Consider African-Americans for top management positions at the paper. (At the time of the dismissals, the highest ranking black news executive, editorial page editor Ellis Cose, announced that he was leaving the newspaper in April to become a contributing editor at Newsweek magazine and also write books.)

• Look closely at the newsroom environment, where African-American employees "do not feel valued and see no possibility for advancement at the newspaper." 9

• Review the newspaper's employment situation in another meeting in 90 days.

Three days later on Feb. 1, the Daily News announced the hiring of three top editors from the rival New York Post: Editor Lou Colasuonno as the News' editor, Managing Editor James Lynch as the News' executive editor and Metropolitan Editor Richard Gooding as the News' city editor.

"Mr. Zuckerman has cast doubt on that (Jan. 29) pledge by moving three of its top editors at the New York Post to three senior editor jobs at the New York Daily News, including the top editor's job," said Dorothy Gilliam, NABJ Vice President/Print.

"The New York Post is no one's sterling example of a newspaper that hires people of color. That raises serious questions about what will happen in the long run to the newspaper owner's commitment to fully diversify his newsroom." 10

Skepticism about Zuckerman's commitment to diversity carried over to a Feb. 10 community forum at New York University sponsored by the New York Association of Black Journalists.

The publisher told the crowd, "I want to work with you to rebuild the newspaper." Zuckerman's words were interrupted by jeers and shouts from fired Daily News workers.

Zuckerman flinched and occasionally bristled. But mostly he was controlled, making vague promises, (but) in the end, saying "trust me," wrote Dorothy Gilliam in a NABJ Journal commentary urging members to "Take a stand against Zuckerman."

Gilliam also wrote, "Mort Zuckerman may be every black journalist's nightmare. What he has done is audacious and offensive. In the annals of journalism there is no precedent for a new owner to christen his acquisition by disproportionately dismissing black journalists – two thirds of the African-American reporters on staff.

"When experienced black reporters are being shut out of the media, it is a crisis for every black journalist. If jobs at the New York Daily News are at risk, all our jobs may be at risk."

Across town at the New York Post, the Daily News' bitter rival was engaged in a bizarre ownership battle involving high stakes for blacks to report, edit, or even own, the newspaper.

In March, real estate developer Abe Hirschfeld assumed control of the New York Post after a decision by a federal bankruptcy judge.

Before Hirschfeld, Steven Hoffenberg, a debt collection entrepreneur, published the newspaper for seven weeks. But Hoffenberg lost control after his assets were frozen and the federal Securities and Exchange Commission filed investor fraud claims against Hoffenberg's Towers Financial Corporation.

Hoffenberg's editor was Pete Hamill, a veteran columnist and author. "In 1960," said Hamill, "I worked with Ted Poston (one of a handful of black journalists working in the white-owned press) at this paper. Thirty three years later, after he walked the back roads of Mississippi putting his life on the line, the fact that we don't have a single black reporter on the city desk is a f------ outrage." 11

When Hamill assumed the editor's post March 8, two black copy aides were promoted to reporter tryouts and two other black journalists were in the newsroom trying out. 12

Hamill lasted four days. Hours after Hirschfeld won the court decision, he fired Hamill then named Wilbert Tatum, publisher of the black-owned weekly New York Amsterdam News, as editor and co-publisher. The Harlem- based Amsterdam News was to continue publishing but also be inserted into the New York Post. Tatum said that development "will mean an opportunity for a newspaper that is not hostile to the aspirations of people of color and other ethnic groups."

The New York Post staff rebelled at the prospect of Hirschfeld ownership. The newspaper did not publish for a day. Staff members vilified Hirschfeld and Tatum in print through the week. 13

On March 26, Rupert Murdoch, the publishing mogul who bought the New York Post in 1976 and owned it until 1988, made a formal purchase offer before a bankruptcy judge. Creditors asked the judge to terminate Hirschfeld's management contract for non-payment of bills.

Hirschfeld and Tatum were out and Murdoch was allowed to run the newspaper for two months and work out terms for permanent ownership. 14

Reporting from Somalia
About two years after the 1991 Persian Gulf war between

Iraq vs. the U.S. and its allies, black journalists once again went overseas to Somalia to make a difference in news coverage.

In that east African country, famine plus anarchy equaled mass death and disaster. Since January 1991, when dictator Mohammed Said Barre was ousted, 1 million Somalis fled their homeland and faced starvation. 15

Heavily armed warlords – Barre among them – used food as a weapon, by starving rivals and by harassing and robbing international relief workers who tried to save the dying.

In September 1992, Walter Goodman, a white TV critic with The New York Times, noted the time it took for the American media to pay attention to the tragedy and wrote, "Perhaps if there were more black television producers and correspondents, the miseries of Africa might have seemed more pressing." 16

On Nov. 11, 1992, Sunni Khalid, foreign affairs reporter for National Public Radio, reported that the United States was considering sending troops to Somalia. In December 1992, the U.S. and other allies sent military units to Somalia to restore order – and journalists chased the story.

Once overseas, Khalid said "most journalists spent their time talking to other white Westerners, and the Somalis resented that. Most white journalists looked down on the Somalis as inferior people. I told them (journalists) the Somalis look down on you as (infidel)."

Khalid and Kenneth B. Noble, the New York Times' Abidjan (Ivory Coast) correspondent, wrote stories that dug deeper than their competitors. 17 Noble for example wrote about returning Somali health workers who were paid less than Westerners. Khalid interviewed a 17-year-old Somali girl who was making $350 a week selling gasoline. 18

Other black journalists headed overseas. They included Charlayne Hunter-Gault of the MacNeil/Lehrer NewsHour (PBS), Gary Reaves of WFAA-TV, Dallas; Arthur Fennell, of WCAU-TV, Philadelphia; Vernon Odom of WPVI-TV, Philadelphia; Lester Holt of WBBM-TV, Chicago; John Johnson of WABC-TV, New York; Ron Allen of ABC News, and print correspondents Keith Richburg and Mary Ann French, both of The Washington Post; Lennox Samuels of the Dallas Morning News; Leonard Greene of the Boston Herald and Nick Charles of the Cleveland Plain Dealer.

These journalists joined Wil Haygood, who had been in Somalia since October covering the turmoil for The Boston Globe. Haygood, Globe photographer Yunghi Kim and three relief workers were even caught in a surprise attack between rival warlords. They escaped and Haygood wrote a detailed Sunday front-page piece for the Globe. 19

Hunter-Gault, a veteran foreign correspondent of the 1991 Gulf War and the South Africa apartheid struggle in the 1980s, finished an exhausting book tour promoting her memoir about desegregating the University of Georgia in 1961. Hunter-Gault was tired, but determined to chase the Somalia story:

"I said, 'I have to go.' My challenge was to try to report it a different way and add some depth to what we didn't know."

She visited a small village where 2,000 people died. The correspondent reported the story by having many villagers speak in their own words.

"By the end of the visit," said Hunter-Gault, "The village elder came running to me saying, 'Wait. Wait. We want you to present the food to the village.'

"People who saw that piece back here (in the USA) said there wasn't a dry eye after watching it."

Fennell of WCAU-TV gave high five's to Somalis he met. Some natives called him brother and pointed to their skin. "We went deep into some villages and were the only ones there in some cases," said Fennell. "We were granted access to some areas that I know we would not have been able to get to had Somalis not felt a kinship with us. They told us that."

Mary Ann French of the Washington Post however found the Somalis color conscious: "Somalis do not consider themselves in the same boat as Bantu people, the ancestors of African-Americans. They see themselves as above that. That's a direct result of colonialism. You see that when average Somalis come into contact with American soldiers.

"The few Somalis of Bantu extraction are the descendants of long-ago slaves, and they are looked at as below the 95 percent ethnically homogenous Somalis."

African-American journalists who reported from Somalia brought home differing perspectives and contexts that explained why the mayhem in East Africa was complex. The U.N. took control of the multinational relief effort from the USA on May 4, 1993. America withdrew its peacekeeping forces March 25. 1994. [20]

In the USA, an NABJ affiliate raised $70,000 for Somalia famine relief. "Somalia Sunday," was two benefit events organized by the Dallas Fort Worth Association of Black Communicators and co-sponsored by the Somali community of North Texas and Muslim community of North Texas. [21]

"I was really surprised that more than 500 people took time not only to make a contribution but to attend the two events we sponsored," said John Yearwood, a Dallas Morning News staff writer.

Sports Journalism and the Color Line

During the winter professional baseball meetings in Dallas, the Rev. Jesse Jackson threatened a boycott of major league sports unless those industries broke up discriminatory hiring patterns. Jackson looked out into a virtual sea of whiteness −100 newspaper, TV and radio reporters recorded his words. After his announcement, he said: "We can play, but when it comes to interpreting and analyzing those actions (media executives) apparently believe only whites are capable of doing that." [22]

Jackson said his new Rainbow Commission for Fairness in Athletics would focus efforts on remedying the dearth of African-Americans in sports media, particularly the minimal numbers of blacks in management and on-air positions in print and broadcasting.

Skeptics dismissed Jackson's push as the civil rights leader's latest grandstanding move, but others were happy that Jackson turned the spotlight on sports media executives.

"You don't have to like Jesse, but you have to listen to him," said NABJ member and USA Today sports columnist Bryan Burwell. "If Jesse shines the light, it's up to us to keep it turned on."

In pro sports, 80 percent of the basketball, 70 percent of the football and 25 percent of the baseball athletes were black, yet the NABJ Sports Task Force reported these numbers on who wasn't playing in the press box:

• There were only three black sports editors among 1,500 daily newspapers, Justice Hill of the Fort Wayne, Ind. Journal-Gazette; Wade Moore of the Pine Bluff, Ark. Commercial and Allen Johnson of the Greensboro, N.C. News & Record.

• There were two other blacks in managerial sports positions at dailies.

• There were seven black sports columnists, including Burwell, William C. Rhoden of the New York Times, Michael Wilbon of the Washington Post, Terry Foster of the Detroit News and Terrence Moore of the Atlanta Journal Constitution. 23

• In broadcasting, Jim Stark of WSVN-TV Miami was believed to be the only black sports director in local television.

• In the big-league sports industry, which included three major networks and a fast-developing fourth (FOX), 28 football teams, 27 basketball teams, 26 baseball teams [that was about to add two more] and 300 Division I colleges, there were only about a dozen black play-by-play announcers. Greg Gumbel and James Brown, both of CBS, were well known and John Saunders and Mark Jones of ESPN were emerging new talents.

• Three professional sports franchises – the Detroit Pistons (NBA), Los Angeles Rams (NFL), and California Angeles (MLB) – employed black play-by-play announcers for over-the-air, cable or radio broadcasts.

Behind the camera or mic, the story remained bleak. Each of the three networks employed about a dozen sports producer-directors and each network had only one black. 24

"Sports journalism doesn't practice what it preaches," said Burwell. "Our sports editors criticize the old-boy network that operates in sports, but never turn those criticisms inward. If they did, they'd be embarrassed."

Since the late 1980s, the NABJ Sports Task Force worked extensively with the Associated Press Sports Editors (APSE) to make recommendations whenever there was an opening at a newspaper or TV station, reiterate the necessity of promoting reporters to major league beats and to columnists, and develop a pool of journalists for managerial positions. 25 Results were uneven. For example, 20 black reporters covered Super Bowl XXVII (27) in 1993; in 1984, only three covered Super Bowl XVIII (18).

The Freedom Forum put $75,000 toward creating a Freedom Forum Sports Journalism Institute designed to integrate newspaper sports departments. The APSE was to run a nine-week summer program for "a multicultural group" of 15 students from the class of 1994.

"In an industry constantly wrestling with issues of inclusiveness and diversity, the sports department remained the last true bastion of white males," said Allen H. Neuharth, Freedom Forum chairman and former Gannett Co. CEO.

Leon Carter, NABJ Sports Task Force chairman and an assistant sports editor with Newsday (Long Island, N.Y.), was an instructor. At the time he was on leave from his newspaper as journalist-in-residence at Norfolk State (Va.) University. In five years the sports institute trained 55 graduates. 26

School Days

Cleo Joffrion Allen read an op-ed article in her newspaper that so infuriated her that she traded the newsroom for a classroom.

The writer of the piece published in the Baton Rouge, La. State-Times wrote that he had been to a minority journalism job fair and could not find qualified candidates. Allen was a 1975 graduate of historically black Southern University and her education prepared her for 15 years of work as a reporter, then copy editor. She remembered fellow black college graduates who were now working at the State-Times, Newsweek magazine, or in public relations. Allen showed the op-ed piece to several colleagues. Why was this tired excuse still being bandied around to keep blacks out of the newsroom?, she wondered out loud.

Then Allen remembered that when she was a student, one instructor taught all the journalism courses at Southern's small journalism department and after she graduated, that instructor (Lucien Salvant) moved to Mississippi to become a weekly newspaper editor.

Allen also read that Southern's journalism department, plus other public college departments, were under pressure to become accredited in 1994 or face dissolution. She decided to become a change agent. Allen would leave her newspaper, earn a master's degree and teach journalism at Southern.

Allen's employer gave her $5,000 per semester award (Manship Fellowship) that helped with school costs. She completed her coursework with a 3.9 grade point average.

Allen applied to Southern and Ted White, a veteran journalist who just became chairman of the department, hired her. Allen sensed hostility from some faculty members. She represented change and tougher standards in the department.

Student hostility also was evident. Allen became known as the "Bitch" because she made them stick to deadlines, learn AP style and read the newspaper for current event quizzes. Many students had severe grammar and spelling deficiencies and Allen incorporated grammar lessons into her instruction. Some students dropped her classes and others said they'd just wait until she left Southern; they assumed she would not stay long.

Allen's struggle reaped rewards. Toward the end of her first semester many students changes their attitudes and their skills improved. Allen was able to place a student in a summer job that turned into a permanent position at the Alexandra, La., Town Talk, the newspaper where Allen began her career.

Two students attended the 1992 NABJ Detroit convention and apparently heard many of the lessons Allen preached because they were more receptive to her lectures that fall. One of those students even wrote a column for her student newspaper in which she echoed some of the comments Allen made about her work during a heated tete-a-tete a year ago. Allen's switch from newsroom to classroom was costly and arduous, yet she was optimistic that she was making a difference in preparing qualified students for journalism careers. 27

Columnist Breaks Barrier

In spring 1993, Bob Herbert became the first African-American op-ed page columnist at The New York Times. Herbert was a columnist and editorial board member of the New York Daily News and contributing correspondent for NBC News. 28

That same year, Los Angeles Times staff writer Ron Harris became "the local in-house columnist." Times management asked Harris to develop a column, months after the L.A. uprising revealed that the newspaper had no black columnists. He began writing pieces in January, however none of them passed muster with editor Shelby Coffey. Harris' unpublished columns, for example, covered why he put money in black-owned banks and criticized women who supported entertainers who called them "bitches and ho's."

Said Harris, "I'm becoming a big underground hit with the reporters at the L.A. Times," yet for the public's eyes, his copy remained sealed in the "velvet coffin," nickname for the newspaper notorious for indefinitely holding or spiking stories.

Chapter 6
Stepping into tomorrow

Convention organizers were optimistic about the Houston meeting. They had an issue-rich and talent laden-lineup:
• Mae Jemison, the first black woman astronaut, would appear;
• Ben Chavis, the new NAACP executive director; best-selling author Terry McMillan and law professor Lani Guinier were keynote speakers;
• Arsenio Hall, Morgan Freeman, Danny Glover and Alfre Woodard were to preview their movie "Bopha!"
• And the convention would open with a forum on hip-hop culture with hip hop poet Reg E. Gaines, Houston's 5th Ward Boyz and the Rev. Calvin Butts of New York's Abyssinian Baptist Church. 1

With the table set, would members come in droves?

Recognizing that many attendees came in conjunction with vacations, convention co-chairwoman Debra Martine-McGaughey said many events were scheduled to get conventioneers out of Westin Galleria twin hotels.

"We've got stuff here we want folks to see," said Martine-McGaughey, like the new Space Center Houston near the Johnson Space Center, and George Ranch Historical Park, "where you get to see demonstrations on how things were done in the West, way back when."

Visitors could also go to the Astrodome to see a Major League Baseball game or drive 45 minutes to the beach at Galveston Island.

The Houston and Atlanta chapters promised spectacular parties.

Said co-chairwoman Sheila Stainback: "If anything, it will be hard to sit in the lobby bar and talk to your friends. If you can't find something of interest each day, then you came only to hook up with somebody."

NABJ needed 1,700 people to attend in order for the convention to be a success, said Treasurer Jackie Greene. Resulting revenues of $334,000 from the four-day meeting would cover 60 percent of the association's operating costs.

Corporate underwriting remained tight despite a post-recession climate. Corporations, said Martine-McGaughey, "have definitely – if not closed their pocketbooks, they've certainly – narrowed the opening."

One bright exception was $25,000 from Time Warner to fund scholarships. 2

Chicago-based National Public Radio correspondent Cheryl Devall gave this account of the Houston convention July 21-25:

Nineteen ninety three turned out to be the year of the woman as the National Association of Black Journalists gathered in Houston.

NABJ had not, like the producers of this year's Academy Awards, chosen women as an official theme, but in ways ironic, infuriating and sometimes triumphant, the theme stuck.

Dorothy (Butler) Gilliam of The Washington Post was elected president, succeeding Sidmel Estes-Sumpter, NABJ's first woman chief executive.

Also present however, was an undertow of contempt toward the idea that women are as intelligent and outspoken as men – and a highlight of the convention was evidence that many women and men resisted the pull of that undertow.

The tone was set at the opening session (Wednesday, July 21) on hip-hop culture during which Houston native and Geto Boys star Bushwick Bill let fly with references to women as "bitches" and "ho's" – prompting many sister colleagues and a few brothers to walk out. When pressed (by Estes-Sumpter) to apologize, the rapper explained that he was "only speaking (his) mind and being (him)self."

Some of the women afterward chided the men on the panel for their failure to challenge the speaker. But also later, a man who had been there suggested that the women who had taken offense were in need of a reality check. "If they can't deal with it here," he remarked, "how are they going to deal with it on the street?" 3

The question might have also been directed toward those men in the room who considered themselves role models to African-American youth.

The battle lines were drawn more sharply in a session entitled "Dis' and Tell," which included panelists Wayne Dawkins, author of "Black Journalists: The NABJ Story" (published four months before the convention); David Hilliard, author of "This Side of Glory," a first-person history of the Black Panther Party; and Kristin Scott-Taylor, author of "The First to Speak: A Woman of Color Inside the White House."

But the heavy artillery was aimed at Jill Nelson, a panelist whose new memoir "Volunteer Slavery: My Authentic Negro Experience," told of former NABJ President DeWayne Wickham's alleged, patently sexist attempt at campaign humor during the 1987 convention in Miami.

At the author's session, two former NABJ presidents, Les Payne and Vernon Jarrett, demanded that Nelson explain why she had named the participants in that episode but had not named in her book all the men she had described having sex with. Without flinching, Nelson replied, "It's my book, and my story. I wrote it and I own it." 4 Earlier in the session Nelson had noted that many male critics had admitted discomfort with her open discussion of sexuality.

Copies of her book sold briskly throughout the convention and square red and black "Volunteer Slavery" buttons sprouted on many lapels like badges of allegiance.

Another woman author, Terry McMillan, was dissed in absentia shortly after she addressed a packed W.E.B. DuBois luncheon. An NABJ founder, Vernon Jarrett, who had been drafted as devil's advocate on a panel about black, lesbian and gay issues, broke from his diatribe against the other panelists to note that, on the 90th anniversary of DuBois' masterwork "The Souls of Black Folk," NABJ had "wasted its time on four women sitting around waiting to exhale," – a reference to the title of McMillan's best-selling novel. 5

A gasp emerged from the listeners who thought they'd had their fill of Jarrett's self-described intolerance toward an equation of black and gay civil rights earlier in the session, when he asserted that many black gay men had chosen their orientation "because they couldn't deal with the new, aggressive black woman."

Joe Davidson, another founding member of NABJ, echoed the attitudes of many in the audience when he approached the microphone asking, "Could you explain what you mean, Vernon? Perhaps I misunderstood you."

One voice that made itself clearly understood belonged to Lani Guinier, President Bill Clinton's former nominee for assistant attorney general for civil rights. More of a strategist than a victim after a high-powered right wing-generated public relations campaign pressured Clinton to drop her, the University of Pennsylvania law professor said the forces against her nomination succeeded in large part because there is not enough racial or philosophical diversity in the nation's newsrooms, and because "too many journalists are stenographers to power." Guinier urged black journalists to "redefine what it means to be fair" and to join her "in a national conversation about race and racism."

That conversation has been stifled in the newsrooms where African-American journalists work, according to an NABJ Print Task Force study released at the convention. "Muted Voices: Fear and Frustration in the Newsroom," indicated a wide gap between the good intentions of white news managers and aspirations of black journalists. William Boyd, an associate at the Poynter Institute, characterized the study's conclusion this way: "Ninety percent of the white people are saying they're committed. Ninety percent of the black people are saying they ain't. But we're not even talking about the same thing." 6

Houston was the first NABJ convention for Frank Blethen, publisher of the Seattle Times. He called "Muted Voices" very useful, well packaged and said it should be a catalyst for creating dialogue and understanding between African-American journalists and their employers. Blethen also said he was "blown away by how political NABJ is. That did surprise me. If that (politics) was all that was there, I would have been disappointed. It's nice to see somebody is providing the leadership and some substance." 7

For Joe Grimm, a Detroit Free Press editor and recruiter, Houston was his third convention: "If I had to bet right now, I'd say we're going to have a hire out of this convention. I spent most of my time at the job fair and talking to prospects. It was very profitable, time well spent. We interviewed 70 applicants. Several are interviewing for positions right now. We did find some people who are well qualified for some hard-to-fill jobs, assistant editors, graphic arts, a few promising interns.

"I heard other recruiters complaining that they were not talking to many people. But if you look around, they were sitting there reading magazines and not getting around to get to know people. I had people out looking for people (in places) other than the job fair."

Grimm exemplified a white editor working earnestly to get to know black journalists and dig deep for talent.

Meanwhile, Richard Leiby, a white editor with the Washington Post and first time convention visitor, revealed his discomfort living as a "minority" for a week. Leiby described his feelings in his Aug. 1 Post article, "White like me." First, Leiby took some offense at Estes-Sumpter's criticism of the hip-hop performer who had called black women "bitches and hos." The president told the crowd it was important that blacks not denigrate each other: "We cannot dog each other out (by now, Leiby writes, he learns that 'dog out' are synonyms for 'dis') because if we dog each other out then *we don't need the white man to do it for us!* "

"The hundreds of people around me are applauding, cheering, chanting 'That's right.' I suddenly feel blonder, paler and more thin-lipped than I have ever been in my life ... Of the 1,400 journalists here, perhaps 100 are white, most of them corporate recruiters like me. For four days we hear black icons ... talk about the perpetual color line in America and the pain of racism.

"NABJ is more than a professional and social event: it is as one attendee tells me, a 'primal scream.' For here, for once, the usual racial ratios are reversed. It is 14 blacks to every white."

Leiby closes his essay this way: "Flying back to Washington, I'm in first class, courtesy of my employer. There are a dozen white faces in first class, one black. I settle comfortably into my seat. For some reason, I feel like I'm already home."

Washington Post columnist Donna Britt responded two days later on Aug. 3 in a piece titled "Dealin' as a minority for a week."

Leiby, wrote Britt, "Failed to notice or at least to mention, stuff that another white recruiter found striking at a previous convention: 'I was surrounded by thousands of smart, well spoken and talented black journalists,' said the other recruiter, 'which showed me that the usual complaint of newspaper executives – 'we can't find qualified blacks' – was bull. I also noticed it at the first conference I had been to where people seemed truly passionate about what they were there for.

'But you know what really got me? For the first time, I knew how it felt to be a minority. It blew my mind.'"

"Leiby's too," wrote Britt. "it wasn't until he was comfortably ensconced in mostly white first class on a plane back to Washington that he felt he was 'home.'

"These days, the word 'entitlement' is increasingly used to describe programs helpful to minorities, women and the aged, but Leiby's piece hinted at a discomfiture over not receiving what some white guys feel entitled to: constant consideration, being made to feel comfortable everywhere they go – even at a black journalists convention." Britt closed her piece this way: "However uncomfortable, his authentic Caucasian experience lasted less than a week. Black folks will be dealin' with this nonsense forever."

In official business, NABJ members re-elected Sheila Stainback as vice president/broadcast and elected Jacqueline Jones as vice president/print. Secretary Vanessa Williams, Treasurer Jackie Jones and Parliamentarian Angelo Henderson, ran unopposed for their positions on the national board.

The membership also reversed last year's decision to admit public relations professionals as full voting members, but grandfathered in those who became full members during the past year. The passage of another referendum on this year's ballot will allow managers from the business or non-news gathering side of publications and broadcast operations to become non-voting associate members of NABJ.

Total attendance was 1,950 according to the August/September NABJ Journal. The number exceeded the 1,700 people organizers projected they would need to raise revenues to run the association year-round.

There was a tragic death in the NABJ family immediately after convention week. Toni Yvonne Joseph, 31, a Dallas Morning News reporter, was not in Houston for the convention but her presence was felt; she coordinated a Saturday breakfast for two dozen Columbia University J-school alumni. Joseph was in the wedding party of a friend that weekend. The day after the convention ended, Monday, July 26, Joseph died from a massive heart attack.

Joseph was one of the nation's leading chroniclers of issues concerning African-Americans. In addition to her Morning News reporting, Joseph was a frequent contributor to Emerge magazine. While her focus was on African-Americans, Joseph wrote about music and literature, AIDS and adoption, finance and fishing, the plight of black farmers in East Texas, and the struggles of parents trying to control their children.

Joseph was a contributor to a Morning News series on violence against women around the world, writing about the ancient African ritual female circumcision, AKA mutilation by Western critics.

The next year, Joseph was a posthumous co-winner of a Pulitzer Prize for International reporting.

Bob Maynard, R.I.P.

Several weeks later, on Aug. 16, Robert C. "Bob" Maynard, 56, died after a battle with prostate cancer. Maynard's epitaph would be first black to be publisher (and before that, editor) of a major metropolitan newspaper, the Oakland (Calif.) Tribune from 1979 to 1992, when the paper was sold to Alameda Newspaper Group. 8

"For a decade, he was best known as the only black owner and publisher of a major daily paper," said NABJ President Dorothy Gilliam. "But in a lesser known role, he affected the entire field of American journalism."

In 1977, Maynard and his wife Nancy Hicks were co-founders of the Institute for Journalism Education, an organization instrumental in breaking down color barriers in the 1980s. The Maynards remained involved with California-based IJE over the years, helping the program integrate newsrooms nationwide by recruiting, training and placing African-Americans, Asians and Latinos in reporting, editing and management jobs. 9

Maynard's Tribune won a Pulitzer Prize for photography during the 1989 Bay Area earthquake. In addition to publishing, Maynard wrote a syndicated column and served on the Associated Press board of directors from 1985-91. He was the 1981 NABJ co-journalist of the year, sharing that award with Max Robinson. 10

Downsized 'Salute to Excellence'

At the fall board meeting in Cleveland, NABJ officers anticipated adjustments they would have to make in order to stage a successful "Unity" convention with Hispanic, Asian American and Native American journalists in July 1994. NABJ voted to significantly cut back its multi-media awards program, a tradition since 1985. 11

Many of the prime Unity '94 time spots were going to be joint association activities. Instead of the customary multi-media, Oscar-like treatment, the proposed alternative was to publish "a very classy and detailed book of the winners and winning entries." New England regional director Gregory Moore said advertising or underwriting could cover the cost of printing and a profit could be generated.

Besides the UNITY '94 time constraints and coalition commitments, NABJ was rethinking the cost of its convention awards programs. The tab had been as much as $65,000 and NABJ paid most or all of it.

Was such cost worth it? "People don't go or they leave early," said Northeast regional director Arthur Fennell. "The program has been too long, too grandiose and too sloppy. Winners don't even show up and people walk away frustrated. We need to scale down and make it less expensive. This year with the Unity format is an opportunity to step away and reformat." 12

Racism Raining Down

That fall, several ugly racial references in mass media fell on African-Americans' heads like acid rain, wrote President Dorothy Gilliam in an NABJ Journal column that inventoried three assaults:

• An AT&T newsletter showing people on various continents making phone calls made an exception for Africa. That continent showed a gorilla with a phone to depict clients. 13

• In show business, actor Ted Danson, ("Cheers") made up in blackface with exaggerated white lips, told nigger jokes and also joked about Whoppi Goldberg's genitalia at the actress' Friar's Club roast. 14

• And the New York Daily News reported that NBC Nightly News executive producer Jeff Gralnick at a news meeting referred to Somali warlord Mohammed Farrah Aidid as "an educated jungle bunny."

In a letter to the New York ABJ, Gralnick acknowledged making the remarks, but said he uttered the words in this context:

"In a staff meeting, I was pressing the point on why I thought it mandatory that Nightly News do a substantive piece of reporting on Gen. Aidid. During that presentation, I made the point that there was far more to the general than the American public understood and were they to understand his full background, they would not be as surprised as many seemed at his ability to confound both the United States and the United Nations.

"Further, and this is where I got into trouble, I said that part of the misunderstanding of Aidid was based in the worst kind of racial and racist stereotyping. I then added, like it or not, for much of America, if you put together the words Aidid, Africa and warlord, they are going to say (the offending phrase) and this is the kind of attitude we have to fight." 15

Gilliam wrote, "Why does this pattern of publicly degrading African-Americans continue to occur in this country? While the easy answer may be that racism is alive and well, I suspect there is a deeper meaning. For all the racial static, misinformation and scapegoating that occur in America, there is very little honest and constructive discussion about race and racism – except in the midst of racially charged situations."

Gilliam rallied members to pro-actively re-examine race and racism in the context of the 1990s and recognize that "this acid rain of insults that keeps falling upon our heads is our painful reminder that we must muster up our courage and do more." 16

South African Exchange

In November, five NABJ members traveled to South Africa in an exchange program funded with a $100,000 Freedom Forum grant.

The five were: Carole Carmichael of the Seattle Times; Phyllis Crockett of National Public Radio; Michael Ottey of the Oregonian; Barbara Rodgers of KPIX-TV San Francisco and John Yearwood of the Dallas Morning News. They would spend a month overseas and bring a group of South African journalists to the USA in early 1994.

This exchange was a continuation of NABJ's aggressive Africa Outreach. Yet the plum assignments for a handful of U.S. journalists was troubling because the process was closed to dozens of journalists who might have wanted to apply if they knew they could apply. NABJ board members questioned the lack of advance notice by the Africa Outreach Committee that included five former association presidents.

Two weeks before departure, five participants and an alternate were selected. Selection criteria included seeking "a diverse group that represents an appropriate gender balance, different parts of the country, varying levels of editorial responsibility, a mix of print and broadcast, and a broad array of story proposals."

Still, said West Coast regional director Andrea Ford, "No one in my region knew anything about this or the selection criteria." President Gilliam explained the hastiness: "We were under real time constraints. It was a one-shot deal with the possibility to expand the program. I felt it was incumbent on me to move or lose the $100,000." There was also urgency to get the U.S. journalists to South Africa a few months before that nation's first multi-racial election in spring 1994. [17]

Election Mischief
Shortly after the November elections, Republican strategist Edward J. Rollins bragged to about 20 Washington journalists that the campaign of newly elected New Jersey Gov. Christine Todd Whitman spent $500,000 paying off black ministers, and Democratic Party members, to suppress the black vote. When Rollins' claim hit the newspapers, he backpedaled and said he made the story up.

Said Herb Lowe, who covered Southern New Jersey for the Philadelphia Inquirer, "The media were too quick to believe Rollins and weren't quick to believe he was telling a lie.

"You couldn't hide $500,000 in cash," Lowe also said. "People would have talked about it." Nonetheless, he said, "There was an effort to uncover every stone." Some ministers' backgrounds were checked for shady behavior and deacons and choir members were interviewed. "After a while it got to be extremely frustrating," said Newsday minority affairs reporter Monte Young, "Because you were asking the same questions every day." Added Associated Press N.J. statehouse reporter Darleen Superville, "After three weeks, four weeks, none of the reporters could find anyone who had been approached." [18]

page 96

Also in New Jersey at election time, the editor of the Burlington County Times resigned, apparently because he was hung out to dry by his publisher over an election story with racial overtones. The newspaper ran a story before the election that Priscilla Anderson, an African-American assemblywoman, missed 59 working days as a high school guidance counselor in Trenton because of her duties as a first-term state legislator.

After the news story, a Times editorial criticized Anderson and the paper did not endorse the legislator from Willingboro, a predominantly black middle-class suburb that was also the newspaper home base.

Anderson lost and prominent members of the black community complained. Publisher Sandra Hardy called a breakfast meeting of community leaders and at that meeting she criticized Bill Newill's news judgment and asked him to apologize to the arriving community members. Three African-Americans who worked in non-newsroom positions at the BCT listened to Hardy's comments and said Newill felt her criticism of him was inappropriate. He resigned the next day.

Was the publisher's public flogging of the editor cover for a greater sin? No people of color worked in the BCT newsroom, a sin of omission deemed inconceivable by African-Americans who were supportive of Newill's tenure as editor. 19

By Design

Rob King, graphics director and illustrator at The Courier-Journal in Louisville, Ky. was pleasantly surprised when he arrived in Detroit in November to help conduct a graphics workshop and was greeted by a crowd. About 140 visual journalists participated in the first Detroit Design Conference for Minority Journalists.

Organizers – The Detroit News, in conjunction with NABJ, the Asian American Journalists Association and National Association of Hispanic Journalists – planned for about 60 attendees so the doubled attendance was very encouraging. Detroit News assistant managing editor Dale Peskin called the conference "an instant network of people with the same needs and jobs who didn't know (each other) existed." Peskin also said that newspaper design and graphics "represent the area of most growth for newspapers but the numbers of minorities were incredibly low."

For example, minorities represented 9.4 percent of daily newspaper journalists, according to the American Society of Newspaper Editors but reporters in that group outnumbered artists by 30-1.

Conference organizers did a good job of spreading the word about opportunities in newspaper design by writing to all minority journalism associations and sending letters to universities with schools of journalism and also writing to about 800 newsrooms. [20]

Chapter 7
Unity '94

In California, three major changes occurred involving black editors and publishers that were celebratory, unfortunate and honorary.

At the end of 1993, Jay Harris was named publisher of the San Jose Mercury News (270,000 circulation), Knight-Ridder Co.'s lead West Coast newspaper.

Harris, 45, joined Knight-Ridder in 1985 as executive editor of the Philadelphia Daily News. Since 1989, he was vice president/operations, based at Knight-Ridder headquarters in Miami and was responsible for the company's newspaper operations in nine cities. For years the question was when Harris would become the top executive at one of Knight-Ridder's 29 daily newspapers. The answer was Feb. 1, 1994. [1]

The unfortunate news was the sudden resignation Dec. 1 of Pearl Stewart as editor of the Oakland Tribune after one year on the job as the first black woman editor of a major metropolitan daily.

Stewart cited irreconcilable differences with boss David Burgin, editor-in-chief of Alameda Newspaper Group. The Tribune experienced numerous traumas over the years, including staff layoffs, its sale by the Maynards to Alameda Newspapers in 1992, more staff layoffs and declining circulation from 101,333 in 1992 to about 75,000 in 1993.

Burgin protested that he took a chance in hiring Stewart, a veteran with no top-level editing experience, yet he was being portrayed as the heavy in Bay Area news accounts. Burgin said he offered Stewart other jobs inside the newspaper, but she declined and left. [2]

Dec. 2, one day after Stewart's resignation, came the honorary news: The Institute for Journalism Education in Oakland was renamed the Robert C. Maynard IJE. Maynard and eight other journalists co-founded the institute in 1977 after moving the Summer Program for Minority Journalists from Columbia University in New York to Cal-Berkeley. IJE later moved to Oakland.

Through 1989, IJE trained and placed 206 journalists of color at daily newspapers – more than any single U.S. institution – and counted among its 600 graduates Pulitzer Prize winners and newspaper executives. 3

"For the first time, a journalistic institute with national stature bears the name of a person of color," said A. Stephen Montiel, institute president. "The name Robert C. Maynard becomes part of ours at a time when there is an urgent need in the news industry for courage, clear thinking and constructive discussion about diversity and portrayal issues." 4

Gender Barriers Fall

In March, USA Today correspondent Jessica Lee became the first African-American woman and first woman of color to become a member of the elite Washington, D.C. Gridiron Club. In 1972, Carl Rowan became the first black member. Women were barred from membership until 1975 when activist women journalists protested.

The club, limited to 60 members, "roasted" presidents and other politicians at annual dinners since 1885.

Another African-American woman journalist first was Sharon Farmer being hired as a White House photographer. Farmer and three other photographers documented every public appearance of President Bill Clinton and First Lady Hillary Rodham Clinton. Farmer free-lanced many years for the Washington Post and her photos impressed the White House. Ironically, her work did not land her a staff position at the newspaper despite repeated attempts. Instead, Farmer managed a photo store in D.C. Some of her memorable photos were published in the image book "Songs of My People." Among those images were a series of shots of a 97-year-old black woman doing the hula hoop. 5

Bee Gets Stung

In California, the Sacramento Bee newspaper was stung by harsh criticism of its Feb. 4 editorial page cartoon showing two hooded Klansmen, one of them holding a newspaper with a recent quote attributed to Louis Farrakhan that said, "you can't be racist by talking – only by acting." The Klansman on the right said to the other, "That nigger makes a lot of sense."

The Bee and parent company McClatchy newspapers was criticized by the media watch committee of the Sacramento Black Journalists Association. "The use of the word 'nigger' was not appropriate – given its brutal historical significance – especially since another word could have been used," said the SBJA statement. Also, members of the Sacramento community canceled subscriptions and boycotted the paper.

Many critics were disturbed by the use of the racial epithet in the cartoon. Yet, did the critics understand cartoonist Dennis Renault's use of irony, not humor, in the cartoon?

Of course words and talking, not simply "actions," could be perceived as racist, as the firestorm over the editorial cartoon confirmed. The Bee printed an apology four days later stating: "The cartoon was intended to be a reaffirmation of our stand against bigotry. Unfortunately, that anti-racism message has been lost in the ensuing controversy. And for that we are sincerely sorry." [6]

Black Columnists Under Fire

Derrick Jackson's Wednesday and Sunday Boston Globe op-ed column was called "the angry black fist pounding reader's breakfast table." Jackson's column had been running in the Globe since 1988 and he was a two-time NABJ columnist of the year. In February 1994, the power of Jackson's journalistic fist faced decline. Globe management changed the op-ed lineup. That meant dropping some staff columnists but keeping Jackson and moving his Sunday column to Saturday (and Wednesday switched to Tuesday).

That meant instead of reading Jackson on the most-read day of the week (814,000 circulation) he was switched to one of the lowest (483,000).

In response the Globe received about 80 letters of protest from black and white readers. In March, a small contingent led by activist Ruth Batson met with editor David Greenway and publisher William O. Taylor. Batson and others said Jackson's reassignment could send a negative message to the black community.

Greenway explained that by opening up the op-ed page, more local leaders and experts, including people of color, could be heard. But Sidney Holloway, a member of the group that met with the Globe bosses, said the other voices were not an acceptable substitute for "a trained, seasoned, award-winning journalist like Derrick Jackson." Holloway also said that "Strong black male writers historically have not been maintained at the Globe," and some of them "have gone on to very successful careers elsewhere, so obviously it wasn't their competence or the quality of their work that was in question. It was some inability of the Globe to maintain them." Holloway apparently was referring to Michael Frisby who departed for the Wall Street Journal and Ken Cooper who moved to the Washington Post.

Greenway promised to try the op-ed changes for six months then reassess. Jackson supporters continued writing protest letters. 7

In New York City, Earl Caldwell, a columnist at the Daily News since 1979, left the newspaper because of a dispute with his editor over the content in a column. In dispute that April was whether Caldwell, 52, was fired or he resigned. On April 12, editorial page editor Arthur Browne refused to print Caldwell's column about a Queens police officer under investigation for allegedly raping five black livery (taxicab) drivers.

During an argument about the decision, Caldwell said that Browne told him he was "through" at the newspaper. Browne denied firing Caldwell and in a prepared statement said, the disputed column was "patently unfair and did not meet Daily News standards. Earl was not fired. However, he has not communicated with the Daily News despite our efforts and he did not file a column for Friday's paper." 8

Caldwell answered that he did not file a column because he did not receive his regular Thursday morning call from his editors. Representatives from NABJ and its New York City affiliate chapter met with News publisher Mort Zuckerman on May 4. And in a follow-up letter signed by Dorothy Gilliam and Yanick Rice, they said "we are outraged by your silencing of one of New York City's strongest black voices." A year ago NABJ officials and local activists met with the publisher to protest layoffs of experienced black journalists at the Daily News.

Caldwell, finished with the Daily News after nearly 15 years, toured black colleges, published a book a year later and talked with investors about launching a global telecommunication operation. 9

In July of 1994, Gregory L. Moore was promoted to managing editor of the Boston Globe. Moore succeeded Helen Donovan, who ascended to executive editor of New England's leading newspaper. Since joining the Globe in 1986, Moore, 39, steadily advanced in a number of editing assignments: assistant metro editor, assistant managing editor and deputy managing editor. Said editor Matthew Storin, "Greg is an unusual mixture of a guy driven to excellence yet also a nice guy of world-class proportions. He is extremely well read and well informed and he gets around town well, so that he's often bringing in good news tips. The bottom line though is this: If I turn something over to him, I know it will be done well. We're lucky to have him."

Moore's promotion was closely watched because the Globe newsroom had been the scene of racial unrest. For example, a white reporter was put on unpaid leave for anonymously faxing a letter to the competing newspaper, to complain about assignments or raises given to black reporters. And Moore was the editor who supervised coverage of the Charles Stuart racial hoax case.

Storin told his staff this about Moore's promotion: "This is a high-profile job we've given him, and when I announced it, I presumed that some people might wonder if he got the promotion because he's a person of color. I said, 'Sure, in a way he did. If you had someone that good and could also add to the diversity of your senior staff, you'd be crazy not to promote him.' People understand what I mean, because they know he's that good." 10

In Milwaukee on a cold night in late March, the NBA Portland Trailblazers finished playing the hometown Bucks and visiting players Clyde Drexler and Rod Strickland were congratulating Garry Howard, a sports journalist. The players learned that Howard was named sports editor of the Milwaukee Journal. That made Howard the only African-American editor of a newspaper in a major league city. Milwaukee was home of the Bucks, Brewers (MLB) and Green Bay Packers (NFL).

Strickland greeted Howard because a dozen years ago they competed in basketball on New York City playgrounds. Howard grew up in the Bronx and was mentored by retired NBA star Nate "Tiny" Archibald.

Drexler sought out the man who brought Howard to Milwaukee from the Philadelphia Inquirer and congratulated him. Journal Managing Editor Martin Kaiser was surprised by the greeting. Drexler told him, "Look, Mr. Kaiser, you've made a bold step," and the editor seemed almost taken aback.

Kaiser explained, "I didn't go out to find a black sports editor just to say we have a black sports editor. I was looking for someone who knew good writing, and Garry's name came up. Some of the top sports writers in the business spoke highly of Garry. Some editor brought his name up. Some people said he was good with reporters and writers.

"Garry's credentials are tremendous. He knows writing, knows people, has enthusiasm, is a hard worker. It's unfair to say he was hired because he was black. That's ridiculous."11

True, but the athletes were keenly aware that though African-Americans dominate pro and collegiate sports and were even making breakthroughs in coaching and sports management African-American sports writers and editors were conspicuously absent.

"Considering that so many athletes in sports are black," said Howard, "diversity in sports departments is almost a joke."

When Howard assumed his post in May, there were six other black sports editors nationally, in Greensboro, N.C., Fort Wayne, Ind., Dayton, Ohio, Shreveport, La. and two Arkansas newspapers.

Before coming to Milwaukee, Howard coordinated Winter Olympics coverage for the Inquirer. At the Journal (circulation of 216,000 daily and 482,000 Sunday) the paper began staffing major events it normally sidestepped, such as the Indianapolis 500 and Stanley Cup Finals. Howard was making bold changes. "The hardest thing to do in this business," he said, "is to get the editors and writers to work together to produce the best possible story. That's what I have to get done." 12

O.J. Simpson, Murder, Race and Media

In June the slain bodies of two white persons, Nicole Brown Simpson and male friend Ronald Goldman, were found in Los Angeles and those discoveries launched a media frenzy that would last for more than a year. The prime suspect was a black male superstar: O.J. Simpson.

This case had every possible element for saturated media coverage: the interracial marriage of a glamorous California blonde and a black NFL superstar turned consumer product pitchman (Hertz); the dead white male as reputed lover of Simpson's former wife, stoking his murderous rage; shock that Orenthal James Simpson, a figure perceived as non-threatening to most whites and a tepid hero/role model to many blacks, was linked to mayhem, despite O.J. and Nicole's record of violent domestic abuse, well known to insiders in Southern California.

The temperature of the case surged hotter when Simpson, sought by police on an arrest warrant, led authorities on a bizarre slow-speed car chase on the Santa Monica Freeway on a Friday evening, about the time that the New York Knicks were playing the Houston Rockets in an NBA Championship round game. 13 That police pursuit of Simpson's white Ford Bronco garnered the highest TV news ratings since coverage of the Gulf War three years earlier in 1991. 14

Surprisingly, for many newspeople and consumers, the first week after the June 11 slayings did not produce the assumed racial hysteria of a case involving a black male suspected of assaulting or killing a white female. Was O.J.'s fame and popularity a shield? Pundits and consumers gave conflicting opinions on whether the media was obsessed or more even-handed than in the past on the racial angle until a June 27 cover of Time magazine became the lightning rod for debate about Simpson, murder, race and media performance.

Time ran a "photo illustration" of Simpson's police mug shot and considerably darkened his face, making the suspect look more sinister.

Rival Newsweek magazine put Simpson on its cover too, but chose the undoctored police mug, showing a brown complexioned defendant. The race issue was out of the closet. 15

"There was no conscious intention to make O.J.'s skin appear darker than it is or make him look any guiltier than he may be," said Time's art director Arthur Hochstein.

Answered Sheila Stainback, an NABJ vice president, "African-Americans are particularly sensitive to complexion. Why did we have to be darker? I think it plays into the whole menacing black male portrayal."

And President Gilliam said in a statement a day later, "[t]he question that must be asked is how does darkening and shadowing this photograph serve the reader?

"Tampering with a photograph in a criminal case is even more serious. The cover appears to be a conscious effort to make Simpson look evil and macabre, to sway the opinion of the reader to becoming fixated on his guilt."

Simpson represented the third time that African-Americans were featured on Time's cover in three years. Before him Clarence Thomas and Anita Hill appeared jointly in a 1991 edition, and minister Louis Farrakhan made the cover in February. 16

"I have looked at thousands of covers over the years and chosen hundreds. I have never been so wrong about how one would be received," wrote Time Managing Editor James Gaines in a "To our readers letter" in the issue after the O.J.

cover (July 4). "To the extent that this caused offense to anyone, I deeply regret it." 17

Unified by Drums

In a powerful opening ceremony inside the darkened Georgia World Congress Center in Atlanta, dancers from four cultures told their peoples' stories to the beating of drums. Amid the swirl of sound and colors, the procession included Chinese lion dancers, Mexican Mariachis and South African drummers. 18 Audience members, some momentarily confused upon receiving drumsticks when entering the ballroom, found themselves swept away into a crescendo of commonality, punctuated by comments from the presidents of each association. 19

"The drum symbolizes the unity and rhythm of all nations," said Paul DeMain, president of both the Native American Journalist Association and Unity '94. "It's beat ties musical notes together. Today, this gathering unites our people."

A convention that was six years in the making was budgeted at more than $1 million and attracted about 6,000 African-American, Latino, Asian and Native American journalists, an unprecedented assembly. 20

The ceremony set the tone for nearly a week of lively discussion – not only about what journalists of color had in common and could learn from one another, but also about ways these journalists impeded each other's progress and perpetuated misconceptions and stereotypes that divided their communities. "Coverage of our communities should not be limited to dance or dysfunction," Creek/Cherokee Gary Fife, host of "Heartbeat Alaska" told a plenary session on myths and stereotypes. "America knows more about our past and dead ancestors than it does about us today."

Fife and Tritia Toyota, a Japanese-American anchor at KCBS-TV in Los Angeles, both urged the plenary to tell about the full diversity of Native and Asian-American communities. Toyota, noting that her family has been in the United States for four generations, reminded the journalists that many Asian-Americans are also recent immigrants, and that the news media should reflect both experiences. "We're talking about class, we're talking about economic differences," Toyota said. "You just can't simplify." 21

Workshops sponsored by Unity '94 and the four associations attempted to steer journalists away from simple conclusions about their complex experiences in this nation. As Ray Suarez of National Public Radio remarked, "We (journalists) do drive-bys too, but we do them with cameras."

Panelists sought to debunk commonly held perceptions of Asian religions, to explore the similarities and differences among Latinos/Hispanics from a variety of cultures, to confront the fact that journalists of color do not always stand up for one another in their newsrooms – and to expose the tensions that can arise when managers of color have to be tough on "their own." Rather than blaming the dominant culture for the perpetuation of all racial tensions and stereotypes, journalists took the opportunity to challenge themselves. "I think we have to not be afraid to go to the Native American communities and say, 'I don't know a damn thing about you. Teach me something,'" said James Garcia of the Austin American-Statesman. "That's part of our responsibility."

It was the kind of discussion for which participants like Dawn Yoshitake came to Unity. Yoshitake, a finance writer for the Orange County Register, said she was eager to talk frankly about cultural differences and the hard work it takes to bridge them. "I wonder where it will propel itself from here," Yoshitake mused between workshops. "I hope we won't just go back to our jobs and lose touch with one another."

For many people at the convention, the issue was not losing touch but making contact with the thousands of friends, colleagues, potential employers or sources gathered for Unity '94. Cheryl Devall recalled when all of NABJ, less than 400 people, fit in the New Orleans Fairmont Hotel with room to spare for its 1983 convention. Eleven years later the immensity of the joint event seemed like a problem many organizations would love to have.

Size came close to spoiling the event. Perhaps because none of the Unity organizers had worked on such a scale before, there were inevitable shortages, hassles and frayed nerves. A surge of on-site registrations Wednesday night (hours after the afternoon opening ceremony) caused convention schedules and souvenir attaches to run out sometime Thursday, forcing the registration staff to substitute photocopies for the glossy 124-page guidebook and bag benefactor The New York Times had to rush down some generic navy blue totes, minus the business card folios that became the most prized freebie in this networking crowd. 22

Thursday's luncheon was also swamped, with 4,800 people straining to hear former UN Ambassador and Atlanta Mayor Andrew Young over an inadequate sound system as they dined on lukewarm servings of chicken breasts with picante sauce.

A large water spill in the Georgia World Congress Center caused a delay. Also, Young was pinch hitting for President Bill Clinton, who did not attend as planned because he was tied up in health reform issues. Clinton addressed the next day's luncheon via satellite. 23

Unity '94 spokesman Lloyd LaCuesta of KTVU-TV in Oakland tried to explain the mishaps. "We are a victim of our own success," he said. "We had more people than we expected ... We don't have a previous (attendance) record." 24

Anticipated demand for this convention caused planners to spread activities between the cavernous Georgia World Congress Center and three hotels. Even with the continuous shuttle buses between sites, the sprawl kept participants from sampling a variety of workshops sponsored by the four journalists' associations.

It was hard to even play catch-up on tape, because only the events at the convention center and in the Westin Hotel (NABJ headquarters) were recorded on audiocassette. Only at the order desk did people find out that most NAJA, NAHJ and AAJA workshops had not been recorded.

Given the hurdles by day, nighttime became the right time for many cross-cultural exchanges. All the Unity organizations were well represented at the AAJA Karaoke party (which featured a now legendary star turn by Los Angeles Times Editor Shelby Coffey III), the NAHJ Salsa Bash and the NABJ Grown Folks Funk Jam.

A number of Unity members joined NAJA members on a trek to New Echota, Ga., about 60 miles north of Atlanta. There they placed a plaque to commemorate the first Native American newspaper in the United States, The Cherokee Phoenix, first published in 1828 in Cherokee and English. Elias Boudinot, a Cherokee, was banned from publishing his newspaper in Georgia. The newspaper and the community it served were destroyed when whites drove Cherokees westward from Georgia in the march known as the "Trail of Tears."

Two summers ago in 1992 as a visitor to NABJ in Detroit, Ruth Denny of NAJA expressed skepticism that the four associations could set aside their differences and mesh their goal sufficiently to pull off a joint convention. A sweet memory from Unity '94 was the broad smile on Denny's face as she swayed to a Latin beat on the dance floor one night, realizing that journalists of color made the vision come true for five days in Atlanta. 25

At the NABJ-sponsored general session, "The Civil Rights Movement: Is it Dead?" seeds of a scandal in the civil rights community were germinating although the audience did not know yet. Benjamin Chavis, NAACP executive director, was on the panel with Joseph Lowery of the Southern Christian Leadership Conference and Maynard Jackson, former Atlanta mayor.

The morning after the session, convention-goers had to be startled when they picked up copies of the Atlanta Constitution from their hotel room doors: The front-page lead story reported that Chavis was the subject of a sex discrimination lawsuit and he allegedly paid Mary Stansel, a former executive assistant, a secret out-of-court settlement – reportedly several hundred thousand dollars – hoping to suppress the story. 26

Four days later at the convention's close, Chavis and other NAACP leaders convened a Sunday press conference at the NABJ hotel that was not sanctioned by NABJ or Unity, but obviously intended to catch some of the 2,000 conference goers attending the closing gospel brunch.

The next month, Chavis was let go by the NAACP after serving for 16 months. 27

Serious About Health

U.S. Surgeon Gen. Joycelyn Elders was the annual NABJ DuBois lecturer. Unlike the previous year's speaker, novelist Terry McMillan, who wondered out loud that she did not know why she was at the podium during a rambling address, Elders was clear in her message since it concerned life and death. Elders told the journalists to use the power of the media to help Americans "save our society as we know it." She warned that because of crime and poverty "we are about to lose a whole generation of our black men."

The first black Surgeon General was credited with doubling the immunization rate of children and supported sex education for all students in U.S. school systems. 28

In the Black

Unity '94 was a financial success for NABJ, although that would not be confirmed until later that fall when receipts were counted and disbursed. NABJ received nearly 60 percent of the proceeds – $178,968 – based on member attendance. (NAHJ received 19 percent, AAJA received 15 percent and NAJA received 6 percent).

Immediately, $120,000 of that share was used to replace stocks and mutual funds that were withdraw the previous year to cover expenses. The remaining money – nearly $59,000 – was spent on maintaining the national office which averaged $60,000 a month in payroll and other operating expenses. 29

Before the July convention, Unity partners feared they would have deficits. Many sponsors, said NABJ treasurer Jackie Greene, did not confirm participation until a week before the event. The partners canceled some events, like a

$300,000 program inside the Georgia Dome, and NABJ spent $15,000 on a modest awards program and saved $40,000. NABJ also raised revenues by charging members $25 additional in convention registration from 1994 and the 1995 convention in Philadelphia.

Before Unity '94, NABJ relied on grants from companies and foundations as its primary source of revenue. After Unity and in early 1995, the association was entirely self-supporting through member dues and convention revenues. At a time when other media associations reduced spending in scholarships, said Greene, internships and student workshops, NABJ maintained its level of funding and in some cases increased spending. 30

Chapter 8
Philadelphia Freedom

In fall 1994, Walterene (Walt) Swanston submitted her resignation as executive director of NABJ, effective Nov. 19. "I have a great deal of respect for this organization," she said. "It's simply time to move on."1 Swanston's exit was announced a year before her three-year contract with NABJ was to expire and suggested she was leaving because of the traditionally rocky relationship between executive directors and the association's president and board of directors. Swanston was the fourth director in seven years.

Previous executive directors had said that NABJ boards hire them but refuse to give them authority that often goes with the title. Board members then expect a level of performance that is inconsistent with what the executive director is allowed to do. "I don't care who the executive director is or who the president is, you get to that conflict eventually," said Carl Morris, the second full-time executive director who served from 1987-90. "You try to do the job and you really can't do the job." 2

Board member and treasurer Jackie Greene said, "We've not really been honest and clear about what we want that position to do. There's always been a conflict." Swanston, he said, "will be sorely missed."

She was hired in October 1992, when Sidmel Estes-Sumpter was president, as coordinator of the Children's Project, which documented African-American efforts to save young people. Swanston became interim executive director in December, succeeding Linda Edwards when her two-year contract was not renewed. She reluctantly agreed to accept the permanent position in February 1993.

page 113

Swanston said she accepted the post with a condition: that a full-time writer/editor be hired to assist with the children's project, NABJ Journal and other activities. However she only got a part-timer who worked for two months. "I felt disadvantaged," said Swanston. 3

Estes-Sumpter believed that lack of the full-time hire contributed to Swanston's departure because she repeatedly raised that issue, said Estes-Sumpter, and "really refused to accept our explanations" about why the position could not be funded. Because of the revolving door history of NABJ executive directors, the board was challenged with coming up with a more stable structure. Said Estes-Sumpter: "We really have not been serious about letting go of the reins of this organization. The president really calls the shots. Well, if the president calls the shots, why do we have an executive director? We really have to come to grips with that.

"Allowing the executive director to exercise real power – a model followed by many organizations, won't happen because the board will not give up control.

"I'm doing a reality check. NABJ presidents are strong-willed, with a hands-on approach. We've reached the point of oil and water. What we say we want and what we really do are two different things." 4

Black Guy Did It?

In late October, Susan Smith, a white mother of two small children, claimed that a black male carjacker kidnapped her children in South Carolina. On Nov. 3, Smith confessed that the black suspect was fiction. She sent her sedan into an isolated lake and drowned her offspring.

Susan Smith's initial claims attracted national coverage. The stereotype of the dangerous black male was powerful. Black men were detained or viewed with suspicion in small-town South Carolina.

Yet in 1994, much of the media was more measured and skeptical in its coverage because it had learned lessons from a similar high profile case. Five years earlier, Charles Stuart, a white Bostonian, claimed that a black assailant fatally shot his pregnant wife and wounded him. It was later learned that Stuart actually killed his wife and shot himself as a decoy.

Gregory Moore of the NABJ media monitoring committee directed coverage of the Stuart case for the Boston Globe. He explained that unlike the Stuart case, reports detailed problems in Smith's marriage and also some neighbor's suspicions that the mother was responsible for her children's disappearance. In the Stuart case, the media relied on accounts from Stuart and police, but family members refused to talk to the media. Said Moore, "You should not just rely on direct statements from the victim, you should not just rely on what the police give you, but give voice to average folks ... who are raising the kinds of questions that are raised when these kinds of high profile cases get into the stranger than fiction." 5

Exodus at the NY Times

Late in 1994 a number of top black journalists left the New York Times. White House correspondent Gwen Ifill joined NBC News Sept. 26. That same day Metro reporter Michel Mariott started work at Newsweek. Assignment editors Mary Curtis and Reginald Thomas left respectively for the Charlotte Observer and New York Daily News. Senior editor Angela Dodson took a leave of absence and Chicago bureau chief Isabel Wilkerson was making plans to leave because of a book deal. 6

Was anything wrong? "It's certainly an indication that we have things we need to work on here," said Dennis Stern, associate managing editor.

The chief problem, according to some of the people leaving, was that many people at the Times – particularly in middle management – view the newspaper as the pinnacle of journalism and believe that journalists of color should consider themselves lucky to be there. Thus, these managers let people drift and did not realize that the journalists of color would receive other offers.

Mariott, 40, said he "got an offer I could not say no to," working as a general editor for the lifestyles section at Newsweek. Ifill, 38, said NBC's enthusiasm made it easy for her to choose a new career path.

page 115

Said Curtis, her move was "less about the Times than about opportunities offered here."

Still, there were concerns because this was the second wave of blacks who recently left the premiere newspaper. In the last two years departures included senior editor Paul Delaney for the University of Alabama, legal affairs reporter E.R. Shipp to pursue a doctorate at Columbia University, metro desk editor Larry Olmstead, who returned to Knight-Ridder Co. to become an assistant vice president in corporate, assistant Styles editor Yanick Rice Lamb, who moved to Child magazine, and Rosemary Bray, a Times Book Review editor, who left to write a book about parenting among African-Americans. 7

Information Superhighway

The November NABJ Journal printed excerpts from a speech by Federal Communications Commission Chairman Reed Hundt about a new phenomenon that was quickly settling into the American mainstream: An "information superhighway" of telephone, cable and wireless systems that were providing e-mail, Internet, video and wireless transmissions.

At issue was whether Americans of color would have equal access to this new technology. In 1994 the White House Council of Economic Advisors predicted that the telecommunications industry would grow from 3.6 million workers to 5 million by 2003 and would also add $100 million to the U.S. Gross Domestic Product.

Hundt said that the FCC took historic action to ensure that minorities were able to compete for licenses to provide the next generation of wireless telephone service, personal communication service or PCS. This opportunity was unlike the past when blacks were virtually shut out of competing for the issuing of television and radio licenses when those technologies began.

New Time Warner president

In fall 1994 Time Warner announced that Richard Parsons, an African-American bank executive, would become president of the world's largest media and entertainment conglomerate and No. 2 executive in the company.

Rivals quickly speculated that Parsons would be a weak executive with little or no role in the corporate operating divisions. But Harry Albright, former chairman of Dime Bank Corp., told USA Today, "The litany of people who have underestimated Richard Parsons are legion. He gives the impression of being terribly relaxed. But if he has to be tough, he'll be tough."

Parsons joined Dime as president in 1988 and reorganized the bank, then engineered the merger of the $10 billion thrift with Anchor Savings Bank. The deal created the fourth largest savings bank.

Time Warner holdings included Time, Sports Illustrated and Money magazines, filmed entertainment, recorded music, cable TV systems and pay-TV, and generated $14.5 billion in revenues in 1993.

Emerge Holds On

Black Entertainment Television owned 44 percent of Emerge magazine and insisted it had to have a larger share of the editorially praised but money-losing monthly. By the fall BET agreed to buy out several investors and increase its stake in the magazine to 80 percent. The remaining share was held by the estate of Wilmer C. Ames, founder of the magazine that began publishing in fall 1989. Circulation of Emerge, "Black America's newsmagazine," was about 150,000, according to certified figures from October. 8

Carl Morris Returns

In December, the month after Walterene Swanston abruptly departed as executive director, Carl Morris, executive director from 1987-90, was named to an interim position called conference coordinator.

Said President Dorothy Gilliam, "We have moved on. The loss of the last executive director was not crippling. We are a very strong and dynamic organization. We have put into place a very sound strategy that will leave us a better organization now and in the future." 9

Gilliam outlined a three-part strategy:
• The board forming a search committee and in the process we are "taking a good look at what we really want the top staff position to be."
• Name an interim conference coordinator to "make sure that our historic 20th convention in Philadelphia is dynamite."
• Greater responsibilities would be given to the national office staff in Reston, Va.

Gays and Lesbians Want Parity

At the quarterly board meeting in Seattle in December, Gilliam announced that NABJ received a $100,000 grant from the Freedom Forum for staging a series of national forums on the impact of the computer revolution on the African-American community. Vice president Sheila Stainback was to chair the committee using the grant. Called Infonet, the project was to produce a segment on New York area African-American experts and put the production on satellite and on-air six times in 1995.

NABJ aimed at expanding its spring "Journalists Across America" outreach program. Last April, 12 chapters held media access workshops. In March 1995 the goal was for all 58 chapters to participate and in 22 of those cities there were opportunities to partner with another journalism organization like NAHJ, AAJA or Society of Professional Journalists. [10]

A hot topic during the Seattle meeting was whether the National Lesbian and Gay Journalists Association should be a full participant in the next Unity convention, scheduled for 1999 or 2000. NLGJA was among many supporting organizations during Unity '94 in Atlanta. A month after the joint convention, the Unity partners voted to retain the same composition of primary partners for the next collaboration.

Immediate past president Estes-Sumpter said she agreed with the Unity vote because, "The industry has yet to deal with race and ethnicity forthrightly. To add sexual orientation would cloud the issues of race and ethnicity."

Also at issue was whether NLGJA, dominated by white males and females, would be responsive to issues that initially necessitated the creation of ethnic journalism organizations.

Midwest Regional director Monroe Anderson attended a fall NLGJA conference as NABJ's representative and he heard concerns about that association not being included in Unity as full participants. "But they showed a movie they intended to use to represent the organization and to educate and fund raise. There were no people of color in the film. They said they would rectify that." 11

'Human Faces on Our History'

In November the Trotter group held its third annual retreat at Stanford University. The three day gathering included a public forum on race, media and fallen icons O.J. Simpson and Mike Tyson. Harvard law professor Charles Ogletree moderated.

Black columnists also assessed the impact of mid-term Congressional elections in which Republicans trounced Democrats and formed a majority capable of stymying Democrat President Bill Clinton.

However, the biggest highlight of the retreat was dinner and a conversation with Virginia Craft Rose, 81, and Ellen Craft Dammond, 78, nieces of Boston Guardian editor William Monroe Trotter.

Trotter member and Oakland Tribune columnist Brenda Payton arranged the surprise meeting. Rose's daughter, Mary Ellen Butler, a Tribune editor, asked Payton if the columnists wanted to meet the only direct descendants of the man for whom the society was named. Rose and Dammond's appearance "put a human face on our history" said a Trotter member, and the nieces spoke proudly of their "Uncle Monroe." Both elders shared these details of their uncle's life.

• "He could have lived the life of an elite," said Rose. "He had a beautiful love affair that ended tragically with his wife before they were married very long and before they had children." Geraldine Pinter toiled alongside her husband at the Guardian, "night and day, to the ruination of her health," said Dammond.

• The nieces acknowledged that Trotter was a troubled man and even suicidal but they did not believe that he killed himself on April 7, 1934. Trotter, 62, and nearly penniless, fell or jumped from atop his house. The nieces said he had a habit of pacing along an outside ledge. His landlady would tell of hearing his tortured footsteps when deadline approached and thinking, "There's poor Monroe, thinking about his editorial." When his body was found he was clutching a piece of the roof, said the nieces.

• Both nieces admitted that they grew up at times unsure of how they felt about their firebrand uncle. "Part of my sorrow was I could have talked to him more and I didn't," said Dammond. "As I've grown older, I've appreciated that we had an uncle who stood for what he believed in and fought for what he believed in."12

Trotter in his day protested the 1915 showings of "Birth of a Nation," D.W. Griffith's crudely racist film lamenting the Confederate "Lost Cause" and showing blacks as dimwitted, shiftless and beasts.

Eight decades later, Trotter's admirers faced another media assault. That fall, "The Bell Curve," published by Charles Murray and the late Richard Hernstein, wickedly suggested that low-IQ blacks were sapping America's resources.

The text zoomed to the top of bestseller lists, but was largely panned by critics as pseudo science. Yet Murray's "social science pornography" – his words – reinforced racist assumptions of many people. 13

Not satisfied with reacting viscerally, many black writers and journalists fired back with facts and logic to straighten out the "Bell Curve." 14

That fall, the Freedom Forum announced its 1994-95 scholarship winners and showed off the recipients in advertisements in journalism trade magazines like Editor & Publisher, Columbia Journalism Review and American Journalism Review. The array of scholars was much more than a token mix of people of color. That bothered John Leo, the white, conservative columnist with U.S. News & World Report.

Leo called the display an affront to white men: "A photo spread of the Freedom Forum winners of journalism scholarships showed 63 beaming faces, only 13 of which belong to non-minority (white) males." The sea or black and brown men and women and white women, wrote Leo, represented a shift that "has more to do with morally dubious moves taking place behind the word 'diversity.'" 15

Leo was blind to cold facts. White males were about one third of the incoming workforce and demographers had been trumpeting the coming change through the 1980s and early '90s. In the journalism field, particularly newspapers, minority college interns and entry-level hires percentage-wise were double the percentage of minorities already working. 16 The newsroom workforce fell short of looking like America, which was approaching 30 percent people of color. But there was concerted efforts among many educators and professionals and foundations to reflect the population at workplaces in the near future.

If young people of color were encouraged to buy into this part of the American dream, it lessened chances of them choosing nihilism, and resentment was being peddled by the disenchanted. 17

In February, U.S. News & World Report stubbornly promoted the myth of news organizations hiring and promoting blacks and browns at the expense of white men. The Feb. 13 cover asked, "Does Affirmative Action Mean NO WHITE MEN NEED APPLY?" and in one of the stories, "A quest for diversity," writers claimed that at the Los Angeles Times, "Young white males ... (were) consigned to distant bureaus, filing stories but lacking staff benefits such as health care and pensions."

Experienced journalists saw right through the deceptive passage. Those "oppressed" white men apparently were not staff writers but stringers or correspondents, explaining why they were in bureaus. Second, USN&WR noted that the white men were young. It was rare then for young journalists – of any color – to make it to the staff of the fourth largest U.S. daily.

A memo from a subscriber and journalist to USN&WR

editors told them that they were wrong to suggest that minority journalists were responsible for the conditions of these young white men unless they could show an egregious breach of employment rules. And as for the cover story, "Does Affirmative Action Mean NO WHITE MEN NEED APPLY?," it weighed in largely as another round of scapegoating racial minorities and women in an uncertain economy, said the subscriber. Co-editors wrote back and said in a postcard that they would share the comments with "appropriate members of our editorial staff." 18

Workplace Upheaval

When the U.S. Justice Department in 1989 allowed the Detroit News (Gannett) and Detroit Free Press (Knight-Ridder) to merge business operations but retain distinct news gathering and editorial staffs, the newspaper preservation agreement guaranteed that the nation's eighth largest metro area would have more than one daily newspaper, but assured there would be war years later. War broke out in July 1995 when unionized workers at the News and Free Press went on strike. The Newspaper Guild, one of five unions, alleged that the management engaged in classic union busting-tactics in possibly the most pro-union metropolis in American. Management shot back that the unions wanted to continue operating under wasteful conditions that were unrealistic in a changed American labor market.

Reporters, photographers and copy editors walked the picket lines. Middle managers and executives worked extra hours and replacement workers crossed the lines to continue publishing both papers. Circulation plummeted and the combatants hardened their positions instead of moving closer to settlement. When the brutal Midwest winter set in, strikers shivered near barrel fires. Many of the journalists were NABJ members who had to decide how long they could stay out of work. 19

In New York, the city edition of Long Island-based Newsday (Times Mirror) appeared to be about to turn the corner and support itself financially. Its initial circulation, circa 1985, was 40,000 then it soared to 300,000 in 1991 when the Daily News went on strike and the New York Post seemed on the brink of extinction. The News and Post survived and New York Newsday circulation retreated to between 216,000 and 231,000 in the early- to mid-1990s. 20

The newspaper had been a consistent money loser, but a high-ranking editor said it was making 7 percent profit in 1995. If true, that was progress, unlike the continuous flow of red ink late '80s and early '90s. Times Mirror executives in Los Angeles did not appear to dispute New York Newsday's success; the paper was just not making enough money, so the executives shut it down in July.

Two Pulitzer prizes in three years could not save New York Newsday. Also lost was a remarkable team, a news gathering staff that resembled the city it covered: About a third of the staff were people of color and 36 percent of the journalists were women. Eight hundred employees were displaced, either absorbed into the Long Island paper, bought out or laid off. Many of the NABJ members feared that they did not have the seniority to stick. 21

Missing in Action: Candidates

A paucity of candidates for National Association of Black Journalists offices prompted some soul searching within the 2,500 member organization. At the same time the group was growing in membership and sophistication and its offices should be more coveted than ever, there were fewer candidates for the board of directors than any time in recent history. There was no competition for 13 of the 17 board offices that would be filled in August when members gathered for the association's 20th convention in Philadelphia. Those offices had only one candidate or none at all. 22

In contrast to the tooth-and-nail battles of recent years, WCAU-TV Philadelphia newsman Arthur Fennell would stroll unopposed into NABJ's presidency. That was the first unopposed presidential bid since 1979.

The treasurer would have to be appointed because no one wanted that position, arguably the group's most influential. Neither did anyone file for student representative. And no candidates stepped forward for four of the 10 regional director positions.

Even board members feel the group needs to examine whether there are serious underlying problems. "For too long, the NABJ has been far too cliquish, particularly when it comes to leadership," said Philadelphia Inquirer reporter Vanessa Williams, who was running for one of the few contested offices – print vice president. She said this feeling of exclusivity may have discouraged some candidates. Others, said Williams, may be turned off by the recent turmoil in the national office, which has gone through four executive directors in nine years.

Some veteran journalists were drifting away from NABJ because they don't need it as much as they once did to learn and advance, she said. "To a larger degree there are questions about what the NABJ is and how relevant it is," said Williams, a reporter for 12 years. That was an assessment in which Williams agreed with her opponent Dwight Lewis, regional editor with The Tennessean. Lewis wanted to see NABJ leaders sit down and develop "a vision for the future." Lewis, 47, faulted the board for not working hard enough to keep NABJ relevant for veteran journalists and to make it relevant to the younger ones. "There are a lot of talented young people out there," said Lewis. "We have to go out and reach them and tell them what (NABJ) is all about. We have to have somebody replacing us." [23]

In the last 10 years NABJ membership doubled and it had a budget of more than $1 million. In some ways, this growth may have hurt the association.

Former president Tom Morgan, also a former treasurer, said in a spring interview with the NABJ Journal that the treasurer's job "has become too hard." Morgan noted that when he was treasurer 10 years ago he oversaw a budget of thousands of dollars. Perhaps, he mused, NABJ needed to hire a professional to handle the association finances and give the treasurer only a supervisory role.

Williams speculated that the growing time commitment demanded by the board positions is discouraging candidates.

Some said the main problem was that NABJ had not welcomed young people and those with less prestigious jobs into the inner circle. Randye Bullock, president of the Detroit Chapter of NABJ, said she would have run for director of Midwest Region 5 – where there are no candidates – but was made to feel unwelcome by some NABJ members because she was not a working journalist. Bullock was in public relations, but was a full member because when she joined NABJ she was a TV program host and free-lance writer.

"There is an air of exclusivity," she said. "You really have to be in the 'in' group. Nobody questions my abilities, or heart or dedication to the organization, but certain people question my eligibility for higher office. I think we can be stronger by being more inclusive." Bullock's complaint was misleading. The cool reception for seeking the office stemmed more from the tradition of full-time journalists holding office. She used to meet that standard but did not during NABJ's leadership crisis.

Campaign literature made it clear that NABJ's direction was a top concern. Fennell pledged to "reinvigorate veteran members." But it would not be that easy to pump up members like Kasey Jones, 43, a copy editor at the Baltimore Sun. Jones was print vice president of the Baltimore chapter, but she wasn't running for higher office or even going to the Philadelphia convention. "The workshops, job fairs and networking are great for people just out of college or struggling at tiny papers in the boondocks who need help getting that next job," she said. "But people like me have our own networks and aren't looking to change jobs, and if we are planning to change jobs are usually already being recruited." 24

Mumia Places NABJ in Hot Seat

A month before its 20th anniversary celebration, NABJ members faced this chilling scenario:

Host journalists.

Execute a journalist.

You have a friend in Pennsylvania. (state slogan)

On August 17, the second day of the convention in

Philadelphia, former Philadelphia Association of Black Journalists (ABJ) president Mumia Abu-Jamal was to be executed for the 1982 shooting death of a police officer.

Gov. Tom Ridge's decision to execute Jamal put NABJ in the hot seat: The association was under fire from various quarters. In New York for example, black talk show hosts vilified NABJ leaders for their decision to distance themselves from Abu-Jamal. And longtime NABJ member C. Gerald Fraser said in a June 26 letter to president Dorothy Gilliam that if the Commonwealth of Pennsylvania stuck to its execution date, NABJ should not conduct business there.

Wrote Fraser, "Will we black journalists frolic in Pennsylvania while one of our ranks is executed, perhaps wrongly, by the state? ... The governor of Pennsylvania expressed his contempt for black journalists by setting the date ... during the convention." 25

On June 30 NABJ issued this statement: "The board of directors at its recent meeting in Philadelphia decided to abstain from taking an official position in the case of Mumia Abu-Jamal. ... As an organization of journalists, the board felt that the complicated issues involved are ones around which individual members in their capacities as journalists may make personal and professional judgments. The organization however, does not see this unfortunate circumstance as an issue of journalism upon which it feels compelled to take a stand at this time."

When Abu-Jamal was charged with the murder of a cop, his primary employment was not as a journalist, but as a taxi driver. Abu-Jamal, whose column, "Live from Death Row," was being carried nationally and internationally by leftist publications and some black newspapers, advocated on-air for the radical group MOVE that had members in prison because of a 1978 confrontation with police.

Two weeks after the June 30 statement, the NABJ board released this: "We choose not to judge the guilt or innocence of Abu-Jamal, based on facts which a judge and jury heard ... however it is within our purview and responsibility to address the First Amendment rights of Abu-Jamal, which we find to be a legitimate issue. ... Disciplinary charges were lodged against Abu-Jamal ... in retaliation for his publishing a book, 'Live from Death Row.'"

The statement demanded that a gag order forbidding the inmate to talk to the media be lifted. 26

Abu-Jamal's supporters were demanding a new trial for the prisoner. They said his 1982 trial was far from fair and a new defense team said that the case had numerous legal errors. Abu-Jamal tried to defend himself and was barred from much of the trial by the judge.

If NABJ did withdraw from Philadelphia in protest, it would expect to forfeit at least one third of $1 million annual revenues, which was raised at conventions. But the city of Philadelphia would stand to lose millions of dollars in anticipated tourist dollars from the 2,500-member association.

Less than a week before Aug. 16, Pennsylvania courts granted a stay of execution for Abu-Jamal. NABJ's convention began. The imposing shadow of Abu-Jamal surrounded, infiltrated but fell short of suffocating the five-day meeting. Nearly 2,500 members and friends attended, participation that exceeded convention estimates.

NABJ was pressured by activists – and a number of members – to call for a new trial for the death row inmate. Many NABJers however worried that an official stand might compromise the journalistic integrity of its members at their respective jobs.

At the annual convention business meeting Gilliam said that the June statement that NABJ would remain neutral on the Abu-Jamal case was a communiqué based on a consensus – not a vote as many people believed – of the 18-member board of directors. Said Gilliam, "I made a mistake."

Abu-Jamal supporters picketed the convention center and Marriott Hotel where conventioneers stayed.

And on the third day, the scheduled 90-minute business meeting instead became a four-hour debate among 250 members about the Abu-Jamal case and what stand NABJ should or should not take.

More than that, the messy but democratic debate was a struggle for the soul of NABJ, a struggle between the nationalistic-activist and professional-establishment wings of the association.

Les Payne, a past president, told members that the black journalist had three responsibilities: to protect its clients in the black community; to raise consciousness and to fulfill the need to know.

"We should always be clear that we are journalists, not activists," said the Newsday editor.

Betty Winston Baye of Louisville, Ky. was among dozens of members from the South and Midwest who felt left out of the building Abu-Jamal debate. "The case shows an East Coast bias," said the native New Yorker and Courier-Journal editorial writer. "The rest of us are trying to absorb the information and do the right thing. The people who knew (about the 14-year-old case) and never bothered to write should bear some responsibility."

Added Sheila Smoot-Scarver of Alabama, "This seems to be a fight between Washington, Philadelphia and New York. We didn't get any information. You want to come to Birmingham? We got plenty of black men on death row who don't want to be there. We got black men in chains, on chain gangs." 27

Gayle Pollard Terry of Los Angeles asked if the Philadelphia chapter's position on the Abu-Jamal case inhibited coverage by local black journalists of the case. Herb Lowe, a Philadelphia Inquirer reporter, said it didn't but he noted that management said it would question newsroom employees who seemed to be doing more than reporting the story.

But Vernon Jarrett of Chicago, a past president, argued, "What is wrong with having a new trial? Are people afraid of upsetting white bosses?"

After 240 minutes of debate and at least three votes, the members agreed on a statement that NABJ favored a "full and fair" review of the Abu-Jamal case. The statement stopped short of calling for a new trial.

The Abu-Jamal furor was covered by the BBC, the New York Times and black media.

Nonetheless, at its peak the business meeting participation involved one-tenth of NABJ attendees. Others were spread out at workshops, major forums and a job fair equivalent to a journalism supermarket.

When the W.E.B. DuBois lecture at the NABJ convention began in 1985 an intellectual was not expected to give a merely entertaining speech but a sturdy historical briefing or blueprint to journalists. At least twice in the 1990s some members became convinced that the spirit of the DuBois event had been compromised. Just ask Vernon Jarrett. The Chicagoan, founder and second president, bogarted the stage at the Saturday night banquet as Johnnie Cochran, O.J. Simpson's attorney, was to give the DuBois talk.

Dorothy Gilliam said that Jarrett asked her to speak before Cochran, but it seemed more than a polite request. Outside the ballroom, 15 minutes before speaking, Jarrett was fuming, displeased that the banquet – which featured a '70s singing duo (McFadden and Whitehead, "Ain't No Stopping Us Now") and Cochran autograph seekers – did not have a more reverent tone. Two years before in Houston, Jarrett erupted because DuBois speaker, novelist Terry McMillan, gave a rambling, self-absorbed talk.

Jarrett told the Philadelphia crowd that he learned numerous lessons "at the knee" of DuBois. He chided members to remember that DuBois was a spiritual ancestor of NABJ – as much as Frederick Douglass, Ida B. Wells and William Monroe Trotter. Jarrett urged them to apply the scholar's lessons as they carry our their work. "I demand that you not go back to your news organizations unless you learn what DuBois stands for," said Jarrett with controlled rage. He cited DuBois' 21 books, that he was considered the father of scientific sociology and, most of all, DuBois was a journalist, the longtime editor of the Crisis, the magazine of the NAACP.

As C-SPAN cameras rolled, two larger than life images of DuBois with his Van Dyke goatee were projected at the ends of the stage.

Jarrett ended his lecture by spurring the hundreds to stand and give the spirit of DuBois a rhythmic ovation.

A noticeably unsettled Cochran moved to the lectern in a counterpoint mode. He said he was familiar with DuBois, and from his prepared text, read the same oft quoted citation – "two ... souls in one dark body" – that Jarrett said earlier.

Shortly after that, Cochran moved from DuBois and fixed on advocating for the acquittal of his client, O.J. Simpson, especially since the Mark Fuhrman tapes had come to light.

The pep rally tone of Cochran's speech divided the audience. Many people stood and cheered lustily, others sat coolly and applauded politely. A few others still, stormed out of the room in disgust. 28

J. Whyatt Mondesire, a Philadelphia journalist, wrote afterward, "DuBois, as Jarrett eloquently pointed out, set the tone and initial high-water mark for all of our collective achievements as he was the 'original African-American intellectual.' Clearly, this dinner should have reflected his spirit and DuBois' philosophy of rigorous intellectual achievement. Instead, we allowed our organization [and] ourselves to be used by a self-serving celebrity lawyer, who chose to mount our rostrum and sell his legal bag of tricks to further the interests of one man, I might add, who has been charged with the most heinous of human crimes – murder in the first degree times two.

"When Cochran ended his remarks saying he would 'take back to LA our (NABJ's) expressions of support' I was angered and sickened.

"I don't care what he takes back to LA as long (as) it comes from some local gift shop or hoagie or soft pretzel vendor. But I do care if he is presumptuous enough to believe that the NABJ somehow sanctioned his client or his defense of same. The invitation to address our dinner does not give him license to transmit some unspoken endorsement for his particular point of view." 29

Unhappy Coronation

Arthur Fennell, 37, succeeded Dorothy Gilliam as the 11th NABJ president and third broadcast journalist to hold the leadership post. Lack of competition did not mean that everyone was happy with a coronation. Members questioned why Fennell was the only candidate for what was a growing, dynamic association. They blamed the lack of competitors on apathy or distaste for contentious NABJ politics. Art Franklin, Fennell's campaign manager and a broadcast journalist in Birmingham, Ala., said vice president Sheila Stainback and Chicago chapter president Art Norman, both broadcast journalists, were potential candidates, but chose not to run because Fennell "stepped forward as a strong candidate" early on. 30

Estes-Sumpter, a behind-the-scenes producer, claimed that Fennell's high profile status as a Philadelphia news anchor would prevent him from speaking out on issues.

"There's nothing to respond to," answered Fennell. "There are no more specific pressures on anyone on-air than there are on journalists in any other capacity.

"The president sets the climate. My job is to be a calming force when we need to be calmed and an agitating force when we need it and know the difference. I think that's good leadership."

One of his first decisions was to appoint Rodney Brooks, a business editor with USA Today, to the vacant treasurer's position, possibly the second most powerful position in NABJ that former president and longtime treasurer Tom Morgan said may have become "too hard."

Competitive races for NABJ office were often heated and at times ugly and distasteful to members. But competition demands passion and the combatants were challenged to show off their best ideas. Even the losing candidates' best ideas lived on to nourish NABJ over the years.

With 13 of 17 offices unchallenged in 1995 it was an early sign of malaise that would sicken the association in future years.

But at present, NABJ appeared prosperous and strong. The 20th anniversary convention in the association's ancestral home drew 2,453 paid participants, said outgoing treasurer Jackie Greene. Only the four-association Unity convention the previous year in Atlanta drew more people to an NABJ gathering. Also, the Philadelphia convention earned $537,886 in net revenues.

Mal Goode, 87

Malvin R. Goode, 87, the first African-American network TV correspondent, died Sept. 12. Goode was a 1978 NABJ

Lifetime Achievement winner and 1990 inductee into the NABJ Hall of Fame.

Remarkably, Goode began his TV career when most journalists are winding theirs down. At age 55, American Broadcasting Company chose him from 37 candidates in 1962. Goode's big break came on a Sunday when he walked into an international crisis: the discovery of Soviet missiles in Cuba, 90 miles from U.S. shores and a doomsday standoff between President John F. Kennedy and Soviet Premier Nikita Khrushchev.

Because the U.N. correspondent was unavailable, trainee Goode became ABC's man: he delivered round-the-clock reports, eight on television and seven on radio. Goode worked for 20 years as a correspondent, interviewing civil rights leader Malcolm X and others for ABC. In the 1970s, he served as a part-time correspondent for National Black Radio. 31

Chapter 9
Acquittal, atonement

On Oct. 3, the 15-month long "Trial of the century" climaxed. 1

"O.J. Not Guilty" screamed headlines around the country, words complemented with above-the-fold photos of a smiling O.J. Simpson.

The announcement provoked man-bites-dog type reactions: whites "rioting," usually in their offices, in a rage over the verdict. In one New Jersey business office for example white workers threw items from their desks, stomped around the aisles cursing in disbelief and black co-workers either cowered in fear or did their best to hide perverse satisfaction that a black man beat white justice.

Despite no murder weapon recovered in the knifing deaths of Simpson's ex-wife Nicole Brown Simpson and her friend Ronald Goldman, O.J. Simpson was on course for a murder conviction until Mark Fuhrman rescued him in late summer. Racist ranting by the ex-cop and the appearance that tainted evidence was planted on Simpson crippled the prosecution and provided enough "reasonable doubt" that discouraged the jury from convicting. 2

Sarcastically, Andrea Ford of the Los Angeles Times observed that the (media) circus left town. As one of the few blacks covering the trial she offered fellow NABJ members seven rules for surviving the next "story of the century":

1. Hang on. You are likely the last kid on the rope in the "crack the whip" game. Don't ask why, but there's an unwritten law in 'mainstream' new organizations that the really, really big stories or really big developments are best understood by whites. A black reporter on such an assign-

ment should be ever watching his or her back – and front, too for that matter, for the long knives. And don't go on vacation; that's like bodily flinging yourself off the end of the whip.

2. Never say anything publicly or even privately that can be construed as favorable to whoever the most news organizations have deemed to be the villain in the story, especially if the 'villain' is black.

Stifle yourself even if such an utterance would be perfectly ethical and absolutely true. Never mind that other reporters can, without much more than a gut feeling for who to instantly hate, vilify anyone they please, anywhere, anytime, and did during the O.J. Simpson trial. They were never accused of having a racial or any other kind of agenda. You are different. Like the Simpson jury, sort of.

3. Don't break too many stories that your editors believe came from black 'villains.' You know you have broken this rule when people start asking you things like, 'Just how long have you known Johnnie Cochran?"

4. Do not be put off when no one pays attention when you reveal, moments after reading mark Fuhrman's old disability file, that you suspect you are in Klan Kountry. Just be patient, in time F. Lee Bailey and Laura McKinny's tapes will vindicate your unpopular opinion. And that profile of Fuhrman you suggested months ago? It will get written, post-haste.

5. Remember, you don't speak for black people, but also remember that you might have to speak up for them.

When editors interpreting polls focus on explaining why so many black people automatically presumed the defendant not guilty, ask them to give equal attention to why so many white people automatically thought he was guilty and did so before any evidence was presented at trial.

6. Refrain from post-verdict discussions in the workplace. Colleagues who hold a different point of view than the jury can really get nasty, so it is not worth your while. But when one of them allows how they are not going to vote for Colin Powell because of the jury, this rule can be ignored and you may reply, 'Excuse me'?

And lastly,

7. Don't be impressed by the celebrities attracted to the Story of the Century like lemmings to the edge of a cliff. When Geraldo (Rivera) damn near runs you over in the courthouse hallway trying to ingratiate himself, pretend you thought he was the has-been guy who played the teacher on 'Welcome Back Kotter.' That'll drive him crazy, but it only partially makes up for the fact that he's way more popular than you are.

Another black journalist who covered the Simpson trial was Dennis Schatzman, the first full-time NABJ executive director (1986-87). His reports for the Los Angeles Sentinel ran nationally in black weeklies. The next year, Schatzman and Tom Elias of Scripps Howard News Service published the "The Simpson Trial in Black and White." Both men shared a seat at the trial but had opposing conclusions about the outcome. 3

Schatzman, 45, disclosed in fall 1995 that he had stomach cancer that gave him about two years to live. He also told the New Yorker magazine (July 17, 1995 issue) that he shot a man in Washington on May 5,1991, "ditched the gun, got my duffle bag and caught a Greyhound" from D.C. to Los Angeles. According to Schatzman, the victim was a casual thug who shot him in the back six months earlier and left him to die. The gunshot took out most of his right lung and was a contributing factor to Schatzman's cancer. Schatzman, 47, died in July 1997. 4

Million Man March
Black men were powerful symbols for evil and danger in America. They were denounced as violent criminals, non-violent drug addicts, school underachievers, oversexed beasts and unreliable parents.

O.J. Simpson, the superstar athlete and pitchman involved in a "trial of the century" for murder, was a lightning rod for debate about treatment of black men in the U.S. justice system.

By 1995, there had been enough "black guy did it" crime hoaxes for the police, press and public to be more skeptical of such claims.

As for beloved black men like Michael Jordan or Colin Powell, whites often claimed that "they did not see" their color, a backhanded comment that stung many blacks.

Black women had a difficult row to hoe too, but there were many public displays of success. A black woman (Carol Moseley Braun), was elected to the U.S. Senate; at one time in 1992 four black women (Terry McMillan, Toni Morrison, Alice Walker and Marian Wright Edelman) were among the top 10 best-selling authors. Black women were succeeding in numerous professions and breaking down old barriers.

Black teen-age, unwed pregnancies were stabilizing and their school achievement scores were rising.

African-American men meanwhile were under siege or guilty of self-destructive behavior. A most alarming statistic among many was the national homicide rate, nine white males per 100,000 but 72 black males per 100,000. 5

Also, women were the heads of two-thirds of black U.S. households. Where were the fathers and husbands? 6

A number of black males decided it was time to make a statement. For much of 1995 people around the nation planned an October "Million Man March" on Washington, D.C. as a show of unity and atonement.

A sea of black male humanity flowed into the National Mall between the Capitol and Lincoln Memorial on Oct. 16. Was the press prepared to cover this story? Million Man March organizers said the mainstream media was predictably biased. Conrad Worrill of the National Black United Front said the mainstream media had trouble separating the message from its most visible messenger, Nation of Islam minister Louis Farrakhan. 7

But journalism watchers said the coverage was remarkably broad and deep, and African-American journalists were credited for that quality.

"A lot of news organizations went beyond covering political figures and interviewed participants with depth and texture," said Washington Post media critic Howard Kurtz. Post coverage included two front page stories and at least five stories featured inside six pages. At least 20 reporters contributed to the coverage. Metro desk political editor Kent

Jenkins said African-American reporters Hamil R. Harris and Michael A. Fletcher brought the march to the attention of editors many months before the event.

The black owned press was noteworthy for rallying people to the march throughout 1995. Many weeklies promoted the event with public service announcements provided by the Nation of Islam. 8

Farrakhan spoke for two hours. His speech included references to the Bible, numerology and black renewal and he included his interpretations of history and denounced white supremacy.

Media outlets relied on the National Park Service for its numbers, and the estimate was 400,000. Million Man March organizers cried foul and insisted at least a million and up to 2 million men participated.

At the time of the event some members of the Trotter Group were on the scene then reported what they witnessed to colleagues at the annual retreat in St. Petersburg, Fla.

Norman Lockman of the Wilmington News Journal said the crowd "churned," newspaper talk for circulation gains and losses. At least 400,000 people were in one place, said Lockman, but with people coming and going all day, attendance was easily double the National Park Service estimate. 9

In addition to black men and boys from all walks of life, Richard Prince of Virginia-based Cities in Schools said that some white men participated: "I am here to atone" read a banner carried by one man. Another carried a picture of his black adopted son. "I am here for him," read his sign.

The Million Man March was peaceful and reverential, unlike many public assumptions of what happens when many African-American men gather in one place.

Goal: Project NABJ Image

At the fall board meeting at the Reston, Va. headquarters, immediate past president Gilliam said her administration left NABJ "at the crossroads to continue to shape the future of the media in America."

During Gilliam's 1993-95 tenure the association realized significant funding and investment increases and strengthened programs even though she had to take on more day-to-day supervision when Walterene Swanston resigned.

New president Fennell announced his goals for 1995-97. They included completing the association business plan; developing a series of professional development seminars for members; improving and expanding NABJ's image among foundations, educators and industry leaders. 10

Fennell and the board announced new committees and task forces:

• Internet connection committee, to develop cyberspace programs and access for members.

• Editorial board, to develop editorial points of view on issues related to the industry and African-American community for publication in media.

• Copy editors and Arts & Entertainment task forces.

• Managerial Think Tank to advise Fennell on managerial issues and concerns.

• Quick response team for pressing organization concerns, and,

• Past Presidents Roundtable for all former NABJ presidents to develop long-range mission plans and provide an overview. 11

Executive Director

At NABJ headquarters, the executive director resigned in 1994 before completing her term and Carl Morris, a former director, filled in as a convention coordinator. In December 1995, the association hired Joanne Lyons Wooten, its fifth director in nine years. Wooten was executive director of the 1,400 member American Physical Therapy Association. During Wooten's five-year stay, APTA membership increased 24 percent and the non-dues revenue base grew 11 percent. 12

Wooten was aware of the conflicts faced by former NABJ executive directors with the elected leaders, but she was confident that she could establish good working relationships: "From what I understand about NABJ history, there are no issues that have been aired that are unique. They are all things that are basic to association management. The answers are available. One of my areas of responsibility is finding answers to some of these ongoing problems."

Wooten was not concerned that she broke tradition by being a non-journalist (Schatzman, Morris, Swanston and Edwards) and the board in hiring appeared to be less concerned.

Wooten's hiring was announced in October. Her initial tasks were flying to Nashville in December for a site visit for the 1996 convention and preparing for next month's winter board meeting. 13

Missing Money

In December the Washington Association of Black Journalists reported that up to $10,000 was embezzled from its holdings and the treasurer, Jeff Ballou, resigned. The missing money came to light when the chapter executive board asked the treasurer to reconcile accounts. Instead, Ballou showed up with an attorney.

"We demanded that the attorney leave," said chapter president Beryl Anderson. "He went into the foyer and the treasurer went out to confer with him. Then the treasurer came back, confessed to taking the money in an attempt to ward off legal action for outstanding student loans and resigned." 14

The WABJ scandal was the third time in two years that a significant amount of money was missing from an NABJ affiliate. In 1993, so much money was looted from the New York Chapter the affiliate faced eviction from its offices and a member had to step in and cover a bounced $500 scholarship check. 15 And in 1995, $10,000 was embezzled from the Colorado ABJ by the treasurer. The Colorado money was recovered. 16

In each case, local chapters did not require that their treasurer be bonded, unlike every NABJ treasurer since 1983 when Tom Morgan began the practice.

Top Detroit Editor

In late fall Robert McGruder, managing editor of the Detroit Free Press, was named as executive editor of Michigan's largest newspaper. He joined the Free Press as a deputy managing editor in 1986. Before that McGruder was managing editor of the Cleveland Plain Dealer.

With his elevation, McGruder's job was guiding the newspaper during a bitter strike involving the Free Press and Detroit News that began in July.

By winter, workers and management were battered but each side showed no signs of surrender. Striking black journalists like Susan Watson and Roger Chesley of the Free Press produced a new paper, the weekly Detroit Sunday Journal. Other journalists who honored the strike but had to work, left the business or left town.

Circulation plummeted at both dailies. The Free Press dipped from 540,000 to 400,000 and the News dropped from 340,000 to 270,000. Retailers reduced or dropped their advertising.

And the strike devastated the local chapter of NABJ. "Print (members) was the heartbeat of our chapter," said vice president Kim Trent. "We lost several people because of this strike and we have about 75 active full members now. But it's not the numbers as much as it is about the quality and strong character of the journalists we have lost. There were people who were dedicated to the organization." 17

Shalit's Scold

Ruth Shalit, a 25-year-old white woman, burst on the scene with elite college credentials and a clever way with words. Her experience level made Shalit a beginning reporter in most newsrooms, yet The New Republic magazine gave her a platform to pen a scathing Oct. 2 attack of the Washington Post and its diversity efforts.

Shalit's scold concluded that the Post lowered journalism standards for the sake of diversity. She also concluded that the paper bent over backward not to offend black political leaders. Moreover, wrote Shalit, the quest for racial diversity exacerbated racial tension in the newsroom. 18

Shalit proved her point, but not in the way she intended.

Critics noted that Shalit was a serial plagiarizer. She was caught lifting other people's work, not once, but twice. Also the New Republic article contained numerous factual errors about the Post. Post editor Leonard Downie cataloged them in a three-page, single-spaced letter. 19

In trying to prove a decline in standards elsewhere, Shalit's qualifications were exposed as shaky. She was obviously bright, but remained still a green weenie in big-league journalism. Yet she had nerve to attack black and Latino journalists at the Post, who worked many years at top regional newspapers in places like Kansas City, Milwaukee, Dallas and Detroit before earning their spots in Washington, D.C. Shalit impugned the character of these experienced journalists.

She made good points, however. One was pointing out an insidious game played by some bosses that went like this: Instead of telling a white applicant that his or her work was not that hot, they could soften the blow by saying, "You're just not the right color."

The affirmative-action card was successfully dealt: Another white job applicant assumed he or she had been cheated out of a gig by a black or brown person. 20

Trotters Meet Clinton

Two weeks after the third annual retreat a dozen members of the Trotter Group interviewed President Clinton Nov. 1 in the White House. The last time NABJ members interviewed a U.S. president there was in 1978 when black journalists, black publishers and black-owned broadcasters met President Carter.

For 90 minutes, the columnists asked Clinton hardball questions about race relations and social policies. 21

Here are excerpts of what two columnists wrote about the meeting in their hometown newspapers:

"I came away feeling that Clinton thinks he knows more than he really does about (race). He is knowledgeable, but he seems as likely to make racial gaffes as most white people.

"(He) said blacks must understand the fear in white America, and not call it racism when parents pull their children close in 'high-crime neighborhoods' or to recoil at gangs or assert that welfarism is bad. Well, hell, Mr. President, we all do those things. To black ears, that kind of comment smacks of the simple-minded excuses some taxi drivers give for

avoiding all black passengers for fear of being robbed ... The president needs to stop trying to sound smart about black folks and start listening – carefully. He may be shocked at the message. It says, 'You too, may be part of this problem.'"
– *Norman Lockman, Wilmington News Journal*

"I went into the meeting expecting Clinton to dodge even our most carefully crafted questions. I came away impressed that he has thought seriously about the way blacks and whites relate in America but wondered whether he has the political resolve to convey that understanding to voters – or white ... Clinton spoke about race with a level of ease and thoughtfulness that George Bush or Ronald Reagan never achieved – or perhaps never cared to achieve. Over glasses of Coca Cola and cookies, Clinton answered the questions that he could, admitted ignorance when he couldn't answer and expressed a willingness to expound."
– *Nichele Hoskins, Fort Worth Star-Telegram* 22

Dodson Charges NY Times Bias

In winter 1996, Angela Dodson, the first African-American woman ever to be named senior editor at the New York Times, sued the newspaper for racial, gender and disability bias.

After 11 years at the Times, Dodson took a leave of absence from July 1994 to August 1995 and did not return. Dodson said she was fired, Times officials said she resigned.

Dodson's absence followed the departure of 10 high-profile black journalists from what was assumed the world's greatest newspaper. The Times' ability to retain black talent was questioned.

Dodson charged that when she was editor of the 42-member Style section she was given neither the authority or upper management support to effectively do her job. 23

Explained Yanick Rice Lamb, an editor supervised by Dodson, "There was a feeling people were making end runs around her, and that typically was not tolerated" by upper management.

Dodson's complaint said that executive editor Joseph Lelyveld and predecessor Max Frankel excluded her from planning meetings.

Moreover, after Dodson and husband Michael Days adopted four boys, Dodson, 44, charged that Times supervisors inappropriately inquired about her family situation and workload. And Dodson suffered from repetitive stress injuries and carpal tunnel syndrome and she charged that the newspaper refused "to reasonably accommodate" her disabilities.

In a statement, NABJ president Fennell said that the association was "troubled" by Dodson's accusations and the case "raise serious questions about the New York Times' commitment to diversity."

Dodson's suit and the NABJ statement angered longtime NABJ member and the Times' highest-ranking African-American editor, Gerald Boyd. Regarding the departures of Paul Delaney, E.R. Shipp, Gwen Ifill and other black journalists, Boyd said "Minorities have left the Times for a lot of different reasons. It's somewhat ludicrous" to think they were all unhappy.

Lelyveld sent a Jan. 22 memo to the staff stating that Dodson's charges filed with the New York City Commission on Human Rights were unfounded.

A black staff member who was generally satisfied at the Times said, "For the most part, I don't find the Times managed by malicious people. But it's the same thing in America – the sins of omission." 24

BET's O.J. Interview

Three months passed since the high voltage O.J. Simpson acquittal. Who would get the first interview with the celebrity who insisted he did not murder his ex-wife and her friend? CBS, CNN, ABC, NBC, FOX?

All wrong. Try BET, a familiar brand in 44 million households but still a mystery to many white viewers and a party crasher to older, larger networks that lost the exclusive.

The losers carped and ridiculed BET newsman Ed Gordon, predicting he would botch the Jan. 24 date with Simpson by asking puffy questions.

Not a chance. Gordon shamed doubters with pointed questions that made Simpson bristle with anger:

Did he kill the two people? What about the abusive relationship? Was he flaunting his innocence with his homecoming party and his golfing?

Why didn't he keep a low profile like Claus von Bulow, the man acquitted of attempting to murder his wealthy heiress wife, who many believe is guilty despite the verdict? 25

Simpson refused to answer specific details about the murder case because of civil suits filed by the families of Nicole Brown Simpson and Ronald Goldman.

The interview produced no revelations. Simpson remained adamant about his innocence. but the public benefited from hearing Simpson speak for himself in a non-circus-like atmosphere. 26

And Gordon did what long-time viewers expected, he conducted the interview firmly, respectfully, *professionally*, despite disparaging assumptions from pundits.

Pike Spiked at CBS

In the January issue of Details magazine John Pike, head of CBS-TV late night programming, reportedly said at a meeting that blacks make good audiences for late night TV because: "First, they have no place to go in the morning – no jobs – so they can stay up as late as they like; second they can't follow hour-long drama shows – no attention span – so sketches are perfect for them. Third, network TV is free."

On Jan. 31 CBS announced that Pike resigned from the network, although the executive denied making the statements. The writer of the Details piece acknowledged that he was not in the room to witness Pike spew the racial insults but the magazine "checked things extensively" after black organizations complained and it stood by its story. 27

Billie L. Greene, president of the Beverly Hills/Hollywood NAACP was not completely satisfied with Pike's departure. She and other leaders wanted a meeting with CBS executives. "This upsets us. CBS feels they can say those kinds of things and get away with them," said Greene, charging that other CBS executives had made racist and sexist comments in the past. "If it happened once – and it's already happened three times – it will happen again. We still want that meeting." 28

NABJ in a statement said it was concerned about the lack of racial diversity in the executive ranks of the network, noting that when CBS was acquired by Westinghouse broadcasting in 1995 it replaced Jonathan Rodgers, the only African-American in the executive ranks. "Regardless of what Pike is shown to have said or not said," said the statement, "the 'appropriate action' for CBS must be a demonstrated commitment to diversity at the top."

Since the fall NABJ, issued several statements on controversies in the news, and these expressions were not accidents. President Fennell kept a campaign promise to appoint a quick response team to speak to compelling issues and an editorial board to issue viewpoints. The association was sensitive to the public relations debacle created by the Mumia Abu Jamal case the previous summer. Association leaders did not want to compromise the neutrality of its newsgathering members but the more visible association did not want to appear indifferent or out of touch on hot-button issues.

"The bottom line is clarity on issues and broader national representation for the organization," said Fennell. I want to eliminate people's question marks about what this organization is and what it's about." 29

NABJ leaders realized it had to toe a tightrope and know when to speak up as a group and stay silent so its individual members could make their own decisions at their jobs.

As an association, NABJ spoke up again at its winter board meeting in New Orleans when Louisiana Gov. Mike Foster called for ending state-sponsored affirmative-action programs. NABJ stated that New Orleans would probably be dropped as a potential 2000 convention site. City officials had been courting the association to meet there at the end of the century.

Cruisin' in Cyberspace

New, but common vocabulary words in 1996: Internet, e-mail, World Wide Web, surfing in cyberspace. The information superhighway no longer was an abstraction for techno-geeks. Were NABJ members equipped to drive? Fennell appointed Condace Pressley, southeast regional director, and Herbert Lowe, secretary, to co-chair an Internet Connection committee.

NABJ showed off its Web site at the summer 1995 convention but the site was flawed. "You had to go through another organization's web site to get to NABJ," explained Pressley. Also, many "hyperlinks" or buttons to take web surfers to other web pages did not work.

NABJ's partner, the National Institute for Computer Assisted Reporting, helped. NABJ re-registered its web address as www.nabj.org and old information was wiped off the site and new pages of organization information were uplinked. 30

A CyberSurvey was included in the February NABJ Journal to find out who was online, at work, home or both and what Internet provider (CompuServe, America Online, Prodigy, others) members used.

Said Lowe, "We want to publish a magazine one day. We must be able to publish our message on the Internet as well as in print. The Journal will be a good start. We will be able to reprint certain articles and columns on the NABJ web site and keep it current month to month."

NABJ-NNPA Fence Mending?

During Black Press Week in March, leaders of NABJ and the National Newspaper Publishers Association (Black Press of America) sought to heal a longstanding rift between both associations. NNPA publishers and editors complained that their 200 mostly weekly newspapers were "the eyes and ears of the black community" and black reporters and editors working for mainstream news organizations countered that the black press did not always practice serious journalism.

The rift was plain in 1991 when former NNPA president Donald Bogle dismissed black journalists who worked in the so-called "white press" as inauthentic and Bogle's former employee, editor Garland Thompson, scolded the Philadelphia Tribune publisher in print for being disingenuous. 31

Five years after the Bogle-Thompson bout, NNPA

President Dorothy R. Leavell invited NABJ representatives to address the NNPA board of directors meeting in Washington, D.C. NABJ Secretary Herbert Lowe and Executive Director Joanne Lyons Wooten gave presentations.

Lowe, who began his career at the black-owned Milwaukee Community Journal and was now a Philadelphia Inquirer reporter, read a statement to the directors that it was time for both associations to sincerely embrace "a spirit of cooperation and brotherhood.

"From our view, it is only distortion that NABJ is the proverbial house Negro, and that NNPA is the field Negro. Both are equal partners in the struggle. There is no elitism."

Lowe criticized a NNPA national news feature that stated its editors and publishers – and not NABJ members – "are the ones who have their ears closest to the ground for what is happening in our communities." Said Lowe, "NABJ strongly disagrees that its members do not have day-to-day contacts with their communities." 32

Jane Woods-Miller, NNPA secretary and publisher of the St. Louis Metro Sentinel, got up from her seat at the end of the hotel conference table to stand less than 5 feet from Lowe and Wooten. Woods-Miller thanked them for coming then said, "I don't think there is a rift. I think the problem is that the roles are mixed up. I'm not a journalist. I'm a publisher. We are the decision makers. We do the hiring and firing. We are two separate entities. You are black folk who work for the white media."

Woods-Miller overlooked the fact – noted in Lowe's statement – that eight of the 44 NABJ founders worked for black-owned media and many of the current 2,500 members worked for black media.

Before Lowe or Wooten could respond, Leavell, publisher of the Crusader newspapers in Chicago and Gary, Ind., stepped in: "She says there isn't a rift. I say there is a rift. This is about building bridges, not burning them up." 33

Black publisher Kenneth Thomas of the Los Angeles Sentinel proposed that NABJ and NNPA hasten to join forces on divisive national issues, particularly the demise of affirmative-action programs.

Chapter 10
Online for the future

In February 1996, the Canadian Association of Black Journalists was established in Toronto by African-Canadian men and women. The time was right, explained magazine editor Angela Lawrence, because in the previous three decades her country's major cities became multiethnic and multicultural, but that reality was not evident in the media. For example, 250,000 blacks lived in Toronto, and Montreal and Halifax had significant communities of color, yet of 41 newspapers surveyed only 67 of 2,000 journalists were of color. Broadcast statistics, said Lawrence, were not much better. 1

The Canadians reached out to NABJ. Lawrence and other Canadians attended the Philadelphia convention the previous summer. President Dorothy Gilliam suggested that the fledging association use the NABJ constitution for guidance in crafting their own. CABJ expressed interest in affiliating with NABJ, which was anticipated later in 1996.

A Pulitzer for Shipp
In April, E.R. Shipp of the New York Daily News received the 1996 Pulitzer Prize for commentary. Shipp's weekly columns were often about racial, ethnic and social issues.

"There are no sacred cows in a Shipp column," said the nominating letter from the Daily News. "She is a fine reporter first, navigating and synthesizing the most complex and emotional issues. But the overriding characteristics of E.R. Shipp's columns are clarity and honesty. Her sheer honesty reveals itself through her willingness to challenge the prevailing line, to bust the myth, to bring her personal experience to bear on issues that touch not only the African-

American community, but all Americans. Shipp's no-nonsense views are rooted in a religious-like commitment to fairness."2

Shipp was a member of Abyssinian Baptist Church in Harlem, yet her affiliation did not stop her from writing a November 1994 column denouncing her pastor, the Rev. Calvin Butts, for the reasoning behind his support of a prisoner early release program.

Butts said there had been many Sundays after the service when people ran up to him. "They'd be screaming, 'Did you see what Shipp wrote?'" and then demand he expel Shipp from the church, burn her in effigy or even worse. 3 But after Shipp won the Pulitzer, the pastor announced it from the pulpit and asked that the members give her a standing ovation.

Shipp was also a professor at Columbia University Graduate School of Journalism, the university where she received degrees in journalism, law and history. She was the third African-American woman to win an individual Pulitzer in the 1990s. The others were Margo Jefferson of the New York Times in 1995 for criticism and Isabel Wilkerson, also of the New York Times, for feature writing in 1994.

Janet Again

Fifteen years after becoming the first black woman to win a Pulitzer in journalism, then return the prize in disgrace, Janet Cooke appeared on "Nightline," and the "Today" shows in May, and made appeals to return to journalism.

First however, she apologized for inventing "Jimmy," the 8-year-old heroin addict and subject of her prize-winning story-turned-hoax, "Jimmy's World."

After Cooke's disgrace, black journalists did penance for her sins. In some newsrooms, black reporters were asked if they were "Cooke-ing" their quotes. Editors called sources to double-check reporters' facts, which undermined the reporters. Also, because Cooke exaggerated on her resume, black candidates' resumes were double-checked and their references were grilled, even before new jobs were offered. Transcripts were required from every academic institution attended, decades after graduation. 4

Cooke created all this wreckage and here she was in 1996, age 41, divorced and supposed to be barely making ends meet in a low-wage department store job. Yet her former lover and Washington Post colleague told her story in the June issue of GQ magazine and there were rumors of a movie deal.

Cooke said she wanted to write again. But in response to tough questions from "Today's" Bryant Gumbel, she said: "Once you really have ruined your reputation, there is never anything you can do to change some people's minds. I have to live with that."

New Journal

The NABJ Journal had been publishing as a tabloid-size newspaper since 1985 and through the 1990s it was scheduled to appear 10 times a year. 5 Secretary Herbert Lowe called the newspaper "arguably our organization's most visible member service." 6

He was appointed to lead a committee to study the short- and long-term visibility of the Journal and by summer, radical changes were made. The newsprint format was converted into a magazine with a color cover that would publish on a bimonthly schedule. The magazine would offer subscriptions to people other than association members. NABJ contracted with The Atwood Group in Kansas to print the magazine. The new Journal would actively seek advertising. Before, the Journal accepted advertising as it came. Lowe, committee members and the board sought to convert the Journal from a valuable but severe revenue drainer to a potential profit center. 7

President Fennell was listed as publisher and the interim editor was Angela Dodson, the ex-New York Times editor. Lowe said that in the future, the new Journal would probably require a full-time editor. 8

The first cover story by Leon E. Wynter was "No Crystal Stair: Fear and loathing that the new technologies will do away with jobs for journalists," and a green skybox teased to an inside story, "How the media covered – or didn't cover – church burnings."

Convention

Nashville is synonymous with country music, but for four days in August, the emerging cyber world and presidential politics were the focus of the NABJ convention.

The convention theme, "Online for the future," could not be clearer that the computer revolution and how it would change newsgathering practices would be examined. Students published online updates of the 21st convention and longtime members hung out at the "Cybersoul Cafe," a kiosk of computers. 9 There were computer-assisted reporting workshops and a plenary session called "Keeping pace in cyberspace."

The message was clear: Get connected or get left behind. 10

"If you can read and point and push, you can compute," Allison Davis, NABJ's founding parliamentarian, assured the skeptical at the "Keeping Pace" plenary session. Davis, a former NBC "Today" producer, coordinated a Web site for MSNBC, the new multimedia newschild sired by Microsoft and NBC. "The future is here," said Davis. "I suggest you get on board now."

Los Angeles Times correspondent Sam Fulwood voiced the fears of many journalists rooted in tradition: "When we hear in newsrooms many people [now] talk about what we do as 'content,' some of us who are kind of old-school like me, we get kind of nervous."

Davis and other panelists insisted that journalism – even if referred to as "content" and "product" – was still in demand in the new online, multimedia world. "When we hire," explained Davis, "what we're looking for are good journalists. I don't care if you know HTML code; I just don't want you to be afraid of the computer. The issue is not whether or not you can code; it is: Can you tell a good and accurate story that people are going to read." 11

Bill LaVeist, online information editor of Phoenix Newspapers, Inc., (Arizona Republic and Phoenix Gazette) said that stories in cyberspace took on a greater life because words in a breaking story could be complemented by pictures, sounds and archival material.

A nagging concern was whether blacks in general would be left behind as the rest of America surged ahead on this information superhighway to cyberspace. "I'm really not concerned about it," said David Ellington, president of Netnoir, "the cybergateway to Afrocentric culture." He said, "Ninety percent of white folks aren't online. I'd really be worried is this were the year 2000 and this few black folks were online." Members became familiar with these new online sources: Netnoir; Black on Black Communications (BOBC.com); The Black World Today (tbwt.com); Africa News Online and the Pan-African News Agency.

Newsmaking Nexus

Nashville was NABJ's most newsmaking convention venue in its 21-year-history. Consider the list of newsmakers: Republican president and vice president candidates Bob Dole and Jack Kemp. Democrat Vice President Al Gore, a native son. Nation of Islam Minister Louis Farrakhan.

Also Jesse Jackson, Olympic Gold medalist Dominique Dawes, assistant attorney general Deval Patrick, Atlanta Mayor Bill Campbell, movie director John Singleton ("Boyz in the Hood," "Poetic Justice"), NBA legend Isaiah Thomas and author and professor Michael Eric Dyson. 12

C-SPAN broadcast live appearances by Dole, Kemp and Farrakhan. Photos of Dole with NABJ President Arthur Fennell ran above the fold on the front pages of The New York Times and Washington Post, firsts for an NABJ convention. 13

Senator Dole made news when he declared that the GOP would aggressively appeal for black votes for the November election. The challenger acknowledged that he made a mistake in turning down a bid to speak at the NAACP convention the previous month. Dole's appearance on the Friday of the NABJ convention was his first before a major African-American audience since the Kansas lawmaker began his campaign 18 months ago. 14 In an answer to a question, Dole said he "will not support" a constitutional amendment to deny citizenship to the children of illegal immigrants, as called for in the GOP platform.

Dole and Kemp said that blacks would benefit most from Republican economic proposals. Dole however appeared to lose many of his NABJ listeners when in explaining his opposition to affirmative action he told the crowd that "you made it on your own" without such programs. 15

Gore spoke the next day to a considerably smaller national press contingent. He previewed themes that he would articulate a week later at the Democratic National Convention. For example, the winner of the November election might be nominating three Supreme Court justices, that 45 African-Americans now serve in key roles the White House, that the Clinton administration supported affirmative action, and that black unemployment during the first Clinton term dipped into the single digits. 16

Gore told anecdotes about his journalist days as a reporter for the Nashville Tennessean in the early 1970s and he pointed out former colleagues – Dwight Lewis, C.W. Johnson and Reginald Stuart – in the NABJ audience.

Wrath of Farrakhan

Minister Louis Farrakhan's Aug. 21 appearance got off to a disturbing start when Nation of Islam security guards made early arriving journalists undergo body searches. NABJ board members said they had agreed that the NOI could use metal detecting "wands," but before the event began, the security officials announced that the wands had not arrived so association members would be body searched.

Men and women were asked to get into separate lines for the "Muslim reception procedure" and were searched in private booths by members of the same sex. 17

During the searches, Julia Cheng of the Greenwich (Conn.) Time was told by security that she could not photograph the searches. Cheng shot her pictures anyway, and an already tense situation intensified.

"Don't touch me," said at least one woman sternly to members of the security detail. Other association members refused to go in. 18 The searches were suspended when NABJ board members complained directly to Farrakhan, pointing out that the Nashville convention was an NABJ, not NOI, event. 19

"I'm very, very honored to have this opportunity to speak to a most influential group of our brothers and sisters," began the minister. He followed with a few platitudes about the importance of the Fourth Estate and its link to American democracy. Then Farrakhan said the owners of newspapers and TV stations don't run them for the good of the masses and black journalists who worked for them were part of the problem:

"You are (a) National Association of Black Journalists that work for white institutions. And white folk did not hire you to really represent what black people are really thinking. And you don't really tell them what you think because you are too afraid of that little cheap gig that you have." 20

Some of Farrakhan's tongue lashing suggested that black journalists in mainstream media did not defend his inflammatory remarks about Jews and Israel, sound bites that had led the news and overshadowed his self-help and self-respect messages to blacks.

Said Farrakhan, "You've known me a long time, some of you. And when you hear them beating the hell out of me, because I'm supposed to be an anti-Semite and a bigot, it would be really nice to hear your brother who applauds you behind the door say something out front – that, 'He's not the man that you think he is. He a lot better than that.'" 21

Farrakhan called NABJ, "a poor group of rich people" because "they said they didn't have no money to give me." 22

The minister also said, "Don't get caught up in the Mercedes Benz, and the image of how you look on TV. Get caught up in what you mean to a democratic society and what you mean to a suffering people." Farrakhan spoke for an hour to about 800 people. 23

When the Q & A session began, moderator Warner Saunders of WMAQ-TV Chicago said, "Well I guess everybody needs a spanking once in a while. Honest to God, brother minister, if I hadn't been searched at the front door, I would have taken that knife I brought in here and cut my wrist."

Saunders then asked what had been tangible evidence of the effects of the Million Man March 10 months ago.

"Fourteen thousand applications have been filed for adopting (black) children," answered Farrakhan. "The crime rate in many cities has indeed gone down. And again, black men went home to their (families) and asked for forgiveness."

During some audience questions, Leah Bennett of the Tallahassee Democrat told Farrakhan that access to NOI spokesmen was difficult, as if a code of silence existed within the Nation. "I want to know," said Bennett, "what's the best way for us who do work for the establishment papers to get some of the information we need to tell the truth?"

Farrakhan's answer: "We don't trust the press and we don't have too much trust for reporters, and I don't see any reason why we should."

Farrakhan's lashing of black journalists in the mainstream media was self-serving. He was a lightning rod that jolted the public, whether he was organizing the Million Man March last year or taking a February "Friendship tour" to Sudan, Libya and Iraq, nations with strained U.S.-government relations, and also links to terrorism, torture and even slavery. Indeed, Farrakhan was scrutinized by the media and he didn't like criticism.

The minister belittled NABJ members for allegedly being intimidated by their white bosses. But wasn't he doing the same thing in Nashville?

"Louis Farrakhan did what he does best. He huffed, he puffed, scolded and intimidated a group of black journalists into not asking him the hard questions that needed to be asked," wrote Gregory Kane of the Baltimore Sun. "He charged black journalists with being cowards afraid to defend him to their white bosses when he's attacked for anti-Semitism.

"He had the coward part right. If anyone heard the faint sound of clucking anywhere in the United States around 5 p.m. on Aug. 21, that would have been the noise of journalists at this convention turning chicken." 24

The minister did score a partial truth: In the 1993 survey "Muted Voices," 32 percent of black journalists responded that they feared "that bringing up race issues – ranging from coverage of the black community to diversity in the newsroom – damages your chances of advancement."

Still, two-thirds of those who responded answered "no" and many of those people became journalists to correct distorted images and to speak up. 25

Michael Eric Dyson, the convention's DuBois lecturer, noted Farrakhan's disingenuousness regarding his digs about "cheap gigs" and alleged obsessions with Benzes and looking good on camera. Farrakhan should have been reminded, said the University of North Carolina professor, when he criticized black journalists who drive Mercedes Benzes, that, "Of course, you're living in the poorhouse up there in Chicago."

Dyson also said that the Nation of Islam promotes anti-democratic discourse within its ranks – "We know about the homophobia and the misogyny and God knows the patriarchy and gender oppression." 26

Deval Patrick, assistant attorney general for civil rights at the U.S. Department of Justice, told a luncheon audience that "race relations is the only social problem we still face that we are attempting to solve by denial." He said that because of his department's work, African-American and Hispanic tenants were living in apartments they were previously blocked from renting. Also, white assailants of blacks and other civil rights violators were put in jail. 27

Clinton nominated Patrick co-chairman of the National Church Arson Task Force in June. Forty-two people had been charged in 26 of the 74 fires that occurred since January 1995. 28

Award Winners

William Brower, recently retired associate editor of the Toledo Blade, was the 1996 Lifetime Achievement winner. He began work as a reporter at the Ohio daily in 1947 and was among a handful of black journalists in the mainstream press at that time. In 1951, 1972 and 1995-96, Brower traveled the USA to write several series on race relations. 29

Ed Gordon was the Journalist of the Year. His signature event was his interview on BET with O.J. Simpson. How did he get that exclusive? Gordon had interviewed Simpson lawyer Johnnie Cochran while covering the trial and he worked every angle to get the interview.

Gordon believed what put him over the top was a necktie. Cochran liked one of his ties, so Gordon bought one for the attorney. After working at BET since 1988, Gordon in July joined NBC as a host and anchor on MSNBC and a contributor to "Today" and "Dateline."

Babacar Fall of Senegal was the Percy Qoboza winner for international journalism. Fall in three years revived the UNESCO-funded Pan-African News Agency and made it the first on the continent to have internet access. He was a key supporter of press freedom and trained many journalists.

The NABJ Sports Task Force honored Olympic gold medalist Dominique Dawes, 19, and raised $1,000 for the scholarship fund. The task force also staged a plenary session on whether high school athletes should jump to the NBA and skip college. Isaiah Thomas, general manager of the Toronto Raptors, was a panelist. The NABJ Visual Task Force raised $5,000 for scholarships with its photo auction.

Strong Finish

In June, only 700 people registered for the Nashville convention and there were concerns that hundreds of members might stay home rather than travel to a mid-size Southern city. Revenues might suffer after a good show the previous year in Philadelphia. The worries vanished when the Nashville convention ended. Attendance was more than triple the amount of June pre-registration and was a few hundred people less than the 2,500 who came to Philadelphia. Nashville revenues were $500,000, and because of lower costs and more money that was raised, the take was comparable to Philadelphia. 30

Drug Conspiracy?

During the convention a story broke in California that would stir black communities through the fall. "Dark Alliance," a three-part series from Aug. 16-18 by San Jose Mercury News reporter Gary Webb, alleged that in the 1980s, CIA-backed Nicaraguan contras helped trigger the crack cocaine epidemic in U.S. cities by selling cheap cocaine to a Los Angeles drug dealer. The sales financed the contra rebels' war against Nicaragua's Sandinista government. 31

The stories fueled conspiracy theories in suffering black communities. Many people probably drew conclusions that were wider than what Webb documented. Webb's credibility was probably hurt by his newspaper's Web site that posted his series with additional content. Online, a man smoked crack against the background of the CIA seal, suggesting that the CIA instigated the crack sales in black communities. After many complaints, the online logo was removed.

Agenda-setting media players like the New York Times, Los Angeles Times and Washington Post produced lengthy critiques questioning the Mercury News series conclusions and accused Webb of sloppy reporting. Editorial boards at large newspapers such as the Boston Globe and St. Louis Post Dispatch called for a full investigation of the allegations. The chorus also included Washington, D.C. talk show host Joe Madison, activist Dick Gregory, California's U.S. Senators, Barbara Boxer and Dianne Feinstein, and Clinton administration drug czar Barry McCaffrey. 32

The uproar produced an extraordinary denial of wrongdoing by CIA Director John Deutch. He faced an angry and skeptical audience in South Central Los Angeles in the fall. 33

Meanwhile, the Mercury News' editors ordered Webb to stop reporting on the reputed dark alliance. The troubling story faded.

Best and Worst of Times

Nineteen Ninety Six showed many signs of improvement in Black America. According to one poll, married African-Americans earned 87 percent of what white couples earned; that was an improvement from 79 percent in 1989. African-Americans who were unmarried were having fewer children but were taking out first mortgages.

The poverty rate for blacks fell below 30 percent for the first time since the U.S. Census bureau began keeping race-based poverty statistics in 1959. And according to the Associated Press and New York Times, the proportion of young adult black high school graduates for the first time was on par with whites. 34

Yet, there were also signs of a widening gap of awareness, compassion and action between American haves and have nots, despite encouraging economic statistics. At the summer convention in Nashville, Atlanta Mayor Bill Campbell had a contrary message for NABJ members: "Not since slavery have things been this bad for African-Americans." He said for journalists, the dilemma is, "do you cover the story or avert the disaster?"

Campbell pleaded, "Find some young child (to help) – sometimes they're right in your own household. It will not happen unless you personally get involved." 35

Chapter 11
Chicago

NABJ held its winter 1997 board meeting in Phoenix, four days after the Martin Luther King Jr. federal holiday. This meeting was special because NABJ canceled a scheduled first meeting in Arizona in 1990 to protest the governor's decision to cancel the state King holiday.

At about the time of the board meeting, host regional director Norm Parrish was homeless, journalistically speaking. He was let go when the evening Phoenix Gazette folded. Parrish landed on his feet at the St. Louis Post-Dispatch in February.1 Colorado-based anchor/reporter Tamara Banks of WGN-TV replaced Parrish as regional director.

Meanwhile, the NABJ board met with news executives of the Arizona Republic, owners of the late Gazette, to discuss the disproportionate number of African-American journalists among the 60 people laid off in the Gazette newsroom. Of four black men there, two were cut and two in management were demoted. 2 Media watcher Richard Prince reported that many NABJ members e-mailed their concerns about the cuts. 3

Struggle for Journal's Soul

About two dozen NABJ members knew about an in-house struggle because they were personally involved. Hundreds of members however were unaware. Behind the scenes, there was a pitched battle for the soul of the NABJ Journal.

"Someone please explain to me how the NABJ Journal became a political football?" asked a contributor to the bimonthly that was written and edited online and then printed as a magazine.

The fight was over who had authority over content: The NABJ board, or at least some of its representatives, or the non-board members who produce it. 4

All heck broke loose in February. A board member asked – some say demanded – that an editor's note be added to Richard Prince's column at the end of an item that was critical of board meeting business.

Editors and contributors argued online that the request – or demand – defined the fight: That the board, which acted politically, could not be allowed to meddle in the editorial process of the Journal.

The redesigned Journal had been mostly praised for its look and content but was under fire for being late. The November/December issue went to press around Christmas eve and did not get into readers hands until early February. In February, NABJ decided to kill the January/February issue and return with a March/April issue.

E-mails whizzing back and forth for weeks were impassioned, at times mean and bitter. President Arthur Fennell pleaded for an end to e-mails that "air dirty linen." The answer instead was a half-dozen replies labeled "don't shoot the messengers."

But like a family fight in which regrettable words get said, some people late in February urged reconciliation and resolution. All involved wanted the NABJ Journal to be a first-class publication. The stakes were raised when it was changed in summer 1996 from a newsprint paper to a magazine with a color cover.

NABJ learned tough lessons about production. Copy arriving at the Kansas-based printer an hour late meant the Journal missed its turn on the press and that meant the magazine had to go to the end of the line and be delayed for weeks.

Candidates Come Forward

At the Feb. 28 deadline, NABJ headquarters reported that two members filed to be candidates for president: Vanessa Williams and Warner Saunders. Dwight Lewis and Robin Stone were competitors for vice president/print, but Sharon Stevens was the lone vice president/broadcast candidate.

Unopposed for treasurer and secretary were Rodney Brooks and Herbert Lowe, respectively. The parliamentarian race was contested: Robin Washington and Roland Martin. By late spring there were three candidate contests for associate representative and student representative.

Yet, a disturbing fact was that in the 10 regions, only one, Northeast Region 2, was a contested race by full members.

Why I Want to Be President

Both candidates for president of NABJ cited a commitment to the association and to black journalists as their reasons for seeking the highest office. 5 Said Williams, "I want to build on some of the successes that we've had in the last few years." The vice president/print cited the association's professional development programs and growing scholarship fund as two examples of successes.

Williams had 16 years of newsroom experience. She worked for 11 years at the Philadelphia Inquirer before joining the staff of the Washington Post in May 1996. Before joining the Inquirer, Williams worked for the St. Petersburg Times. She had covered neighborhoods, social issues, politics and city government. At the Post, Williams covered the city politics beat.

"I have the experience," said Williams. "I know the game. I know most of the people." 6

Saunders said, "I want to see if I can put the group back together and have us live out our commitment and be a little more focused on those goals." Saunders was president of the affiliate Chicago Association of Black Journalists and he had 28 years in the business. He started in the late 1960s working on several broadcast public affairs programs for Chicago stations. In 1982, he joined the staff of WMAQ-TV-5 as a sports anchor and reporter. He was anchor and reporter for the 5 p.m. broadcast. Watchers of the NBC drama "ER" recognized Saunders as the sometime telecaster on that show.

"We all have the same problems," said Saunders, adding that a strong NABJ could provide the type of support system blacks in journalism need.

The Williams vs. Saunders presidential race promised to

be livelier than two years ago when only Philadelphia newsman Arthur Fennell stepped forward to take the reins of the organization. 7

Destroying Records

And what was the subject of the item that started a fight over who should control the NABJ Journal? Prince said that Secretary Herbert Lowe had articulated to the board that he disagreed with the long-held principle that the Journal was a product of the members, not the board, and that the board should therefore keep its hands off.

Prince said he went to executive director JoAnne Lyons Wooten's house to transcribe Lowe's board comments. There, he learned about the board policy of destroying board meeting tapes after a certain amount of time had elapsed. 8

At the April board meeting in Chicago, the board voted 9-7 to continue erasing audio tapes of its meetings. 9 Lowe said the vote during the April 11-13 weekend narrowly defeated a motion to end the recent practice of destroying the records.

Proponents of erasing said other associations do this as protection against lawsuits. After the policy began in January 1996, tapes were erased after minutes from board meetings were approved, usually three months later. 10

Opponents said it was contradictory for a journalists organization to destroy records while its mission was to fight for the free flow of information and for robust debate. 11 "We hold ourselves to one standard, everybody else to another standard," Linda Waller of Dow Jones Newspaper Fund, and an opponent of the policy. 12

Vanessa Williams said she was concerned that members believed the board was trying to hide something by quickly erasing tapes: "Journalists don't want to hear that," she said. "They get really righteous." 13

There was another issue, explained Barbara Ciara, then the Region 3 director: NABJ was running out of storage space. Erasing tapes was a necessary and an innocent act, not a sinister plot. 14

Candidate Bails Out

Two months before the NABJ election, Warner Saunders

withdrew as a candidate for president. That left vice president/print Williams as the only declared candidate.

"It is with a deep sense of regret that I must withdraw my candidacy." wrote Sanders in a May 16 statement. "Today I was named the new 6 and 10 o'clock anchor of our newscast here at NBC-5 Chicago. As you can imagine, this new position also demands a tremendous time commitment that will inevitably prevent me participating in other activities."

Blame Jerry Springer for Saunders bailing out on NABJ.

When the trash talk show host was hired to do news commentaries, WMAQ-TV's lead anchors resigned in protest. Springer meanwhile did two commentaries in one week, then resigned after receiving nonstop criticism from journalists and viewers. 15 Saunders gained a huge promotion, NABJ lost a competitive presidential contest.

Could Williams overcome the curse? Arthur Fennell assumed the presidency without competition for the first time in 16 years. The last uncontested election before 1995 was in 1979. The Morris Memo, an industry newsletter edited by a former executive director, Carl Morris, said Williams "will inherit most of the do-nothing, big-spending Fennell administration when she takes office."

Lack of a clear challenge to Fennell's vision left the Philadelphia TV journalist open to broadsides. Yet the fact remained that no other member stepped forward to run in 1995, so were most of the criticisms of the outgoing president fair?

Williams was characterized as forthright, outspoken, cold and abrasive in a May/June 1997 NABJ Journal profile by Joe Davidson. Williams defined herself as direct and honest. "I've gotten better," she said about knocks that she can be impatient, volatile and sharp-tongued. She was going to need every ounce of patience and guile to lead a growing association that was dynamic but had weak spots that must be fixed. 16

Tigerized

A big story that spring was golf phenom Tiger Woods winning the Masters tournament in Augusta, Ga. Celebratory news accounts noted that Woods' feat occurred two days before the 50th anniversary of Jackie Robinson desegregating Major League Baseball. Derrick Jackson wrote in the NABJ Journal that Woods was the latest comic strip figure "in America's never-ending search for a black Superman."

Jackson wrote, "At the very moment America praises Robinson and Woods for smashing barriers, it is building new walls that will leave most African-Americans segregated and shattered." A relatively harmless, apolitical corps of black pro athletes made up .0006 percent of the African-American population and most of the 99.9994 percent that remained were feeling the effects of anti-affirmative action initiatives, increased school segregation and hostile work environments, for example, audio tapes that exposed racist practices at Texaco.

Jackson wrote that "Race relations will not improve as long as white people stand safely on the other side of the wall, cheering the precious few who can leap them with a single bound. The people of Metropolis have no right to claim Woods as their new superhero when they hand black people so much Kryptonite. The best celebration of Woods' victory would be to ensure that the 50th anniversary of it is not a weak chip shot against a never ending barrier." 17

In that same edition, columnist Wiley Hall catalogued white male terroristic acts in "The pathology of white males: Major methods needed to protect Fortress America."

After noting the Oklahoma City bombing case, the pipe bomb explosion at the Olympics and a handful of other recent cases, Hall slyly wrote "Obviously, white American males have spiraled out of control. They have become a serious threat to domestic tranquility, and something has to be done."

On May 27, NABJ office workers discovered that a central processing unit was stolen and another computer was damaged. Three other offices at Taliaferro Hall at the University of Maryland were burglarized, too.

The break-in was the second at NABJ headquarters that year. On Jan. 28, NABJ jackets, plants, coffee mugs and other items were stolen and a computer was destroyed.

Damage was estimated at $7,600. Most of the expense was recovered through insurance claims and restitution from four teenagers who were charged with theft.

Financial records that were deleted from the computer were replaced from a backup financial management system maintained offsite. The damaged computer was replaced in March. [18]

In May, Bennie Ivory was named executive editor of The Courier-Journal in Louisville, Ky., advancing from the same position at the Wilmington, Del. News Journal. The C-J's publisher said Ivory would continue to stress strong local and regional coverage, watchdog journalism and public service.

Ivory pledged that the newspaper's reporting would be "aggressive, aggressive and aggressive." As managing editor at the Clarion-Ledger in Jackson, Miss., Ivory directed reporting that led to the re-indictment of white supremacist Byron De LaBeckwith in the murder of civil rights leader Medgar Evers 26 years earlier. DeLaBeckwith was convicted in 1994. [19]

Anticipation in Chicago

NABJ appeared positioned to set new convention attendance records in Chicago July 16-20. In June, at least 80 percent, or 1,600 of 2,019 rooms at the main convention hotel, the Hyatt Regency, were reserved by NABJ participants on the peak nights, Thursday and Friday, said DeOtis Fields, certified meeting professional at the Hyatt Regency. [20]

Capacity was also high and filling up fast at Swissotel and Fairmont, spillover hotels, said CABJ hosts. Hosts Lynn Norment and Warner Saunders projected 4,500 to 5,000 people coming to the convention. Even a conservative projection based on hotel occupancy meant at least 3,000 attendees. [21] Last summer in Nashville, 2,200 attended. [22]

Record Convention

The 22nd convention was huge, highlighted by an in-person address by Bill Clinton – the first sitting U.S. president to visit NABJ – and an earnest plea from just-released political prisoner Geronimo Pratt to fight for justice.

A record crowd of 3,300 people – at least 50 percent more

than last year's convention – set an association record. The national office said the count eclipsed the 2,500 who came to Philadelphia in 1995. Attendance also topped at least 3,000 NABJ participants who were the largest delegation at Unity '94 in Atlanta with Hispanic, Asian and Native American journalists.

On Saturday night Arthur Fennell passed the leadership of NABJ to Vanessa Williams. The longtime board member promised a 1997-99 administration of "Straight talk, hard work and no bullshit.

"I am grateful, I am humble and I am ready," said Williams. "Our race is now beginning.

"NABJ must secure its place in cyberspace. We must push the industry. We will not wait for ASNE (editors), RTNDA (news directors) or NAA (publishers) to set an agenda for our future.

"We will establish an NABJ Institute and bury the lie that qualified black journalists can't be found."

Two thousand people applauded in the banquet hall at the Hyatt Regency. 23

Williams' remark about the institute was poignant because its current fate was decided by 50 members who participated in a sparsely attended but contentious business meeting Friday morning.

Plans to move the Media Institute forward were tabled when members voted 23-18 to require the board to make a 70-page strategic plan available to members. Fennell and other executive board members said they did not have the plan at the meeting.

Members also voted 37-2 with six abstentions to end the practice of erasing tapes of board meeting action. "If a school board did this we would be all over them," said former president and treasurer Tom Morgan. Before the vote, he urged the end of the procedure because "we are journalists, not lawyers. We pay lawyers to keep us out of trouble." 24

Some members feared that the derailed approval of the strategic plan spelled trouble for NABJ. Morgan called the 23-18 vote to table "a strong repudiation – close to impeachment."

Southwest Region 7 director Warren Bell disagreed and said the strategic plan "could have been easily worked out, but now the board members' hands are tied for a full year. It was deliberate." 25

Sidmel Estes-Sumpter said she had been asking the same tough questions about the strategic plan six months before the meeting. Melanie Burney of the Associated Press said she was appalled by the tone of the meeting: "Much of it was personal and not for the good of the organization. While we should disagree, we should be respectful." 26

Williams was elected president with no opposition. In contested races, Robin Stone of the New York Times was elected vice president/print, 441-347, over Dwight Lewis of the Tennessean. For parliamentarian, Robin Washington of the Boston Herald edged out Roland Martin of KKDA radio in Grand Prairie, Texas 363-359.

In the only contested regional director race among 10, Roxanne Jones of the New York Daily News defeated incumbent Mark Griffith 110-55 for the right to represent Region 2 – New York, New Jersey and Pennsylvania.

Voter participation was about 47 percent of 1,700 working journalists who were eligible. Nearly half of those who voted did so by absentee ballot.

President Clinton

The president spoke July 17, hours after addressing the NAACP convention in Pittsburgh. He was warmly received. Clinton solicited black journalists' help in bridging the racial divide in the United States.

"If you look through all of human history," said Clinton, "societies have been defined by people in coherent units who pit themselves against one another. We shouldn't kid ourselves. This is not an easy task, but there is hardly anything more important."

Four black journalists, including a college student, asked Clinton one question each. One question from a San Francisco radio reporter was what can be done about the dismantling of affirmative action in education, specifically Proposition 209 in California. Clinton said he hoped to find a way to restore the programs. "There may be some ways to get around it," said Clinton. "I think we can reverse it in a couple of years."

Many NABJ members, the general media, viewers and readers were perplexed that none of the four questions was about the debate on whether white U.S. political leadership should apologize to African-Americans for two centuries of slavery and its residual impact 130 years after the 1860s. That summer, U.S. Rep. Tony Hall, D-Ohio proposed that Congress apologize for slavery. 27

The Chicago Tribune reported the next day that the question was anticipated, but not asked. Some NABJ members who also belonged to the Trotter Group – columnists who met twice with Clinton at the White House in 1996 and last spring – were beside themselves. They concluded that the interviewers did not prepare well.

Immediately after the president's visit, a few members interviewed at random gave mixed reviews on the relevance of the slavery apology question. "I was surprised that they did not ask it," said Lisa Dandridge of WREG-TV3 in Memphis. "I thought at NABJ, that would be the question that we would ask. I'm not disappointed, but I'm shocked it didn't come up."

David Pollard of the Chillicothe (Ohio) Gazette said, "I think it's kind of silly to ask one man to apologize for something that happened for 400 years. I think it's about time a president brought up the race issue and said we need to talk about it." This was a reference to the race relations commission that was led by African-American historian John Hope Franklin.

Five hours before Clinton addressed NABJ, Washington, D.C. radio host and activist Joe Madison said, "If the president wants to apologize (for slavery) have him apologize for a U.S. that culturally conditioned itself to believe that black people are inferior."

Madison accepted an NABJ service award on behalf of Gary Webb, the San Jose Mercury News reporter who wrote a series last summer on alleged crack cocaine smuggling into minority communities that subsidized guerrilla wars in Central America, conducted as the CIA looked the other way.

The series was ridiculed by some of the major media and it sent a jolt through large segments of the black community, who demanded vigorous investigation.45

Senator Moseley-Braun

U.S. Sen. Carol Moseley-Braun, D.-Ill., was politely received at the closing banquet July 19. Congress' only African-American senator had a tumultuous first term that included an ill-advised trip to Nigeria to meet with leaders who canceled democratic elections and executed opposition leaders. In her address she made a plea to advocate for the interests of young Americans in a climate of social program cutting. "Welfare became a code word for race that corrupted the debate, no matter that the facts contradicted the assumptions," she said. "We're holding children hostage. The national commitment to the poor has ended," said Moseley-Braun, who was dissatisfied with the final drafts for welfare reform.

Regarding the media industry, the senator told NABJ members that in a whirlwind of legislation that year, minority ownership of broadcast properties fell from 2.5 percent to 0.5 percent because of changes in the broadcast certificate program. "The optimistic vision of the generation before us," said Moseley-Braun, "need not be lost. It's our patriotic duty that our children do better than us ... Our generation must be creative and disciplined," and not succumb to pessimism.

Salute to Excellence

Less was more. A scaled down "Salute to Excellence" awards program was held in a caberet-like venue, Park West, and was near capacity.

Award presentations moved quickly, unlike recent years when excess turned people off and away.

Even the entertainment worked. Six Bryant Ballet dancers emerged from darkness then mist to open the program. At the midpoint, Toronto pop star Deborah Cox sang her hit tune "Sentimental" for a grooving NABJ crowd. Cox flirted with the teenage male escorts and they almost melted off stage, much to the amusement of the crowd.

USA Today corresponded Gary Fields received the Journalist of the Year award for exhaustive coverage of the burnings of dozens of black churches in the South. "The amount of history you lose if a 100-year-old church burns is tremendous, not to mention the disconnect," said Fields. "When churches are gone, the center place is gone."

The Lifetime Achievement winner was Samuel L. Adams, associate professor of journalism at the University of Kansas since 1973 and curator of the Ida B. Wells Award. "My greatest accomplishment is keeping the faith and overcoming obstacles that were usually placed there because of race," said Adams. "If you're going to conquer the tiger, you must first know its ways."

The Percy Qoboza winner for international journalism was Marie-Roger Biloa, director general of Paris-based AFRICA International magazine. The Cameroon native said her magazine began with a cover story on the first Africa-African American summit in 1993 in Abidjan, Ivory Coast. Circulation was 100,000 and readership was 500,000.

A sour note in a mostly upbeat awards program was the ironic success of BET News, with the winners accepting a handful of prizes then noting that the network canceled its news programming. 28

DuBois Lecture

If W.E.B. DuBois were alive it is likely he would cast President Clinton as an actor in a "theater of the absurd," Pulitzer Prize-winning biographer David Levering Lewis told about 75 NABJ members Saturday morning July 19.

Lewis answered a question about Clinton's claim that his push for honest, open discussion about race relations could be the "third great American Revolution." Said Lewis, "Clinton makes passionate, eloquent speeches to the people who are not the problem. He is preaching to the converted."

Lewis, distinguished professor of history at Rutgers University, was the 1997 DuBois speaker. He wrote "W.E.B. DuBois: Biography of a Race, Volume I (1868-1919)" in 1993. The book covered the first 50 years of the scholar's life. "Biography of a Race" received the 1994 Pulitzer Prize for biography. Lewis was working to complete volume II, covering 1920 to 1963. DuBois died in Ghana at age 95 during the week of the March on Washington. 29

During a 45-minute lecture and about 20 minutes of questions Lewis said:

• DuBois tried many strategies including scholarship, journalism and propaganda to promote the interests of black Americans.

• During many evolutions of DuBois' development, 1935-1948 was a period of "Talented Tenth Marxism mixed with liberal optimism."

• DuBois' Harvard peer, journalist William Monroe Trotter, "jump-started DuBois' public career" by forcing him to confront the accommodationist political strategy of Booker T. Washington. Trotter's Guardian newspaper was "reckless as it was principled" said Lewis, and DuBois and Trotter "were under the rubric of principled journalism," regardless of the risks.

• The proposal that the U.S. Census Bureau add a biracial category to count Americans seems "harmless" but Lewis was aware that politicians feared losing a percentage of their followers.

David Levering Lewis said African-Americans need to be "more ecumenical" when debating because unlike the past when many positions were clear, current debate in the black community is fragmented. "Do we go it alone or in coalitions?" Lewis asked. "The fact that we pose more questions means there will be more answers for them." 30

Black and White Movie Experience

It was just a movie – or so E.R. Shipp thought as she scrounged up tickets to the special screening of "Soul Food" at the convention. But "Soul Food" became a lesson in how cultural differences pose challenges that were difficult for even professional communicators to overcome. It was a sobering reminder of the distortions that can transpire when journalists interpret the world through different prisms. 31

"Soul Food," scheduled to open in theaters that fall, was a comedy-drama about a family that observed a 40-year tradition of elaborate Sunday dinners at the home of matriarch Mother Joe. Tragedy strikes, and in scenes both humorous and poignant, even a few macho guys at the NABJ screening grabbed their hankies. The question was whether the Sunday dinner – and the family – would survive.

The screening was an interactive, communal experience. Some in the audience talked back to the characters on the screen. There were laughs en masse, screams, rooting for the good guys, boos for the bad guys.

Shipp took two freshly graduated Columbia University J-school students, Wendell, who is black and Mark, who is white. Wendell fell right into the spirit of the evening, like Shipp. Mark was a bit taken aback, especially at a scene in which the haughty character played by actress Vanessa Williams lost her ice princess cool and, at a family party, went after her philandering husband with a knife. The audience whooped it up, laughed, applauded and egged her on. Mark was perplexed – and appalled.

Vanessa Williams' character, a successful lawyer, having been forced to come off her high horse and finally demonstrate passion about something other than her career, had done so in a quintessentially lowbrow manner. It was fairly clear to Shipp, given the tone and texture of the rest of the film, that there would be no actual violence, and there wasn't. But where she, and probably Wendell, saw a funny scene, Mark, already discombobulated by the interactive experience in the theater, saw black people cheering for a violent act.

When Mark and Wendell discussed the movie then brought Shipp into the debate, it was as if they'd seen two different movies with two different audiences. Neither could fathom the other's reaction. Mark and Wendell, both armed with master's degrees awarded to them in May, were about to begin interpreting the world for readers and viewers. They could not even agree on what happened at a movie. One might have produced a story about the good time had by all, the other, a piece on the callous attitude of blacks toward domestic violence. Neither would have conveyed the whole story. That journalists of different racial and cultural backgrounds could view the same thing so differently proved that they were like most people. But the consequences were more far reaching. At a time when greater diversity of the journalistic workforce was demanded to reflect varied perspectives, there was a slight decline in the number of black reporters and editors at newspapers, as well as the number of stories by minority reporters that made it onto television. The decline was worrisome because often, what was in question was more than a review of a movie. 32

At the convention, Yale University political science professor Martin Gilens presented his study, "Race and Poverty in America: Public Misperceptions and the American News Media," published in the Public Opinion Quarterly. Gilens' study reported that from 1988-92, although African-Americans accounted for 29 percent of the nation's poor, national newsmagazines Time, Newsweek and U.S. News & World Report illustrated stories about the poor with images of black people 62 percent of the time. Network TV newscast distorted reality further. When stories involved the poor, 65 percent of the people shown were African-American.

"By implicitly identifying poverty with race," said Gilens, "the news media perpetuate stereotypes that work against the interests of both poor people and African-Americans."

On July 16, the opening day of the convention, Dennis Clyde Schatzman, NABJ's first executive director, died in Ontario, Calif. at age 47. He served less than a year until early 1987 and a decade later most members probably recognized him as a black press correspondent covering the O.J. Simpson trial in 1995. He was also co-author of "The Simpson Trial in Black and White" with Tom Elias. 33

Some people called NABJ President Vanessa Williams bold; others would say she was straightforward. While backstage with President Bill Clinton, she said to the commander-in-chief, "I'm president-elect. Do you have any advice for me as president?" Clinton told her, "Always act like you know what you're doing." 34 Despite her perceived audacity, Williams said her new role as NABJ president was "very humbling because so many people have high expectations." Indeed. Membership was growing in an ever-expanding age of technology, but there were troubling signs of detachment among members, local chapters and the national organization that could leave the association flailing in rugged waters.

Chapter 12
Strategic plans

In September, two months after 41 members convinced the board to delay the release of a strategic plan, a summary of the plan for a proposed institute was distributed to all members.

The strategic plan studied 10 areas in which the 17 member board and staff was to improve planning, implement programs and services and ensure financial stability. 1

Areas and highlights from 38 recommendations included:

• FINANCE: More authority and autonomy should shift from the treasurer to the executive director, including drafting and formation of the annual budget.

• FUND RAISING: Develop a group of national funders who will move with the annual convention from year to year.

• MEMBERSHIP SERVICES: Better market the association programs to local and national members. Most members forget matching grants are available for chapters, and an Infonet project and other programs exist.

• PROGRAMS: Increase community outreach programs such as "Journalists Across America" and urban journalism workshops.

• CHAPTER RELATIONS AND SUPPORT: Immediately resume the annual recertification process as called for in the constitution and operating procedures.

• OFFICE STAFF AND STRUCTURE: As of June, the association's $1.5 million budget supported five full-time staff members. The American Society of Association Executives recommended about a dozen full-time staff.

• BOARD STRUCTURE AND GOVERNANCE: Recommended a modified ladder system for NABJ executive officers and have staggered terms to ensure continuity in leadership.

• TECHNOLOGY: Already implemented were links from the NABJ home page to affiliate and student chapter Web sites.

• MARKETING: Enhance the marketing and sales of association identity items and create a catalog of items.

• NABJ INSTITUTE: It would stand alone as a center dedicated to developing skills and leadership potential of African-American journalists and compiling, disseminating and chronicling information on African-Americans and the media industry. Five program areas included archives and entrepreneurial development.

Also in September, Linda Florence Callahan, North Carolina A&T University professor, was named associate member representative to the NABJ board of directors. Also, Cindy Lynette George, a junior and journalism major at the University of Florida, was named student representative.

More Money and Responsibility

At the October NABJ board meeting in Denver, the Chicago convention report stated that 3,211 people registered. That represented about a 32 percent increase over the previous convention in Nashville.

Revenue numbers were fatter. Total revenues were about $1.4 million before $833,000 in expenses. The net profit or surplus for NABJ was $561,700 – a record. The affiliate Chicago ABJ made $65,000 from fund-raisers and its share of convention program advertisements. 2

More money, more members meant more challenges in managing the volume. The board talked about better management of dozens of chapters. Although they were run by journalists, it was critical that they operate like businesses.

"For everybody's sake, get some management," said President Vanessa Williams, who also admitted, "We need to give our chapters some guidance on getting operations in order and also how to do it." 3

What many chapters needed was 501(c)3 status, incorporation as non-profit organizations like NABJ, and bonding of the officers who handled money. Some chapters met all of the criteria, others met some or none.

Board members debated how quickly all chapters should be uniform before penalties were necessary. Southeast Region (IV) Director Condace Pressley spoke for urgency: "Everybody is thinking and talking about it. It's time for chapters to start doing it." Northeast Region [II] Director Roxanne Jones urged more time and guidance. She said that chapters need "a step-by-step 'this is how we do this.' We need more of an instruction sheet of how they do it." Vice President/Print Robin Stone said that chapters should know that meeting all of the criteria should be a priority for them and board members must "be clear that this is the making of a new policy." 4

The urgent need to operate all chapters efficiently was illustrated in the lead story of the inaugural NABJ Update newsletter in November. Joe Davidson reported in "Missing Money" that former officers of the Indianapolis and New Orleans chapters acknowledged taking $10,000 and $1,800 respectively from chapter accounts for personal use.

Glendal Jones paid back the $10,000 to Indianapolis and apologized for the theft at an August meeting. Karen Cestelan apologized to members in New Orleans for making out chapter checks to cash in order to make payments for her daughter's school. Cestelan had begun restitution, said current chapter president Pearl Stewart.

The Indianapolis and New Orleans scandals were a new round of incidents after financial irregularities that came to light in 1995 in Denver and Washington, D.C. The incidents exposed sloppy operating procedures. For example, in New Orleans, the treasurer at the time of theft had no access to the chapter's books. Eddie Francis told chapter members in a letter, "he does not have and has never had any financial documents." With dozens of chapters and high expectations to attract members and raise money, the Indianapolis and New Orleans embarrassments were warnings that all NABJ chapters must have their organizational structure and financial records in order.

By October 1997, 137 of NABJ's 3,000 members were using the online Listserv, a vehicle for driving on the information superhighway, or Internet. Members sent e-mail to NABJ@UMDD.UMD.EDU. This was called "sending mail to the list." The Listserv made copies for all the people who subscribed.

Many people posted job openings. In another instance, members offered advice to black journalism students at Louisiana State University who complained that LSU was not making a serious effort to let the NABJ student chapter function. At that time, accreditation representatives were examining the school of journalism. 5

Trotters Return to Harvard

In late October, the Trotter Group returned to Harvard University for their annual retreat, the place where 18 columnists established the society in 1992. At the Harvard Kennedy School of Government Arco Forum, nine Trotter members critiqued the Clinton race initiative before a packed auditorium of 300 people. Here were some of the columnists' observations:

• The Clinton race initiative could also be called "better living through denial" because it is nice words that lack action, said Lewis Diuguid of the Kansas City Star.

• "Racism exists at 30,000 feet but not on the ground," said Les Payne of Newsday, because whites including President Clinton "can acknowledge racism but cannot name a white racist."

• "Black and white (relations)," said Betty Winston Baye, "is a story of a dysfunctional family. This black and white thing is a fight in the family." As for the affirmative action conflict, the columnist from The Courier-Journal of Louisville, Ky. said the quiet beneficiaries of affirmative action were white women.

Based on what you've written and said, can Clinton do anything right? asked Harvard law professor Charles Ogletree, the moderator.

"We are critiquing President Clinton," said Payne, "because we have a chance to influence the policy," unlike previous administrations when black opinion writers did not have opportunities to sit down with a U.S. president, like the Trotters did in 1995 and June 1997. 6

Vernon Jarrett, retired Chicago Sun-Times and Tribune columnist, said the tone only seemed harsh because "Black America walks a tightrope between disaster on one side and near disaster on the other."

Triumphs and Traumas

In summing up 1997, it was a significant year for a number of high-profile black newsmakers:

• Michael Jordan led the Chicago Bulls to another NBA championship and Tiger Woods repeated as Masters golf tournament champion. Both men pursued lucrative product endorsements.

• Oprah Winfrey continued to be a daily guest in countless American homes.

• Wynton Marsalis was awarded the first Pulitzer Prize given to a jazz composition for his oratorio "Blood on the Fields."

• Kenneth "Babyface" Edmonds and crew topped the pop charts and crossed over from music to film production with "Soul Food," which filled theaters from coast to coast with black folks talking back to the screen.

• Meanwhile, producer Debbie Allen shepherded an inspiring, underreported chapter in American history, the Amistad rebellion of 1839, toward the big-screen treatment it deserved. 7

But prominent individual black success was tempered by dismal news affecting the masses. Many people were still hurt by a dearth of jobs, the torpedoing of the federal safety net, inadequate education and shorter life expectancy.

In February, African-Americans in Miami staged a "blackout," taking off from work and school to hold a peaceful downtown rally.

In October, a Million Woman March took place in Philadelphia with demonstrators pressing a wide range of grass-roots causes. Organizers did not court the media like the Million Man March organizers did in 1995, yet that should not have been an excuse for the light coverage by many news outlets.

In New York City, the near-fatal beating of Haitian immigrant Abner Louima by police showed that some residents paid disproportionately for the lower crime rate other New Yorkers enjoyed.

New Yorker Hazel Dukes was among four people removed from the NAACP national board for alleged financial misdeeds.

And the Rev. Henry Lyons, president of the National Baptist Convention, was under investigation for obscene misuse of church funds to buy a luxury house, cars, jewelry – done with a woman other than his wife. Despite damning evidence and a "Waiting to Exhale"-like torch job of the disputed property by the preacher's wife, representatives of the 8 million member black denomination stood by Lyons. 8

Regarding affirmative action, there were losses, a significant win and even a more significant stalemate. Courts upheld the elimination of race as a factor in admissions to state universities in Texas and California. The imposition of Proposition 209 in California was widely regarded as the reason only one African-American accepted admission to the University of California Law School. Admissions officers nationwide scrambled to determine ways to defend attracting racially diverse pools of applicants to their schools.

There was victory in Houston when voters chose to maintain minority and female set-asides in city contracts after the mayor and other civic leaders argued that racial and gender inclusion was good business.

The standoff was a potential landmark Supreme Court case over affirmative action hiring and firing in Piscataway, N.J. public schools that was settled with cash from civil rights organizations eager to fight before the high court another day. 9

Perhaps the saddest convergence of crises familiar to black Americans ended with the death in June of Betty Shabazz, widow of Malcolm X. Shabazz, who had demonstrated great persistence and courage in the public eye during the 32 years since her husband's assassination.

She also fought many private battles shared by countless, unsung black women – maintaining her faith and dignity, getting an education, rearing her own children and then a grandchild.

When that 12-year-old grandchild, Malcolm's namesake, set the fire which eventually killed Betty Shabazz, black women and men responded with the prayers and tributes and grief of people who know too well how close to the edge all of us still live. 10

Staff Changes

At the end of 1997, NABJ Executive Director Joanne Lyons Wooten announced that she would be leaving in order to develop and manage land that her family owned in North Carolina. Wooten, who began serving the association at the end 1995, promised to stay through March or until a successor was chosen. NABJ moved its headquarters from Reston, Va. to College Park, Md. and developed a strategic plan on Wooten's watch. And at the time of Wooten's announcement, additional staff came on board: Communications Director Deborah Randolph Chase and Fund Raiser Patsy Pressley. 11

In March the NABJ Media Institute and Pew Center for Civic Journalism co-sponsored a workshop called "Reporting the Nuances: Civic Journalism and Communities of Color." About 70 members participated in weekend workshops in College Park, Md. The sessions were opportunities to ask more meaningful questions and expand coverage of communities of color.

Pew Center Director Jan Schaffer explained, "Civic journalism and covering the nuances is a call to return to our roots and good habits that we have lost along the way. We have to be better listeners. Get away from 'bipolar' journalism that covers the loudest voices on opposing sides of issues." 12

A week after NABJ held its Media Institute seminar in Maryland, the association staged a workshop at New York University. That event made a very good impression on

Columbia University journalism student Leticia Theodore.
She said, "It seems when 'blacks' and 'media' are
mentioned in the same sentence, it is almost always
patronizing or disastrous. Not this time. I realized for the
first time that quite a few blacks held prominent roles in the
media. It was a good feeling. We were represented
everywhere, from reporter to editor-in-chief.

"These busy and I'm sure exhausted people gave up their
Saturday for us students. They were committed to helping
future journalists and each other. On that day, every
workshop facilitator and every speaker became my personal
mentor.

"I have never belonged to a formal organization. I am
now a member of NABJ." 13

In March, Yvette Walker of the Kansas City Star was
named editor of the NABJ Journal. She succeeded Gracie
Lawson, a Detroit-based writer and editor and former
Chicago Tribune editor who stepped down to pursue full-
time graduate school study.

In her farewell column in the Winter 1998 Journal,
Lawson announced that the magazine had just switched from
bimonthly to quarterly publication. Association news and
membership information was to be published eight times a
year in NABJ Update, a newsletter edited by Deborah
Randolph Chase. 14   The Winter NABJ Journal quietly
dropped a regular feature, the editorial that was written by an
editorial board during the Fennell administration.

Executive Director Chosen

On May 6 Antoinette "Toni" Allison Samuel was
introduced as the new executive director. Samuel had held an
executive level position at the National League of Cities since
1994. She was director of the Center for Education and
Information Resources and spearheaded programs that
provided leadership, management and budgeting for four
major operations at America's largest organization of
municipal officials.

"Toni impressed us with her management skills, her knowledge about what makes an effective membership association and her enthusiasm about joining NABJ," said President Vanessa Williams. "We think she will make an excellent addition to our team."

Samuel began working for NABJ on June 1. JoAnne Lyons Wooten, who had served since December 1995, completed her service in March. 15

Dream Maker in Detroit

Crystal Mayo, one of the few black women publishers of a newspaper, the Metro Star in Detroit, was also a children's dream maker. Mayo used journalism to help children discover their potential. In 1996 Mayo began running the Detroit Free Press Journalism High School Program with journalists who served as mentors. Mayo arrived at a difficult time. Twenty one schools used to participate, however none were active during a bitter strike. Gradually, Mayo persuaded union-oriented Detroit school officials to bring schools back into the program for the sake of the children. Said Mayo, "I was able to get four schools back. From that four I got nine, from nine I have 12," said Mayo in winter 1998. 16

The high school program started in 1985 as an answer to school cutbacks that affected high school newspapers. Students were taught how to produce a high school newspaper that was published in the Free Press and distributed to participating high schools and feeder middle schools.

There also was a paid summer apprentice program. Free Press parent company Knight Ridder awarded four $20,000 scholarships annually, Ford Motor Co. (where Mayo once did creative marketing) gave a $24,000 scholarship and the Free Press awarded three $1,000 scholarships.

Mayo was able to increase sponsorship support and she broadened the high school program beyond newspapers and added radio broadcasting, graphic design, electronic media and photojournalism.

Josephine Belford, supervisor for the Detroit Public Schools Office of Communication Arts, said many students were unaware of their talents until Mayo helped uncover them. Because of this Mayo played an important role in boosting high school retention. 17

Joyce C. Ingram, the highest-ranking African-American journalist in the history of the Virginian-Pilot of Norfolk, died June 2 after a sudden illness. Ingram, 42, was a deputy managing editor of national news and directed coverage that affected Hampton Roads, Va. That coverage included military, medicine, environment and business, sports and features.

Before joining the Virginian-Pilot in 1994 she held various editing posts for a decade at the Philadelphia Daily News. Ingram conceived and directed the "Children and Violence" series, a three-year crusade that resulted in reforms, solutions and state and regional awards.

As a features editor she came up with a new name for the section, YO! It added more sass to an already spunky tabloid.

Ingram was a key line editor of the NABJ Journal when it changed from a newsletter to a tabloid-size newspaper in 1985.

Ingram was an avid art collector and devotee of the widest range of jazz from blues, bop, cool, to Brazilian rhythms. Tall and statuesque, she was at times a living Monet. In a newsroom sea of light blue and khaki, she favored rich colors in elegant designs.

Ingram was mercurial, sharp-tongued at times, painfully shy at others. She was decisive and demanding as an editor. A Virginian-Pilot staff member said Ingram was even manipulative sometimes "if the greater good was better journalism." 18

Capital Anticipation

Washington, D.C. hosted back-to-back NABJ conventions in 1979 and 1980, but the association waited 18 years to return to the nation's capital. After a well attended and profitable Chicago convention there was optimism of rising higher at a venue that was within convenient reach of the core of members from the Northeast corridor and Southern states. Seventy workshops plus plenary sessions on Race in America, Color and Coverage and the Africa No One Knows were scheduled July 29 to Aug. 2. 19

Big, Brassy Convention

Another annual attendance record was set at the Washington, D.C. convention. At the closing banquet on Aug. 1, President Vanessa Williams announced that 3,500 registered, surpassing the nearly 3,300 people who came to Chicago the previous year. 20 The last time the convention was held in Washington, D.C., 200 people participated and NABJ then lacked a national office, scholarship program, publication and many other services. 21

More than record attendance, many participants were struck by the overwhelming volume of activities – plenary sessions, workshops, reservation-only super workshops, job fair and exhibit area, gala receptions and a handful of film sneak previews and premieres.

With about a dozen scheduled activities occurring at once, every hour from 8 a.m. to 6 p.m., and a full plate of social activities all night, attendees coped with too many people to see, places to go and not enough time. 22

Attendees staying in the Grand Hyatt and Renaissance hotels went to sessions in the cavernous Washington Convention Center across the street.

In addition to professional development, job hunting, networking and reuniting with family and friends, many NABJ members focused on the future of black and other minority journalists in America. That was because of recent news industry, government and judicial decisions.

Seattle, FCC and ASNE

Members were divided on whether to withdraw from the scheduled Unity 1999 convention with Hispanic, Asian American and Native American journalists in Seattle the following July. A Washington state referendum banning all forms of affirmative action was scheduled for a November vote. The referendum, called Initiative 200, was similar to California Proposition 209 that eliminated affirmative action in that state in 1996.

A scheduled 90-minute association business meeting was extended two additional hours so the Seattle question could be discussed and debated by members. Pulling out of the convention and breaking hotel and assembly hall contracts meant forfeiture of $600,000 to $900,000 in deposits, said officers and members. Others said that if NABJ bolted, the move could bankrupt one of the smaller minority journalist associations.

Nevertheless, many members argued passionately that NABJ should not meet in a venue that was attempting to dismantle affirmative action. The board of directors decided to wait for the November vote in the state of Washington before deciding whether to stick with the plan to participate in Unity '99.

The association also agreed to file a friend-of-the-court brief in support of the Federal Communications Commission appeal of a federal court decision to eliminate equal employment opportunity hiring rules for broadcast journalism.

"Diversity in America today is under legal assault," FCC Chairman William Kennard told NABJ members at the July 30 newsmaker luncheon. "African-Americans bring a unique perspective (to broadcast coverage). I bring that unique perspective to the FCC. It matters because race matters."

Kennard said that nearly 20 percent of full-time broadcast news employees in 1997 were minorities; women of all races amounted to 41 percent. Compare that to 1971, three years after the equal employment opportunity rules were in effect. Then, minorities were 9 percent of the workforce, women 23 percent.

In the newspaper business, Vanessa Williams and other officers urged members to speak up and lobby the American Society of Newspaper Editors to stick to a commitment to strive for racial parity in newsrooms.

ASNE conceded that it would not reach the goal it set 20 years ago to achieve parity by 2000. Minorities represent 11.5 percent of the workforce; the general population was 27 percent people of color.

Robin Stone, vice president/print, told 150 people who attended the July 31 business meeting that ASNE wanted to extend the deadline to 2010 and lower the percentage goal. "Some in ASNE are trying to distance itself from its very noble mission," said Stone. "Some recommended setting different goals in big cities and letting small cities off the hook."

Sidmel Estes-Sumpter, NABJ president from 1991-93, said ASNE members were divided on what minority goals should be in the 21st century. "We need to work with forces in ASNE who want to put out a much more progressive report," she said. 23

The Africa No One Knows

Africa, said MacArthur DeShazer, executive director of The National Summit on Africa, "is one continent Americans know least about, but one we have the most opinions about, mostly negative. Journalists often reinforce those views."

At a plenary session called "The Africa No One Knows: Changing the Image of a Continent," diplomats and policy experts attempted to broaden understanding. About 300 members attended the session that was going on the same time as the contentious business meeting on July 31.

Seven African ambassadors sat in the audience and Ugandan ambassador Edith Sempala was among the six panelists.

Susan Rice, assistant U.S. secretary of state for African Affairs, said two-thirds of Africa's 50 nations were instituting economic reforms. "Today," said Rice, "a new generation of Africans are coming of age, raised in democracy and relieved of Cold War divisions."

Rice said the 1998 Africa Growth and Opportunity Act was the most important legislation regarding Africa in 1986 when economic sanctions were placed on former apartheid South Africa. The 1998 trade bill "was based on a controversial premise," said Rice: treating Africa like the rest of the world. She urged the Senate to remove fast-track conditions that were tacked on the bill and pass it, like the House of Representatives. 24

Actor Danny Glover, U.N. Goodwill ambassador to Africa, said he accepted the role in 1998 to extend the tradition of artists such as Paul Robeson and Harry Belafonte. Glover briefed the audience on his two-week visit to urban areas and rural villages in South Africa and Namibia.

"I saw people attempting to build and learn and change their lives," said Glover. "These were stories that were profound. You as journalists need to tell these stories."

DeShazer said a Georgetown University survey reported that African immigrants in America had the highest level of income and education, second only to Canadians. 25

At the Movies

A limited number of convention goers – 800 tickets were dispensed – were treated to a sneak preview of "How Stella Got Her Groove Back," Terry McMillan's novel turned into movie. The near-capacity audience couldn't stop talking about the friendship between Angela Bassett's character Stella and Whoopi Goldberg's Delilah. Nor could the women get enough of Taye Diggs, the young man with whom 40ish Stella grooved. 26

But what really got tongues wagging was McMillan's performance after the film preview. The picture ended close to midnight and it was clear that McMillan did not want to engage in idle repartee with her fans, people who adored her books and paid money to see her films.

During the 45-minute Q & A, McMillan rolled her eyes at questions she deemed silly or inappropriate. Some reporters acted like groupies, prefacing every statement – one could hardly call them questions – with kudos for the actors and the film. The last straw was when a young reporter began her question with "lush, lavish ..." Two journalists in the middle row groaned loudly and got up to leave. McMillan rested her head on the table in apparent agony.

Still, McMillan should have remembered she was there in a professional capacity. Most people will forgive the temperamental nature of an artist, but rudeness is the exception. While McMillan was impatient and even rude, co-panelist Bassett performed with grace. She made the best of a bad situation, answering trite questions with diplomacy and treated each reporter/fan with dignity they did not earn or deserve. 27

There were other fine film premieres:

"John Henrik Clarke: A Great and Mighty Walk," was a documentary on the life of the Afrocentric historian, 82, who died two weeks before the convention.

"Linc's" was the new cable-TV sitcom about a black-owned bar directed by Tim Reid ("Frank's Place" and "WKRP in Cincinnati").

"Down in the Delta," was a new film directed by Maya Angelou and starred Alfre Woodard and Al Freeman Jr.

"Sister, I'm Sorry," was a docudrama presenting testimony by women who were sexually assaulted, abandoned and mentally and physically abused. It featured actors Blair Underwood and Michael Beach and was hosted by Margaret Avery. 28

Avoid Dubious Alliances

Kimberly Crenshaw, professor of law at Columbia University and UCLA, was the annual W.E.B. DuBois lecturer. She urged 50 attendees Saturday morning not to let skin color define allegiances.

U.S. Supreme Court Justice Clarence Thomas was Crenshaw's model of a harmful black leader who won broad support based on his race rather than his ideas. "We made Clarence Thomas in ways we did not realize," she said. "Senators were unsure how to vote. They told us: Do the math. Conservative Republicans lined up behind Thomas; so did senators with black Democratic majorities.

"Three votes could have gone either way.

"There was a 'Pinpoint (Ga.) strategy': How to get a black person to the court without being 'Borked.' 29

"We got played on this."

Crenshaw counseled against repeat mistakes. "We have to distinguish our Mandelas from our Buthelezis," she said, comparing Thomas to the duplicitous rival of Nelson Mandela. Instead, she advised, "Treat our political capital like hard-earned money. Make sure our capital is well spent."

She also urged attendees to contest reactionary ideology, regardless of race. "Reactionary politics," said Crenshaw, have legitimacy in the black community where once they did not." She cited people who defend the existence of black Confederates and slaveholders and are opponents of civil rights. 30

Demographic Changes Serve as Warnings

David Seals of WTMH-TV in New Haven, Conn. was attending his first NABJ convention. "I'm here to network and meet some folks in the business I haven't met before." Seals said he did not attend previously because it was too expensive. This time he was looking for work and decided that attending was a good investment. 31

Caril Fernandes of WKMG-TV in Orlando, Fla. was a first-timer like Seals. Cost had been a factor for her too, but the 1998 site made it easy for her to attend. She stayed with family members who lived in the Washington, D.C. area.

Barbara Rodgers, reporter/anchor with KPIX-TV in San Francisco started coming to conventions in 1981. Rodgers said fellow black journalists comforted her as she dealt with difficulties on her job. She had watched the association grow and she was concerned about the change of focus.

Rodgers worried about the future of NABJ: "No one wants to run the organization. No one wants to work." The deputy Region 10 director (West coast) cited uncontested races for major offices, including president.

Rodgers said if younger journalists are willing to take advantage of current opportunities, but aren't willing to work at the national and local levels to ensure they will continue, there may not be much of a job fair, convention, or association in the future.

Noluthando Crockett, the former National Public Radio correspondent known as Phyllis Crockett, attended the convention for the first time since Unity '94. She was president of a South Africa-based media management and training and consulting company. Her attendance coincided with other business in Washington.

Crockett said she missed a number of conventions because "It was not 'it' anymore for me."

She called herself a "young elder," not old enough to be old, but too old for the job fair and many workshops.

Crockett recommended that NABJ programmers start looking at doing workshops on retirement and have programs for members like her making the transition out of traditional news. 32

Chapter 13
Ethical challenges

At the convention business meeting, the NABJ board announced that it was time to increase member dues. Since the last hike in 1991 it was $60 for full members, $35 for associates and $20 for students. Member dues funded only 8 percent of the $2 million association operating budget, reported regional directors and membership committee co-chairs Courtis Fuller and Roxanne Jones. Sixty percent of the association – 1,800 of the nearly 3,000 members on the rolls before the convention – were full members. 1

In October at its meeting in Seattle, the board approved increases to $80 from $60 for full members; $50 from $35 for associate members, and $25 from $20 for student members, effective Dec. 31, 1998. The increases were projected to raise members' share of funding of the operating budget from 8 to 10 percent and generate $46,545 in additional revenue.

What would members get for the additional cost? Nine professional development programs; five media services; four awards and recognition programs; five member programs and services, and five publications or online services. 2

Affiliate Trouble
In fall 1997, board members agreed that it was time for dozens of chapters to operate professionally and have mandatory bonding insurance in order to protect the financial integrity of affiliates. Months later, the July 1998 NABJ Update reported that only 34 of the 74 professional chapters appeared to be in compliance and 40 chapters risked

suspension. Penalties could be loss of NABJ affiliation and loss of privileges, such as the privilege to host regional or national conferences or receive funding or matching grants.

A March 31 deadline was extended to June 30, yet 40 chapters did not purchase the bonding insurance necessary for compliance. "For some reason there's a gross miscommunication between us," said Glenn Rice, Region 8 (Midwest) director and board liaison to the NABJ Council of (chapter) Presidents. "It's unfortunate that we haven't learned from other chapters' previous mistakes." 3

Globe Columnist Resigns

Patricia Smith, a black metro columnist at the Boston Globe, resigned after admitting that she fabricated people and quotes in four columns that year. Globe Managing Editor Gregory Moore confronted Smith about the veracity of her sources after a routine check by the paper found discrepancies in six of Smith's columns. 4

"From time to time in my metro column," wrote Smith in her farewell, "to create the desired impact or slam home a salient point, I attributed quotes to people who didn't exist.

"I could give them names, even occupations, but I couldn't give them what they needed most – a heartbeat," wrote Smith, 42, a published poet and past NABJ award winner.

"Patricia was never asked if she was making up things," said Moore. "In 1996 and 1997, things seemed to be fine.

"She wrote some pretty powerful columns. In May (1998) there was some reason to spot check her columns. It was a couple of quotes that were really poetic in the mouth of a regular person." 5

For example, Smith's source "Claire," a cancer patient, reacted this way to news that a cancer therapy showed promise in mice: "I'm not proud. Right away I said, 'Rub it in my skin, pop it to me in a pill, shoot me up with it. If I could find a way to steal it, I would. Hell, if I could get my hands on it, I'd swallow the whole ... mouse.'" But when asked, Smith could not prove that "Claire" existed. After initial defensiveness, Smith became reflective then confessed to juicing, or in Smith's words, "tweaking" her columns.

Smith's indiscretion rocked the Globe and saddened or infuriated many black journalists working in the mainstream press. Philadelphia Daily News columnist Linda Wright Moore wrote that Smith's "note of apology" was mostly "a compendium of excuses, tied up with a ribbon of arrogance." This was because Smith tried to explain her inadequacy away by claiming she did not have the "correct" start in journalism because she didn't "pop out of J-school in a nice, neat, byline-ready package."

In fact, Smith was an experienced journalist who had been working at newspapers since the 1970s, first in Chicago, then she became a feature writer at the Globe in 1990. She had worked in the business long enough to know right from wrong.

The fallen columnist was one awful case in an ethically challenged 1998 of too many journalistic indiscretions.

Two months after Smith's fall, Mike Barnicle, also a metro columnist at the Globe and a fixture for a quarter century, was fired. In August he was suspended for lifting one-liners from comedian George Carlin's book and giving the appearance that they were his words. Barnicle, who is white, resisted a call from the editor to resign and was initially suspended instead.

Before the crisis subsided, a new one arose: A retired Reader's Digest editor recalled a 1995 Barnicle column the magazine wanted to reprint but did not because fact checkers were unable to verify details of the columnist's story. According to Barnicle, a rich, white Connecticut couple sent a $10,000 check to a black family whose late son befriended the donor family's boy at a hospital.

"In light of his failure to follow the most basic reporting requirements, as well as the duplicitous way in which the story was written," said Globe Editor Matthew V. Storin, "It is clear Mike Barnicle can no longer write for The Boston Globe.

(In a curious coincidence, Barnicle received an NABJ "Thumbs down" award for dubious achievement in 1991. Barnicle told a TV interviewer, "I know more about being black, being under siege in this city, than any other black writer or black TV person you can name or find.")

Losing two star columnists at the same major newspaper because of ethical lapses were devastating blows in the press, yet there were more embarrassments:

• Stephen Glass, a contributing editor at The New Republic magazine, admitted to making up quotes and sources in 27 articles. Glass' habitual lying was especially troubling because he used elaborate schemes to trick the magazine's fact checkers.

• Mike Gallagher, a Cincinnati Enquirer reporter, was fired for committing what amounted to burglary for tapping into the Chiquita Banana Co.'s voice mail system to get tapes of alleged shady activities by the company in Latin America. The Enquirer apologized, paid the company millions and disavowed itself from the reporting.

• Time magazine and Cable News Network reported then later apologized for printing and airing reports that claimed lethal sarin gas was used against U.S. deserters during the Vietnam war.

• Also, "Primary Colors," the political novel that was released as a movie in 1998, deserved to be linked to the above cases. The author called himself "Anonymous," but was subsequently confirmed to be Joe Klein, a political columnist with Newsweek magazine.

When it was first alleged that he was "Anonymous," Klein assured his editor that was not the case and continued to cover Beltway politics. Then Klein was exposed. Although he wrote fiction in the literary world, Klein was a liar in the journalistic world. 6

An Emerging Problem

Chicago Tribune reporter Jerry Thomas experienced a career disaster – he was fired by his newspaper because of a free-lance article he wrote. Thomas' problem however had nothing to do with plagiarism or presenting fiction as non-fiction, like many embarrassments of 1998. He was a victim of bad timing that exposed a conflict of interest and also the changing rules of free-lancing, and because of the growth of the Internet. 7

Thomas wrote a piece for the Chicago Tribune (Sunday) Magazine on flamboyant boxing promoter Don King. The cover story ran June 21. Meanwhile, Thomas did a free-lance article on King for Emerge, the black- oriented news magazine. Editor-in-Chief George Curry promised that the Emerge piece would run after the Tribune piece in the July/August issue. However, the printer mailed that edition of Emerge in mid-June, weeks ahead of schedule, said Managing Editor Florestine Purnell.

The Emerge story arrived before the other story could be published by Thomas' employer. As a result, Tribune management fired Thomas. Also, Tribune photographer Ovie Carter received a one-month suspension because of a photo that accompanied the Emerge article. 8

Thomas did not seek permission from the Tribune to do the free-lance piece. His black colleagues in the Tribune newsroom were saddened by his exit, but did not protest. "Thomas brought a voice to the paper that nobody else had, doing stories that even black journalists shy away from," said Dahleen Glanton, a features writer and 10-year veteran. "But the consensus among the blacks here seems to be there was nothing to protest ... there clearly was a violation, and I don't know how you get around that."

Many reporters free-lanced for other media, but because of Internet growth, newspapers began tightening rules on which publications their employees could contract with. Curry said after the Thomas dismissal that future Emerge contracts with free-lance writers included a clause in which the writer stated that he or she obtained permission from their employer to write for the magazine.

Within hours of being fired by the Tribune, Thomas was hired by Jesse Jackson – a former source – as his spokesman and media adviser. 9

E.R. Shipp, Ombudsman
E.R. Shipp, the 1996 Pulitzer Prize winner for commentary, took a leave of absence from the New York Daily News and from teaching journalism at Columbia University to serve a 2-year-term as ombudsman of The Washington Post.

Post executives approached her for the job, so Shipp did research on the newspaper that attracted steady criticism from both the federal establishment and the District of Columbia's black majority population.

"I don't go into this blindly or naively," said Shipp. "I think the ombudsman (defined, it means reader representative, internal critic and guardian of accountability) has a chance to look into all the concerns that have been raised and have some say into issues that need to be addressed."

Her appointment couldn't be more timely.

Shipp said, "There's been an explosion of issues where some kind of monitor could have helped news organizations avoid the problems we've seen." For example, the fabricated quotes and stories of Stephen Glass at the New Republic, Patricia Smith and Mike Barnicle at the Boston Globe, CNN's repudiation of its nerve gas story and the Cincinnati Enquirer's retraction of its Chiquita Brands investigation.

Shipp regarded her new job as an opportunity to influence the craft beyond the Post as did her predecessors – Geneva Overholser, who spoke frequently to journalism organizations, and, during the Watergate era, the late Robert Maynard, the only other African-American to have held the position. 10

Back to School

In January, Dorothy Gilliam ended the twice-weekly column she had written for The Washington Post for 17 years in order to take on the job of cultivating young journalists of color for the newspaper. Gilliam became director of the Young Journalists Development Project at the Post, geared to identify and train young people in the Washington metropolitan area who showed potential as journalists. Gilliam developed the proposal for the project, although she originally did not commit to running it.

"But," she said, "I really, really realized that if this was going to get done, it was going to have to get done by somebody who really cared."

At a time when the American Society of Newspaper Editors said their organization would not reach its goal of parity of America's minority population in newsrooms by the year 2000, the Post was seeking another way to reach parity in its newsroom. ASNE reported there were 11.6 percent journalists of color in U.S. newsrooms. The Washington, D.C. metro area was 30 percent people of color, said Gilliam, and about 17 percent of the Post's more than 500 newsroom professionals were people of color, said Milton Coleman, deputy managing editor and Gilliam's superior.

Said Coleman, "What we're doing is very, very long-range recruiting."

Initially, Gilliam coordinated a program for University of Maryland and Howard University students. Post reporters and editors taught for a semester at each school. The program encompassed 14 topic areas from visual journalism to reporting.

During the 1997-98 school year, the project moved into Washington-area high schools. For the high schools involved, the partnership often provided the only opportunity for students to work on a school paper. "High school newspapers are becoming an endangered species in America," said Gilliam, noting that few schools in the district had newspapers because printing costs were prohibitive. Said Gilliam, "Most of us got our start on high school newspapers. If those aren't being printed, where are the journalists, especially minority journalists, going to come from?"

Fortunately, Gilliam was armed with ample resources from the Post. Students produced newspapers that were printed at the Post. 11

New NABJ Office

On Sept. 7, NABJ headquarters moved from Taliaferro Hall at the University of Maryland in College Park to Adelphi, Md., about three miles west of the campus. NABJ had been in College Park since the summer of 1996. The association opened its permanent national office in Reston, Va. in November 1985, then moved to College Park, Md. and now Adelphi, Md. 12

Trotters at Stanford

From Nov. 8-10 the Trotter Group held its sixth meeting since 1992 and second meeting at Stanford University. Thirty African-American opinion writers had a frank discussion about how the Boston Globe handled the sins of two of its most popular columnists, one black (Patricia Smith), and one white (Mike Barnicle).

Authors Ishmael Reed, Arnold Rampersad and John Rickford led a panel on the power of language. The trio discussed the use of black vernacular from a historical perspective and concluded that African-American writers should be able to make use of "both the black and white keys."

Condoleezza Rice, provost of Stanford, and former Bush administration special assistant to the president for national security affairs, spoke about "American Foreign Policy in the 20th Century."

Wade Henderson, executive director of the Leadership Conference on Civil Rights, did a post mid-term elections critique of Congressional and Senate races with an emphasis on the politics of affirmative action.

And Angela Davis, activist and professor at the University of California at Santa Cruz, discussed "Critical Resistance: Beyond the Prison Industrial Complex." 13

At a public forum at the Stanford University Annenberg Auditorium, the topic was "Why African-Americans are Bill Clinton's Bridge Over Troubled Waters."

At the start of 1998, Clinton was embroiled in a scandal because of his sexual encounters with intern Monica Lewinsky inside the Oval Office. Clinton sought counsel from black clergy such as the Rev. Jesse Jackson. Also, a key black Clinton adviser was Vernon Jordan, the well-connected lawyer and ex- National Urban League president.

And according to poll data, much of Black America, which benefited from a strong economy and believed they had more access to Clinton than previous administrations, were more forgiving of his sins and also suspicious of partisan attacks from the predominantly white, Republican right-wing.

Initiative 200 Decision

On Nov. 3, 1998, 59 percent of voters in the state of Washington agreed to end government-sponsored affirmative action. In racially diverse Seattle, the majority of voters supported retention of existing affirmative action but voters from the state's biggest city could not overcome the will of a majority of Washington voters. 14

NABJ members had waited anxiously for the decision. Would the choice affect whether they would participate in the Unity '99 convention in eight months, or withdraw in protest?

NABJ could not make this decision alone. Whatever was decided would affect the fates of smaller Unity partners, Hispanic, Asian American and Native American journalists.

Foundations had invested $2 million in Unity. John Funabiki of the Ford Foundation called the four partners "the foot soldiers of diversity." He told the New York Times, "They hold job fairs. They have high school and college scholarship and program aids. They have management training programs." The Ford Foundation committed $500,000 to the Unity effort.

Yet this advance support was at risk because the coalition looked like it would fracture over Initiative 200. Blacks journalists like Robert Pierre of the Washington Post suggested a boycott of Seattle. In April, seven months before the vote, NABJ President Vanessa Williams proposed looking at alternative sites. The other Unity partners rejected the idea.

Paul DeMain, a former president of the Native American journalists group, said NABJ boycott proponents were ignoring American Indians' sensitivity to broken agreements. "We've had people rip us off for decades, signing agreements then tearing them up," he said. "NABJ's saying, 'You don't hear our concerns.' We're saying, 'You don't hear ours.'" 15

Williams pressed for new options at a September Unity meeting. The partners agreed to sponsor an October public forum in Seattle on affirmative action. On Oct. 10, the Unity partners met. Hispanic and Asian Americans sought a compromise in vain. A vote was called to explore other convention sites and the board deadlocked. Asians sided with the blacks, explaining that any group's request for information should be honored. Hispanics sided with the Native Americans.

The next day the board met again. At the last minute, Native American representatives agreed reluctantly to have Unity explore other sites.

Alternatives that were discussed included holding the convention on a battleship so that participants would not touch land, or holding the event on an Indian reservation, or in essence in another nation. Both ideas died. 16

The day after the Initiative 200 vote, NABJ's board voted 12-6 to go to Seattle.

"If we had pulled out, there would be no Unity. We had a commitment," said Region 5 director Monroe Anderson of WBBM-TV Chicago, who voted yes.

On Nov. 5, the Unity board reaffirmed its original decision. Some black journalists vowed quietly that they would not go to Seattle.

Top Job at Newsweek

At the end of 1998, Mark Whitaker was named editor of Newsweek and became the first African-American to lead a major newsweekly. Whitaker, 41, advanced from managing editor and succeeded Maynard Parker, who died in October after a battle with leukemia.

Whitaker told the Washington Post, "My aim is to be the very best editor of Newsweek I can be, and not just the best black editor. I'm very interested in the racial question here in America, not just between blacks and whites, but Hispanics and Asians and the changing demographics of the country. Perhaps I have a little more sensitivity to that issue than other people might have." 17

Sensitivity definitely was lacking with news that the editor of a new hip-hop magazine was beaten in his New York office Nov. 16 by a rap music producer and another man.

Jesse Washington, 29, editor of Blaze, a spinoff of Vibe magazine, accused Deric "D-Dot" Angelettie and Anthony Hubbard of barging into his office, kicking him repeatedly in the face and head, and beating him with chairs.

Washington told The Associated Press that Angelettie was upset that Blaze published a photograph that identified him as the "Madd Rapper." The assailants were charged with assault and criminal possession of a weapon. Washington was treated for fractures of his face and lacerations.

In August, Washington had a run-in with Fugees guitarist Wycliff Jean, who allegedly pointed a gun at the editor because of an unfavorable review. The incident was not reported to police and Jean denied the gunplay on MTV.

"Some rappers need to be educated about how to deal with the media," said Newsday reporter Curtis Taylor, who was also president of the New York Association of Black Journalists. "We're hoping that we can sit down and create a dialogue where journalists doing their jobs does not result in violence." 18

Chapter 14
Unity '99

After collecting $2.05 million in total revenue, NABJ ended 1998 with a $216,395 surplus. Leaders then predicted that the association would have a successful 1999. To meet the goal, board members projected that most of the revenue – 47 percent – would come from 1999 convention registrations, followed by:
- Contributions (23 percent);
- Investment income (12 percent);
- Member dues (11 percent);
- Miscellaneous income (3 percent), and
- Regional and program income (2 percent each).

NABJ faced several challenges in meeting its fiscal projections. First, a number of its members vowed to boycott the July Unity convention in Seattle because anti-affirmative action Initiative 200 succeeded in Washington state. Second, even if Initiative 200 were not an issue, traveling to the Pacific Northwest for a number of East Coast members would be a reason to sit out Seattle.

Then there were concerns about declining membership. After peaking at 3,321 members in August 1997 shortly after the Chicago convention, membership shrunk to 2,899 in October 1998, then 2,733 in January 1999.

Executive board members and regional directors agreed at their fall meeting to devote more energy to member recruitment. 1

Competition, Finally

After four years and two uncontested presidential elections, the summer of 1999 promised a contested race for president. Robin Stone, vice president/print and deputy editor of Essence magazine, and Will Sutton, deputy managing editor of the News & Observer in Raleigh, N.C. and former NABJ parliamentarian and regional director, were candidates. 2

NABJ had become lethargic because of one-candidate presidencies. This was no fault of Arthur Fennell and Vanessa Williams, the members who stepped forward and led the association from 1995-97 and 1997-99 respectively. Nevertheless, competition in the first two elections of the early 1990s invigorated NABJ. Candidates had to match their best ideas against opponents. Oftentimes, the best ideas of losing candidates were adopted by the winner.

Many members complained that they were turned off by the politicking and mudslinging that occurred during campaigns. Yet what had been missing from recent NABJ elections was passion that burns naturally from competition. Too many single- candidate or even no-candidate elections, in which other officers had to be appointed by the board, sapped NABJ's strength.

The Stone-Sutton competition marked the first NABJ election waged in cyberspace. Both candidates had Web sites to reach new voters and keep supporters up to date. Stone and Sutton were chasing about 1,800 full-time working journalists, at least 60 percent of the total membership.

By springtime, there was also a contested race for vice-president/print: Herb Lowe, secretary and reporter with the Philadelphia Inquirer, vs. Rochelle Riley, associate editor of The Courier-Journal in Louisville, Ky. and a chapter president in Louisville, Dallas-Fort Worth and Washington, D.C.

There was competition for the associate board member and student board member seats, but associates and students voted for their representative only, not the 16 journalists in the six executive board and 10 regional director seats.

Except for a contested regional director race in the Southwest, where incumbent Warren Bell Jr. of New Orleans was challenged by Cheryl Smith of Dallas, most of those board seats were uncontested or vacant.

Cracks in an Exalted Image

Florida A&M University's School of Journalism, Media and Graphic Arts was the first J-school accredited at a historically black institution of higher learning. FAMU was named "College of the Year" by Time magazine and the Freedom Forum honored the journalism dean as "Administrator of the Year." Yet a dispute over faculty hiring and credentials revealed a crack in the university's exalted image. 3

Renewal of J-school accreditation became questionable in 1999 because of a very public fight between Journalism Dean Bob Ruggles on one side, and FAMU President Fred Humphries and Provost James Ammons on the other. In an effort to raise the profile of the university, the president and provost insisted that all professors hold doctoral or other "terminal" degrees. FAMU journalism professor Gloria Horning was recommended for tenure by a faculty committee and the dean, but was denied. Horning, a white woman, sued FAMU for discrimination, and alleged that the institution was run "by and for black men." A black woman, former Detroit Free Press columnist Louise Reid Ritchie, was also denied tenure, even though she held a Ph.D. in clinical psychology.

The clash at FAMU was similar to battles at other campuses where administrations pressed journalism programs to staff them with Ph.D. instructors rather than long-time working journalists. FAMU journalism faculty feared losing many well-regarded members from a department that boasted alumni at leading news outlets.

One of them, Joe Oglesby of the Miami Herald, remarked in a column about the contrast between FAMU's image and its problems: "the trouble with flying high is that it's so easy to fall." 4

Countdown to Unity

Unity organizers performed more unified fund-raising than the inaugural event five years ago. Jackie Greene, Unity '99 co-treasurer and a former NABJ treasurer, explained: In

1994, NABJ, NAHJ, AAJA and NAJA held separate fund-raisers in order to finance their mini conventions, and the Unity '94 organization secured donations for joint activities such as the opening and closing convention ceremonies. That strategy brought in $1.9 million. After the event, $400,000 was divided among the associations based on attendance. Remaining money went toward operating the Unity office. 5

In 1999, Unity conducted about 90 percent of fund-raising in order to pay for a shared convention. Unity Executive Director Walterene Swanston said $3 million was raised in financial contributions and donations of equipment and services. 6

The projected convention cost was $3 million. About 20 percent of the funds, or $600,000, were expected to go to the opening and closing ceremonies, and $500,000 would go to student projects. About $100,00 was budgeted for workshops. Big media sponsors included The New York Times and the Seattle Times. Prominent non-media underwriters included Canon, State Farm and Coca Cola. 7 DaimlerChrysler, another major non-media sponsor, promised to underwrite a "Literary Lounge" where featured authors like Connie Briscoe, who wrote bestseller "A Long Way Home" would read and sign copies. DaimlerChrysler also underwrote a "Spirit in Words" poetry event.

Tourism and trade groups recognized opportunities to gain exposure. The Black Dollar Task Force and Seattle Chamber of Commerce Urban Enterprise Center promoted a Community Endowment Fund Walk in the Central Area of Seattle, a place where Quincy Jones, Ray Charles and Ernestine Anderson began their music careers. 8

Conventioneers were urged to visit the Web site unity99.org for information.

Unity '99 in Seattle

Would Unity '99 live up to its name, or would so many members from the largest of the four partners stay away and severely weaken the convention? NABJ planned for 1,700 of its members to come to Seattle July 7-11, far fewer than the 2,500 or more people who came to the last two conventions. Nevertheless, NABJ attendance exceeded the conservative estimates. In all, 1,960 members registered, exceeding the projection by 260 people. And of those, 200 members registered on site. Because 1,600 people came to the NABJ banquet, again exceeding projections, an overflow room had to be set up. 9

In all, about 6,800 journalists and friends of color registered for Unity '99, numbers that surpassed the 6,000 people who came to Unity '94 in Atlanta. For National Public Radio correspondent Cheryl Devall, Unity '99 often meant heading to a panel, workshop, speech or tour and never quite making it because she kept running into old friends and colleagues.

Devall's experience could confirm a widespread observation that Unity – and even NABJ – had become too big. This was a good problem. Unity '99 by many accounts had become America's largest gathering of journalists. Although the numbers of people of color were too small in the journalism industry, for one week in Seattle, the combined gathering of journalists of color were too great to be ignored by national and local news media. 10

Merchants noticed, too. Many an instructive conversation began when a merchant took note of the umpteenth $2 bill handed over the counter by a convention goer. Unity '99 organizers encouraged attendees to change their spending cash in $2 bills as a tangible demonstration of the convention's impact on the local economy.

Tonya Wiley of Convention Services Northwest changed $15,000 into $2 bills. Wiley said she could have easily changed more because demand among convention goers was so great. The money talked and the city of Seattle listened – and usually responded with a smile.

Small change sent a bigger message about how many attendees felt about Initiative 200. Many NABJ members probably debated whether to come and spend their dollars after feeling the sting of the anti-affirmative action referendum. Apparently many members decided it was better to come and engage the issue rather than boycott.

Said association President Vanessa Williams, "I am proud of the way NABJ members debated the issue, made a decision and then followed through by attending the conference in such large numbers. I also respect those members who stood firm in their convictions and chose not to come to Seattle. It's clear the so-called 'controversy' has not diminished NABJ's presence in the industry." 11

The large gathering provoked additional discussion of the Initiative 200. A memorable convention week front-page headline in the Seattle Times was "What Do Whites Want?"

The Seattle crowd also caught the attention of four U.S. presidential candidates. Texas Gov. George W. Bush, a Republican, initially declined an official invitation to Unity, although he was in Seattle for another event.

U.S. Senator John McCain, R-Ariz., gave an impromptu speech and held a news conference. He orginally declined an invitation to participate but changed his mind after reading in the Los Angeles Times that Bush did not plan to attend and that no Republicans were scheduled to speak.

"When I saw the story, I was unhappy than an oversight had taken place," said the senator. "All I can tell you is I do the best I can."

Choosing his words carefully, McCain said he supported affirmative action and defined it as a way to level the playing field in America. He said more could be done to open doors of opportunity for people of color. "We do not have sufficient equal opportunities," said McCain. 12

Democratic front-runner and Vice President Al Gore spoke at the most well-attended Unity plenary session. Nearly 3,000 attendees came to hear Gore speak on "Race, Technology and the Future of the United States."

Gore attacked the notion of anti-affirmative action advocates that minorities had already received social and economic parity with whites. "How in God's name," said Gore, "do some people in our nation get the impression that one generation after Brown vs. Board (of Education) ... less than one lifetime after aggressive fights to combat discrimination, that all of a sudden you have a colorblind society?" The vice president also said that the future success of America could only be guaranteed through education: "How long can this nation generate one-third of the world's economic capital when one-third of our students continue to fail in the most basic reading skills?"

Gore said the Internet would become as important to society as the book was 400 years ago. He wanted to connect schools across the nation with Internet and e-mail access. 13

An hour later, about 400 people remained to hear former U.S. Senator Bill Bradley, D-N.J. speak on race then answer journalists' questions. 14

A black journalist wisecracked that Bradley probably was the presidential candidate most comfortable when talking about race relations because the former New York Knicks basketball champion had showered with more black people than any other contender.

But Bradley took a serious tone and told the audience that racial unity was a fundamental push of his campaign: "It's an issue I care desperately about." He added, "You have to be your brother's keeper. If morality or world leadership does not concern you, consider self-interest. By 2010, less than 60 percent of the work force will be native-born white Americans." 15

Bush scrambled to make an appearance at the convention after declining the official invitation, but said he would not answer reporters' questions. When organizers told him he could not make a speech without responding to questions, Bush decided to do a walk-through in the Exhibit Hall where many non-Unity members of the press were there to recruit for employers. NAHJ President Nancy Baca called Bush's glad-handing visit a "drive-by photo opportunity." 16

Bradley, one of the three presidential candidates who put Unity on his to-do list, pointedly told his audience, "Let the record show I did not have to change my calendar to be here; I was already planning to be here." 17

With 250 panels and workshops to chose from spread over five days, many attendees struggled to live up to the Unity theme. Even the plenary session most closely tied to the Initiative 200 controversy, "Balance or Bias: Affirmative Action and the News Media," was not well attended. The 3,000-seat convention hall was two-thirds empty.

Where were all the "Affirmative action babies," as ABC News senior correspondent Carole Simpson identified herself, and likely, many colleagues?

Donna Lacy Marshall, an African-American anchorwoman from WHAS-TV in Louisville, Ky., suspected that many people were talked out on the subject. "Just to keep talking and fussing about it and getting angry about it isn't going to change how white America feels about it."

Kristina Heath, a Native American student journalist, theorized that people who deal with affirmative action on a daily basis probably wanted to concentrate on other matters. Unity workshops were as varied as "Climbing the Magazine Ladder of Success" to "How to Apply Computer-Assisted Reporting to Mexico and Latin America." 18

At the "Balance or Bias" session, a nine-member panel gave a report card on news coverage of affirmative action in Washington state and California. The ideologically diverse collection of experts agreed that the phrase "affirmative action" upset most people because it was synonymous with race. They also agreed that the phrase was hard to define but easy to distort.

John Carlson, chairman of the Initiative 200 movement, said discussion of race should be minimized, not maximized. Carlson also said that "Affirmative action as a concept is great, but it goes too far."

Interesting. During the audience Q & A segment, someone asked Carlson, if he had no problem with the concept, what kind of affirmative action was satisfactory?

Carlson's answer: What black, Hispanic, Asian American and Native American journalist associations were doing at Unity '99 worked, that is, the training and mentoring of students and professional development for others.

Yes, the associations prepared young people rigorously to compete in the professions and society. Carlson however, dodged the question. Understanding the flaws and virtues of affirmative action was difficult. At fault were gaps in public discourse and media presentation.

It was telling that Roger Clegg, a fierce opponent of affirmative action and head of the Center of Equal Opportunity, a conservative think tank, said he had no major problems with coverage of the issue. Clegg said that was because he had low expectations that coverage would have any depth.

In essence, the more ignorance, the better chance that affirmative action would die.

"Media coverage reflects the debate itself," said Faye M. Anderson of the Douglass Public Policy Institute, a nonpartisan education and research organization. "Both sides ... are polarized camps and every player has a vested interest in being for or against it."

Frank Blethen, publisher of the Seattle Times, supported affirmative action. He editorialized against Initiative 200 as vigorously as John Carlson rallied for its approval.

"For us the issue is inclusion, not arcane language," said Blethen. "If we don't do a better job of inclusion, our democracy will collapse." 19

Authentic Unity?

Attendees wondered whether journalists of color spent too much time isolated at the association events or made efforts to mix during Unity week.

"People have really segregated themselves into groups and there (wasn't) a great deal of mingling among the different organizations," observed Monique Nation, a reporter for KRIV-FOX in Houston.

"At the convention, I really (didn't) talk with people from different minority groups," said Radford University student Aqeelah Abdul Ra'uf. "The people of different races that I did see talking and mingling together were already friends or co-workers."

Eunnice Eun, a reporter with WPRI in Rhode Island, said the concept of unity went beyond mingling: "Most of us come to the convention to see our friends that we only get to see once a year. I (hung) out with my black, Hispanic and Asian friends. We all (came) for the same cause and purpose."

Michelle Dunham of Washington, D.C. added, "You have to make a special effort to mingle with people. You just can't expect UNITY to force people to talk to each other. I took it upon myself to talk to other people because I wanted to know what they are doing and what kind of things they are faced with in the industry." 20

Comparing notes was important because while the general population of Americans of color increased to about 30 percent and continued to rise, journalism industry numbers declined. Minorities in TV journalism were 19 percent in 1999, down from 20 percent in 1998, according to a Radio and Television News Directors Association/Ball State University study. Minorities in radio journalism were 11 percent, down from 16 percent in 1998.

In the newspaper business, minority employment increased to 11.5 percent, according to the 1999 ASNE report, up 1.5 percent from 1998. However, that report noted that minority interns were down 2 percent to 31.3 percent, and first full-time minority hires was also down, 18.7 percent in 1999, compared to 21.5 percent the previous year.

ASNE counted women for the first time in the census and females made up 36.9 percent of newsrooms, and 34 percent of supervisors were women. Sixty three percent of minorities were concentrated at papers of 100,000 circulation or more.

Integrity is Challenged

The Unity convention did not sit well with at least two white male critics in the mainstream media.

U.S. News & World Report columnist John Leo asked July 18, "Is it a good idea for professional associations to organize themselves by pigmentation?" Another Leo criticism was "If the four groups of nonwhite journalists organize around a diversity agenda, how can their editors expect them to cover diversity fairly and objectively when they get back to their newspapers, magazines, or TV and radio stations?" 21

The other critic was William McGowan, writer of a July 16 Wall Street Journal op-ed piece called "Among the Believers: Diversity, yes. Diversity of opinion, no."

Of the 6,800 people to chose from, McGowan, who attended the Seattle convention, and Leo, who did not attend, both quoted Michelle Malkin, a Seattle Times columnist and Asian American of Filipino decent.

"The fatal flaw of Unity '99 was its unspoken mandate of strict political conformity," McGowan and Leo quoted from Malkin's column. "If you don't accept the left-leaning agenda of advocacy journalism, you're enabling racism. If you don't support the pursuit of racial hiring goals as a primary journalistic goal, you're selling out."

Malkin chose not to be a member of any of the four associations of color, but she was a panelist at Unity '99. She sounded like an outsider who knew little if anything about the associations.

In response to the Leo critique, Wayne Dawkins of Newport News, Va. wrote in a letter, "Now, what is the alternative for the daily press? Retreat to the narrow coverage of decades past when blacks and other people of color were ignored or covered routinely as victims or suspects? Yes, I'm an activist. I'm on the march for high-quality, well-informed, inclusive media."

Dawkins used as an example the growth of NABJ in nearly 24 years from 44 men and women to 3,000 was the result of activism – training aspiring journalists, experienced members teaching each other new tricks, and intense collaboration with mainstream industry associations.

Leo sent Dawkins a lengthy e-mail rebuttal. He wrote that integration of the media was accomplished, therefore activism in 1999 was unnecessary.

Furthermore, Leo said if he had his way, journalists of color *would not* be allowed to join associations of color.

Vanessa Williams of NABJ and Kara Briggs, former president of NAJA and Unity: Journalists of Color, were given space Aug. 2 to answer McGowan's Wall Street Journal critique. Williams wrote, "The accusation that diversity proponents intimidate and shout down those who disagree with them is ungrounded and unfair.

"People who believe in their convictions, and possess the skills and vehicles to articulate them, have no excuse not to speak up ... Mr. McGowan and I do agree on this point: Diversity must also include diversity of opinion. There is no challenge, and no fun, in debating one's self."

Jim Naughton, president of the Poynter Institute in St. Petersburg, Fla., wrote in the July 6 Seattle Times that talk about diversity was indeed uncomfortable: "We don't want to have this conversation. We must.

"It is the unresolved American issue. It will not be

resolved unless people talk about and through their differences. Citizens will not talk through their differences unless someone helps them understand why they should, why there are practical reasons to understand diversity.

"That's where (you) journalists come in."

Naughton also wrote that "the future of mass communications depends on mass, and the mass is changing dramatically.

"The most recent audited circulation data shows, for instance, that The Miami Herald has gone down 12,561 in the same year that El Nuevo Herald has gone up 13,000. This was not a surprise to Al Tompkins of the Poynter's leadership and management faculty. His demographic studies show that by the year 2020, minority populations are projected to reach 42 percent in Arizona, 45 percent in New York State, 49 percent in Texas, and 62 percent in California. Practical reasons include self-interest.

"Some of us would contend that the notion underlying civic or community journalism – that newsgatherers ought to know what their audiences care about – cannot be honored without paying heed to diversity of those audiences. Practical reasons." 22

NABJ Election

The Robin Stone vs. Will Sutton competition for president of NABJ was the first contest waged in cyberspace, and on the ground in Seattle, there was also a spirited and sophisticated media campaign.

Stone supporters posted TV monitors in the Washington State Convention & Trade Center and influential members gave on-camera testimonials that praised the Essence magazine editor. Sutton supporters posted dozens of billboard-size posters of the Raleigh News & Observer editor along a city block leading from the hotels to the convention center. 23

Supporters from both camps cheerfully courted undecided voters in the corridors of the convention center. For the first time in six years, journalist members could choose from two candidates, Stone, an incumbent board vice president and former chapter president, and Sutton, a former board member in the 1980s and a Unity founder.

On Friday night July 9, the announcement was that Sutton captured 55 percent of the votes and out-polled Stone 552-436. Competition probably resulted in a record voter turnout; 1,230 full members cast ballots, which meant at least two thirds of the eligible members voted.

(In 1993, the last competitive race, 782 full members voted for three presidential candidates. In 1991, 665 full members chose from two presidential candidates.)

An unusual statistic was that only 447 of the 1,230 voters cast ballots in Seattle; 783 votes were absentee ballots, yet many of these votes were from convention goers who voted *before* coming to Seattle. This oddity suggested that many members wanted to choose their leader, but avoid the campaigning and politicking.

After the announcement in front of 1,600 people at the NABJ banquet, Sutton told his supporters to take their campaign buttons off because NABJ would move forward as one family. Regarding integration of the news industry, he said, "We will negotiate when possible, we will holler when necessary. We will not wait 25 years," for newsrooms that reflect American newsroom diversity. Internally, Sutton promised that the new board and association staff would encourage chapter creativity, not stifle it.

In the other major competitive election, Herb Lowe of the Philadelphia Inquirer and incumbent secretary, was elected vice president/print, edging Rochelle Riley of the Courier-Journal of Louisville, 492-458.

In addition, Meta Mereday of the NY/NJ Minority Purchasing Council, Inc., defeated incumbent Linda Florence Callahan of North Carolina A&T State University for associate member board representative. Dena McClurkin of Clark Atlanta University was elected student member board representative after a three-candidate race.

A constitutional amendment that would have rescinded associate member and student member voting power on the board was defeated 578-342 by the full members who voted.

The rest of the nationally elected officers were unopposed: Vice President/Broadcast Condace Pressley of WSB-AM, Atlanta; Secretary Greg Lee of the Washington Post; Treasurer Glenn Rice of the Kansas City Star, and Parliamentarian Robin Washington of the Boston Herald.

In Southwest Region 7, challenger Cheryl Smith of Dallas beat incumbent Warren Bell of New Orleans. Otherwise, the other nine regional elections were abysmal. Only three of them had candidates seeking the positions. This meant that representatives had to be appointed during regional caucuses in Seattle. [24]

Said Sutton, "We have to do a better job of recruiting and identifying a leader. Leadership is not an accident. It's a process." The lack of candidates to fill seats, let alone compete against an opponent for positions on the NABJ board, were problems that surfaced four years ago in 1995 when 13 of the 17 seats, including the presidency, were unapposed or unfilled.

Outgoing president Vanessa Williams said the lack of involvement by many NABJ members was across the board, whether it was running for national office or participating at a local chapter level.

Morieka Johnson, a designer at the Detroit News, said that many people were afraid of "biting off more than they could chew." She preferred to see people not run for positions than take them and not perform their jobs well. [25]

DuBois Debate

Instead of an annual W.E.B. DuBois lecture by an outstanding black scholar, NABJ changed its format in Seattle and staged a Saturday morning debate between two public intellectuals, conservative Shelby Steele and liberal Cornel West. The pairing was an update of the DuBois vs. Booker T. Washington debate of a century ago on what was best for African-Americans: civil and political rights, or economic development and self-sufficiency? Agitation or accommodation?

In 1999, the issue was affirmative action, and Seattle was the ideal venue because of Initiative 200.

Hundreds of members were bused from downtown hotels to Mount Zion Baptist Church in the Central District, the heart of Seattle's black community. Moderator Michele McQueen of ABC News described Steele and West as two men "divided by background and tactics, united by their love of their people."

Most of the 400 people who packed the church favored West, a Harvard University professor, theologian and author of "Race Matters." West spoke in cadences that had the rhythm and poetry of great jazz saxophonists. At Mount Zion, West preached self-love and hope to an approving audience.

But the winner of this debate appeared to be Steele, and it wasn't because he was a crowd pleaser. The Hoover Institution senior fellow and author of "The Content of Our Character: A New Vision of Race in America," and "A Dream Deferred: The Second Betrayal of Black Freedom in America," grudgingly earned the respect of a audience that often grumbled and gasped at his blunt indictments delivered in monotone. Steele played offense during most of the debate; West played defense.

For example, Steele accused many blacks of validating racial profiling by demanding it for affirmative action, but bitterly protesting it when used in crime prevention. "When we keep thinking strictly of race," said Steele, "then we are not asking enough of ourselves. We have lost track of our own ingenuity." Steele acknowledged that racism made life harder for blacks, yet he said that should not be used as an excuse for blacks to stop progressing. 26

West disputed Steele's other charge that "contingent thinking" by blacks confused white guilt with black power, and that blacks had become complacent. Said West, "We are not making an excuse. We are pointing out a reality, so we can keep track of that reality. Most black people are pointing out the racism and are still trying to do something." 27

Although much of the audience became agitated over what Steele said, there was acceptance of a painful truth: "Don't," Steele advised, "put our faith in policies that can be voted out in a single afternoon." He spoke directly to Initiative 200 in Washington state and before that, Proposition 209 in California, both cases in which affirmative action was rolled back at the polls.

Through groans and shouts of audience members, Steele said he was proud of black achievement and innovation over generations because, "it defined our humanity despite white supremacy and racism."

Then Steele issued this challenge: "In sports, music and literature, we ask for no government programs, but we enforce excellence with a degree of cruelty." Therefore, why not up the ante and try harder in business and other fields?

About a minute after those choice words, someone in the audience shouted. "We still love you Shelby."

It was grudging respect for Steele's strong medicine.

The debate was great theater. Both men began at opposing podiums. It looked like the setup for a presidential debate. But West's microphone distorted his voice. Without hesitation, West walked over to Steele's podium and for 90 minutes both men carried on their debate shoulder to shoulder. The closeness of their bodies symbolized unity of purpose. 28

Award Winners

NABJ recognized two Ron Allens. First, NBC foreign correspondent Ron Allen was honored as 1999 Journalist of the Year. Based in London, Allen covered the war in Kosovo; the fall of dictator Mobutu Sese Seko in Zaire (Congo) and continuing ethnic violence in Rwanda.

Second, Fort Lauderdale Sun-Sentinel reporter C. Ron Allen received the Community Service Award for waging a victorious effort to steer 18 African-American boys ages 7 to 17 away from trouble and into a twice weekly mentoring program called the Knights of Pythagorus.

The Percy Qoboza award for International excellence went to Fred M'membe, editor and publisher of The Post in Zambia.

Belva Davis, the first black woman TV reporter on the West Coast, received the Lifetime Achievement award. She began with KPIX-TV in San Francisco in 1966 and her career spanned 33 years. Davis won six local Emmys, interviewed five U.S. presidents, and reported from Cuba, Kenya and Tanzania. 29

A sorrowful episode during a mostly festive convention was the disappearance and apparent death of Joe Wood. A New York-based free-lance writer and editor of the New Press. Wood, 34, attempted to scale Mount Rainier. His body was reported missing July 8. Much of the upper reaches of the trail where Wood was last seen was obscured by several feet of snow. Wood attended the first Unity convention in 1994 as an NABJ member and met his companion, Somini Sengupta, a New York Times reporter. Sengupta attended Unity '99. 30

Unity Finale

During convention days at Unity '99, Sheila Stainback wrote in Columbia Journalism Review, most of the journalists moved in groups of their own racial and ethnic background. In the evening, she said, there was more cross-cultural sampling, and the journalists danced and partied to new sounds and dance moves. A graying, white journalism professor, for example, earned the respect of the crowd at the NABJ "wild wild west" hip-hop party for vaguely but bravely trying to locate the beat as he contorted on the dance floor. Hispanic and Asian American journalists co-sponsored a combined salsa-karaoke night. 31

The closing celebration of the four groups featured the 1970s soul group the Spinners. Journalists of all colors sang along to the words of many of the Spinners' hit songs.

At the closing, Unity presidents Kara Briggs (NAJA); Vanessa Williams (NABJ); Nancy Baca (NAHJ), and Catalina Camila (AAJA) smiled, clasped hands, then raised them in triumph. The coalition that only months before threatened to fracture into disunity and even bankrupt one or two associations, instead worked through differences of opinion and tactics and exceeded attendance of Unity '94.

At least 28 percent of the Unity '99 attendees were NABJ members. Add 1,176 people who registered but were categorized as "outside of the organization" and the NABJ piece of Unity pie swelled to 45 percent of convention participants. NABJ job fair revenue from Unity '99 was $267,000, based on a Unity formula. The association also received about $50,000 in advertising revenues. 32 Total NABJ convention revenue was $691,940, about 20 percent less than $871,833 raised the previous year for the Washington, D.C. convention. 33 Organizers began plans for the first Unity convention of the 21st century. The partners agreed on summer 2004 in Washington, D.C.

Chapter 15
Recover, thrive, or perish?

At the end of 1999, did NABJ meet the financial goal its leaders projected at the beginning of the year?

In 1998, the association brought in $2 million in revenues, but in 1999, projections were downgraded: $1.625 million in revenue was anticipated. By early 2000, Treasurer Glenn Rice reported that the association slightly exceeded the goal and collected $1.63 million. 1

A scholarship endowment drive moved forward. In September, a report said $639,000 was raised toward the $1 million needed to establish the endowment. By January 2000, the endowment exceeded $800,000. 2

President Will Sutton and the new board that began work in the summer sailed NABJ toward a battering storm.

The first blow was membership. In December 1999, the numbers plummeted to 2,456, down 26 percent from an all-time high of 3,321 members in August 1997.

In October 1998, when members anxiously watched the Initiative 200 anti-affirmative action battle in Washington state, there were 1,893 full members, the working journalists of NABJ. In December 1999, five months after the Unity '99 convention, those numbers sunk to 1,462 full members, losses of more than 430 bodies or 23 percent.

These losses could have been the result of members who boycotted Seattle and did not renew their dues, or journalists who left the business, voluntarily or involuntarily. Either way, NABJ was bleeding, and the association faced a daunting challenge: A return trip to the West, away from its member base, to a 2000 national convention in Phoenix, Ariz.

Phoenix was approved in the mid-1990s, and like the months before the Seattle convention, many members grumbled privately that they would not come because of the distance from many Atlantic coast cities where members lived. Another excuse to stay away was the withering August heat.

Leadership Crisis

Sutton's mantra was that NABJ had to change and become chapter focused. Also, the association needed to strongly encourage more members to pursue new growth sectors for journalism jobs: copy editors, photographers, graphic artists and supervisors.

Sutton's suggestion was to go where the lines were shortest. Lines for reporting and anchor positions that many members wanted were longer.

"As we consider our options," said Sutton in 2000, "we have to consider the need." 3

Initially, it was difficult to tell if board members and most of the general membership approved of Sutton's focus.

Phoenix convention attendance was a little better than Seattle. Paid attendance was 2,250, and total attendance was 2,600. 4 The convention occurred shortly after the Republican and Democratic National conventions.

Three conventions in four weeks put a strain on some veteran NABJ members who fortunately had top political assignments. For example, Gwen Ifill of "The News Hour with Jim Lehrer," passed on Phoenix. "It would have been too much," she said during a break from the Democratic convention in Los Angeles.

Kevin Merida of the Washington Post, NABJ's Journalist of the Year, left Los Angeles for Phoenix immediately after he filed his story on the presidential nomination of Al Gore.

Gayle Pollard Terry of the Los Angeles Times stayed up for a Congressional Black Caucus event until 2:30 a.m. that Friday, went home and packed, then caught a 7:30 a.m. flight to Phoenix.

"I was brain dead Friday, she said "but by Saturday, I was up again and playing cards." 5

The Phoenix convention was promoted as the 25th anniversary celebration of NABJ. Officially, the association would reach its silver anniversary four months later in December.

At the end of the Phoenix convention, Sutton felt heat from what at first appeared to be a harmless and exciting announcement, that at the convention next year in Orlando, Fla. members would receive free multi-day passes at Disney World.

Many members complained that the pass could violate journalism ethics as well as run afoul of many news outlets' guidelines on accepting such gifts.

Mike Woolfolk, a Southeast regional director, told members in an e-mail that the passes, valued at $250, were "valuable benefits" and part of an effort to sign up new members and "reclaim the many folks who dropped off the roll." 6

Fiscal Crisis

NABJ received another jolt in October. Executive Director Toni Samuel announced her resignation in order to become chief operating officer of the International Association of Employee Assistance Professionals, an association twice the size of NABJ.

"I joined NABJ out of ethnic pride and a desire to give back," wrote Samuel in her resignation letter. "I trust I have brought results and honor to that notion. However, I leave with having received so much, from the staff, the board and the beloved members. I am sure I will work very hard and give my all to my new organization, but never will I work for so much, nor for a mission so honorable."

Samuel stayed 17 months, from May 1998 to November 2000, and was the sixth executive director in 14 years. Tangie Newborn was appointed interim executive director.

At the fall meeting in Hampton, Va., unofficial convention revenue and expense figures were incomplete, which was unusual. In January, NABJ leaders acknowledged that 350 people who attended the Phoenix convention received complimentary registration or "comps."

Some members had complained immediately after the Phoenix convention that total attendance (2,600) was exaggerated because of "comps," and the free registrations represented thousands of dollars in lost revenue. NABJ leaders answered that many of the comped guests were sponsors and job fair exhibitors, who donated or paid thousands of dollars to support the convention. 7

There was little dispute that consecutive Western conventions in Phoenix and Seattle substantially lowered attendance and potential revenue. In the winter of 2001 the NABJ board reduced the operating budget by one third from $2 million to $1.34 million.

A major budget casualty was the NABJ Journal. The fall 2000 and winter 2001 editions were killed. Publishing did not resume until spring 2001. As an alternative, NABJ put more of its information online on its improved Web site. Yet that decision was not satisfactory. Hundreds of members were online, but hundreds more were not. The printed Journal connected members and allies and adversaries in the journalism industry.

For seven months, there was woeful silence.

NABJ was also hobbled by ineffective leadership. President Will Sutton acknowledged that there was validity in assessments that he not did get the board of directors to completely support his vision for the association.

"I think it's true that some people chose not to work with me," he said, "but as to why, I think it's a two-way street."8

Despite his long involvement with the association, as a board member in the 1980s and as a Unity pioneer, Sutton was considered an outsider by many people the 1990s. "I would have done more team-building with the board," said Condace Pressley, vice president/print. "I'm concerned that there wasn't significant buy-in to his agenda and his vision, which is why he didn't accomplish as much as he would have liked." 9

Shortly before the Phoenix convention in August 2001, reluctance to work with Sutton turned into a near revolt. Members complained bitterly upon learning that the association accumulated between $200,000 to $500,000 of operational debt, and $436,000 in stock market losses, the latter largely attributed to the collapse of tech stocks that rocked the U.S. economy. To cover expenses that exceeded the association budget, NABJ closed the financial hole by borrowing from its reserves.

On July 27, about three weeks before the convention, a letter signed by more than 100 members who called themselves the Concerned Members of NABJ, urged creation of a financial oversight committee with veto power on significant NABJ expenses.10 Signees included incumbent treasurer Glenn Rice and immediate past president Vanessa Williams. Sheila Brooks, another signee, former board member and owner of a broadcast company, said, "You need to have people who are capable of making hard decisions. ... We are worried that some of our board members can't read a balance sheet."

At first, Sutton balked at the notion of forming an oversight committee. He said it would undermine the association's constitution.

At the Orlando convention and during the business meeting, former president Sidmel Estes Sumpter (1991-93) asked how the financial situation could have worsened so much since the time she served on the board. "We had a Journal that printed 10 times a year. We had the (NABJ) Update and student newspapers," she said. "The regional (conferences) used to make money. The Ford Foundation gave us $400,000. How could things change so much?" 12

Sutton apologized for not being more vigilant.

"In hindsight," he said, "I wish I had asked more questions of our executive director and our treasurer, and for that I apologize."

Most of the 100 members who attended that business meeting approved a financial oversight plan by the Concerned Members of NABJ. A compromise that Sutton accepted said the ad-hoc committee would advise the board about financial matters, including the annual budget, and make quarterly reports to the membership. The committee did not have veto power over board decisions.

New Leadership

That month, both incumbent vice presidents competed for

the NABJ presidency, and Condace Pressley defeated Herbert Lowe.

The good news was like 1999, there was competition for president. The bad news was that despite concerns about shrinking membership and out-of-balance finances, less than 60 percent of eligible members voted. Two years before, 80 percent of the members voted in the first competitive presidential race in six years. 13

In his USA Today column, former president DeWayne Wickham (1987-89) noted that while 386 people voted at the convention, 1,500 people showed up for an Eric Benet concert staged for members in one of the Disney theme parks. Wickham needled NABJ members to reorder their priorities.

Recover, Thrive, or Perish?

By 2002, association finances stabilized, and future conventions were scheduled in cities that were in close proximity to most of its members. The Journal was almost back to its quarterly publishing cycle.

Still the association has a lot of work to do in order to regain the energy and power of the early to mid-1990s.

In May 2003, Jayson Blair, a 27-year-old black reporter with the New York Times, was exposed for plagiarizing substantial parts of a news story from the San Antonio Express-News. Blair's violation exposed a broader record of shoddy work and deceit: He claimed to be on assignment as a national correspondent when in fact he made up stories while writing from home. The Times ran dozens of corrections because of Blair errors. And it was learned after the fact that Blair had not graduated from the University of Maryland; The Times didn't check.

Right-wing critics who had attacked journalists of color and diversity efforts in the late 1990s predictably leaped in and claimed that Blair was the poster child for failed affirmative action. And a number of black journalists wrung their hands and wondered if Blair would cause damage as great or greater than Janet Cooke did in 1981.

Fortunately, many black columnists pointed out correctly

that Blair's damage was less about race and affirmative action and more about ethical problems in the media that needed fixing. Like Stephen Glass and Patricia Smith five years earlier, why were some journalists willing to make up quotes, people, even places in order to win approval from editors? While there were numerous journalists of color who were more experienced and respectful of the sacred traditions of ethical journalism, why was a young and reckless reporter like Blair allowed to make a fool of one of the world's greatest newspapers? People searched for answers as this book was in production.

Roy S. Johnson competed for NABJ president in 1991 and 1993. He was a major player in the Sports Task Force. When Emerge magazine folded in 2000, Johnson became editor of the new magazine, Savoy. In September 2002, Johnson, an informed NABJ watcher, gave this assessment of what the association had to do in order to recover:

"NABJ remains a broad-based, well known, and respectable organization.

"It's no longer feared; it's not a must-belong organization for younger journalists. Those are two critical areas that must be addressed if the organization wants to do something to prevent it from becoming extinct or obsolete.

"It should be an inspiration for young people considering this career and continue to be a nurturer for young journalists who see 'big brothers' and 'big sisters' (at the convention) so they're better prepared for the other 51 weeks of the year. (NABJ must) be a resource for veteran journalists to take their skills and platforms to higher levels or skills, reaches and other mediums.

"NABJ should be a magnet for every prominent black person. We should be turning people away from speaking at our conventions.

"NABJ should be the largest collection of 'taste influencers' of color in existence. For every black book author, producer, politician and corporate executive, NABJ should be the place to be.

"That it's not should be an embarrassment."14

Notes

Chapter 1   Westward

1. Wayne Dawkins, "Black Journalists: The NABJ Story," page 131
2. Katti Gray, 'Committed to the Cause,' (2000) page 27.
3. Dawkins interview with Morgan Aug. 27, 2002
4. Allegra Bennett, January 1990 NABJ Journal
5. Ibid. Also, Earlene McMichael, February 1990
Black Alumni Network newsletter
6. March 1990 Black Alumni Network
7. February 1990 NABJ Journal
8. May 1990 NABJ Journal.
8a. Fall 2002 interviews with Tom Morgan, DeWayne Wickham,
Carl Morris and Sidmel Estes-Sumpter
9. Black Alumni Network, April 1990.
10. Clem Richardson, June/July 1990 NABJ Journal
11. Dan Holly, Black Alumni Network, August 1990
12., 13., 14. and 15. Ibid
16. Cheryl Fields, August/September 1990
NABJ Journal, from the NABJ Monitor
17. Ibid
18. Sandy Ross, August/September 1990 NABJ Journal.
19. Wayne Dawkins column, September 1990 Black Alumni Network
20. Dan Holly, September 1990 Black Alumni Network
21, Ibid
22. Wayne Dawkins column, September 1990 Black Alumni Network
Also, Jocelyn R. Coleman, August/September NABJ Journal
23. Wayne Dawkins, "Black Journalists: The NABJ Story," 172-173
24. September 1990 Black Alumni Network
25. Wayne Dawkins, 1990 notes
26. Ibid
27. Mandela was released Feb. 11, 1990.
From "Long Walk to Freedom," Nelson Mandela, pages 484-491
28. Wayne Dawkins, Black Alumni Network, September 1990
29. The first meeting of the four associations was in Baltimore in 1988
30. Dan Holly, Black Alumni Network, November 1990
31.Wayne Dawkins, Black Alumni Network, December 1990
32. November 1990 NABJ Journal
33. Ibid

Chapter 2 Survival lessons

1. The 1990 Los Angeles program book listed 21 activities each on
Thursday and Friday.
2. Wayne Dawkins/Sherry Howard/Linda Wright Moore,
NABJ: The First 20 Years, (1995) pages 12-13
3. "NABJ: The First 20 Years," Wayne Dawkins/Sherry Howard/Linda
Wright Moore; August 1992 NABJ Journal, Oct. 5 episode.
4. Anthony Twyman, January 1991 NABJ Journal.
5. Wayne Dawkins, February 1991 Black Alumni Network
6. Anthony Twyman, January 1991 NABJ Journal
7. Vincent Taylor, February 1991 NABJ Journal
8. Ibid
9. March 1991 NABJ Journal
10. Richard Prince, February 1991 NABJ Journal
11. Copies of the handwritten list were obtained
from Mal Johnson and later, Chuck Stone
12. ASNE census, with the new census about to be released that April.
13. Cornelius Foote Jr., March 1991 NABJ Journal
14 . Ibid
15. Ed Wiley III, March 1991 NABJ Journal, "Up to us to monitor
J-schools: NABJ members can influence accreditation"
16. and 17. Ibid
18. The Sentinel, Detroit Chapter of NABJ, reprinted in the April 1991
Black Alumni Network
19. Richard Prince, April 1991 NABJ Journal
20. Ibid
21. Circa 1999, the FCC dropped the requirement. Some companies
said they would continue to diversify its workplaces voluntarily.
22. Donald Scott, April 1991 NABJ Journal
23. Ibid
24 . Sharon R. King, April 1991 NABJ Journal
25. The Daily News was at Kansas City jobs fair
26. Dorothy Gilliam, June/July 1991 NABJ Journal
27. Wayne Dawkins, "Black Journalists: The NABJ Story," page 150
28. Wayne Dawkins, "Black Journalists: The NABJ Story," 68-72
29. Cheryl Devall, Black Alumni Network newsletter, September 1991.
30. Richard Prince, NABJ Journal, September 1991
31. Cheryl Devall, Black Alumni Network newsletter, September 1991
32. Wayne Dawkins, September 1991 Black Alumni Network
33. Richard Prince, June/July 1991 NABJ Journal

34. Workshop Roundup, July 27, 1991 NABJ Monitor.
Also, Betty Anne Williams, June/July 1991 NABJ Journal
35. Richard Prince, September 1991 NABJ Journal
36. Election results chart, page 10, September 1991 NABJ Journal
37. TaNoah Sterling, September 1991 NABJ Journal
38. Gail Stephanie Miles, July 26, 1991 NABJ Monitor
39. Richard Prince, September 1991 NABJ Journal. Also,
Wayne Dawkins, Black Alumni Network, September 1991
40. Ibid
41. Richard Prince, September 1991 NABJ Journal. Also,
Lewis Diuguid, Sept. 6, 2002 interview, and Wayne Dawkins,
Black Alumni Network newsletter, September 1991.
42. Valerie Gray, July 27, 1991 NABj Monitor
43. Richard Prince, September 1991 NABJ Journal
44. Andrea Ford, "NABJ's boot to the FBI is
grounded in history," September 1991 NABJ Journal.
45. Lionel McPherson, October 1991 NABJ Journal.
46. November/December 1991 Columbia Journalism Review
47. Desda Moss, November/December 1991 NABJ Journal
48. Ibid
49. Sam Fulwood, November/December 1991 NABJ Journal
50. and 51. Ibid
52. Aug. 25, 2001 Los Angeles Times: David Brock,
Angela Wright and Anita Hill
53. Tammerlin Drummond, November/December 1991 NABJ Journal
54 Note: Special awards were presented before 1981
55. Richard Prince, NABJ Journal, February 1992. Also Tammerlin
Drummond, November/December 1991 NABJ Journal
56. Richard Prince, November/December 1991 NABJ Journal
57. Ibid
58. Wayne Dawkins, January 1992 Black Alumni Network
59. Ibid. Also, "Three Blind Mice" by Ken Auletta

Chapter 3 Crusading for diversity

1. Kimberly Hayes Taylor, January 1992 NABJ Journal
2. Ibid.
3. Michelle Johnson, January 1992 NABJ Journal
4. Ibid
5. March 1992 Black Alumni Network, briefing by Arthur Fennell
6. February 1992 NABJ Journal

7. Richard Prince, February 1992 NABJ Journal

8. Ibid

9. Reference Derrick Z. Jackson commentary,
"Say 'no' to Disney," February 1992 NABJ Journal

10. In addition, eight of the 44 founders had ties to the Philadelphia region when Sandra Dawson (Long) of Wilmington, Del.; Marilyn Darling of Wilmington and Mal Johnson, a founding member of Black Communicators and the Association of Black Journalists were included.

11. Richard Prince, February 1992 NABJ Journal

12. March 1992 Black Alumni Network. Also, Richard Prince, February 1992 NABJ Journal

13. Tony Moor, February 1992, NABJ Journal

14. Ibid

15. The phrase was introduced in 1969, at the end of Johnson and beginning of Nixon administrations

16. Sidmel Estes-Sumpter, February 1992 NABJ Journal

17. Tony Moor, February 1992 NABJ Journal.

18. Kenneth Walker, March 1992 NABJ Journal

19. Wayne Dawkins, BET Weekend, summer 1998. Reeves left the Atlanta Journal and Constitution and Cox Enterprises in 1997 to run the family owned Atlanta Daily World

20. Garland Thompson, March 1992 NABJ Journal

21. Bridgette Lacy, March 1992 NABJ Journal

22., 23. and 24. Ibid

25. "Days of Grace," Arthur Ashe, and Arnold Rampersad page 7

26. Edward L. Heard Jr. and Richard Prince, April/May 1992 NABJ Journal

27. NABJ Journal story erroneously says Aug. 8

28. "Days of Grace," Arthur Ashe and Arnold Rampersad

29. April/May 1992 NABJ Journal

30., 31. and 32. Ibid

Chapter 4 L.A. uprising

1. Don Terry, March 25, 1992 New York Times;
Seth Mydans, April 30, 1992 New York Times.

2. Ibid

3. Pamela Newkirk, "Within the Veil," page 19.

4. Ibid

5. Sharon King, June-July 1992 NABJ Journal,

6. Ibid

7. The Los Angeles Times staff did win a Pulitzer Prize in 1993
8. Linda D. Williams, May 9, 2003
9. June/July 1992 NABJ Journal.
10. Jerry Thomas, June/July 1992 NABJ Journal
11., 12. and 13. Ibid
14. Lisa Baird, July/August 1992 Columbia
Journalism Review
15. Janice Hayes, June/July 1992 NABJ Journal
16. Ibid
17. Wayne Dawkins, "Black Journalists: The NABJ Story,"
pages 79, 81
18. Richard Prince, August 1992 NABJ Journal.
19. Richard Prince, November 1992 NABJ Journal
20. Cheryl Devall, September 1992 Black Alumni
Network newsletter
21. Ibid. Also, Clinton criticized rap singer Sister Souljah for saying after the Los Angeles riots, "If black people kill black people every day, why not have a week and kill white people?" Clinton repeated the remarks that were published in the Washington Post at Jesse Jackson's National Rainbow Coalition convention
22. Ibid
23. "Reporter offers no apology for gaffes,"
Paulette Walker, Aug. 22, 1992 NABJ Monitor
24. Richard Prince, November 1992 NABJ Journal
25. and 26. Ibid
27. Cheryl Devall, Black Alumni Network
Also Richard Prince, 1992 November NABJ Journal
28. Dan Holly, October 1992 Black Alumni Network
29. Ibid
30. "Nine people," November 1992 NABJ Journal
31. Denise Johnson, August 1992 NABJ Journal
32. Ibid
33. November 1992 NABJ Journal, page 12.
34. Ibid

Chapter 5 Bruised in Big Apple

1. Richard Prince recollection, 2002
2. Example, a coffee shop meeting held at one of
the early 1990s conventions.
3. Trotter Group Journal introduction, 1992
4. Ibid

5. Founded in 1901, NABJ Story; birthdate from
The Black Press USA, Roland Wolseley
6. Derrick Z. Jackson profile in 1992 Trotter Group Journal
7. Curtis Taylor, April 1993 NABJ Journal
8. Circulation numbers from 1993 World Almanac.
9. Unattributed quote in NABJ Journal story.
10. Curtis Taylor, April 1993 NABJ Journal.
11. Often called the dean of black journalists, Poston was a reporter
with the New York Post in the 1930 through the 1960s and he was part
of FDR's "Black cabinet" in the 1940s,
12. Richard Prince, April 1993 NABJ Journal
13. and 14. Ibid
15. Adriane Wilson, April 1993 NABJ Journal
16. Richard Prince, April 1993 NABJ Journal
17. John Yearwood, April 1993 NABJ Journal
18. Ibid   19. Ibid
20. World Almanac
21. April 1993 NABJ Journal
22. Roy S. Johnson, April 1993 NABJ Journal
23., 24. and 25. Ibid
26. Gracie Lawson, September/October 1997 NABJ Journal
27. Cleo J. Allen, April 1993 NABJ Journal
28. in the late 1970s, Roger Wilkins briefly wrote an urban affairs
column that appeared inside the A-section of The New York Times.

Chapter 6 Stepping into tomorrow

1. Paulette V. Walker, June-July 1993 NABJ Journal
2. Ibid
3. The Geto Boy insulted 60 percent of NABJ membership,
a well-educated, middle-class constituency.
4. Richard Prince "Journal-isms," October 1993 NABJ Journal.
5. Cheryl Devall, August 1993 Black Alumni Network
6. Ibid
7. Betty Anderson, August/September 1993 NABJ Journal.
8. Letters to My Children, Robert C. and Dori J. Maynard, 1995.
9. Raleigh News & Observer editorial, Aug. 20, 1993.
10. Bill Drummond, August/September Journal
11. Journal story says 1984, but the theater and
Oscar-like treatment actually began in Baltimore in 1985.
12. Don Williamson, November 1993 NABJ Journal.
13. Dorothy Gilliam, November 1993 NABJ Journal

14. Ibid
15. Annette Walker, November 1993 NABJ Journal.
16. and 17. Ibid
18. Kevin Merida, December 1993/January 1994 NABJ Journal.
19. December 1993/January 1994 NABJ Journal
20. S. Yvette Durant, December 1993/January 1994 NABJ Journal

Chapter 7 Unity '94

1. December 1993/January 1994 NABJ Journal.
2. William Drummond, December 1993/January 1994 NABJ Journal
3. and 4. Ibid
5. Ken Cooper, March 1994 NABJ Journal
6. Michelle Johnson, March 1994 NABJ Journal
7. Michelle Johnson, May 1994 NABJ Journal
8. Curtis Taylor, May 1994 NABJ Journal
9. Lisa Baird, December 1993/January 1994 NABJ Journal
10. Summer 1994 NABJ Journal
11. Gregory Clay, Summer 1994 NABJ Journal
12. Ibid
13. NBC split the screen to show car chase and basketball action live.
14. Unattributed claim in Summer 1994 NABJ Journal.
15. Richard Prince, Summer 1994 NABJ Journal
16. and 17. Ibid
18. Cheryl Devall, August 1994 Black Alumni Network
19. Robin Washington, October 1994 NABJ Journal
20. NABJ Journal says nearly 10 years in the making, but black, Latino, Asian and Native American leaders initially met in 1988. The first meeting of black and Latino leaders was in 1986.
21. Cheryl Devall, August 1994 Black Alumni Network
22. Ibid
23. Antoinette Parker, October 1994 NABJ Journal
24. Cheryl Devall, August 1994 Black Alumni Network
25. Ibid.
26. Robin Washington, October 1994 NABJ Journal
27. The secret out-of-court settlement could be as much as $330,000, wrote Ron Walters in zmag.org. Chavis was dismissed from NAACP Aug. 20, 1994.
28. Joycelyn Elders, after 15 months on the job, resigned at the end of 1994. Elders left because she was under siege by the Clinton

administration critics due to a controversial remark she made at a medical conference about sex education. Elders returned to the University of Arkansas Medical School as a professor of pediatrics, then retired in 1998. (surgeongeneral.gov/library).
Also, Antoinette Parker, October 1994 NABJ Journal
29. Vicki Parker, December 1994/January 1995 NABJ Journal
30. Ibid

Chapter 8   Philadelphia Freedom
1. Joe Davidson, November 1994 NABJ Journal
2., 3. and 4. Ibid
5. Melanie Eversley, November 1994 NABJ Journal
6. Richard Prince, November 1994 NABJ Journal
7. Ibid
8. Ken Cooper, November 1994 NABJ Journal
9. Rick Blake, December/January 1994-95 NABJ Journal
10. Don Williamson, December/January 1994-'95 NABJ Journal
11. Ibid
12. Lisa Baird, December/January 1994-'95 NABJ Journal
13. New York Times magazine, 1994
14. Wayne Dawkins, January 1995 Black Alumni Network
15. February 1995 Black Alumni Network
16. According to ASNE, 11 percent
17, Wayne Dawkins, February 1995, Black Alumni Network
18. Wayne Dawkins memo, and "Distortion: Newsmagazine piece examining media and affirmative action," April 1995 Black Alumni Network newsletter
19. Kimberly Trent, Summer 1995 NABJ Journal
20. Wayne Metz, Summer 1995 NABJ Journal
21. Ibid
22. Dan Holly, August 1995 Black Alumni Network
23. and 24. Ibid
25. Wayne Dawkins, August 1995 Black Alumni Network
26. Full statement on page 21 of Summer 1995 NABJ Journal
27. Richard Prince and Wayne Dawkins, Fall 1995 NABJ Journal
28. Wayne Dawkins, Fall 1995 NABJ Journal
29. J.W. Mondesire letter, Fall 1995, NABJ Journal
30. Melanie Eversley, Fall 1995 NABJ Journal
31. Wayne Dawkins, Fall 1995 NABJ Journal

Chapter 9 Acquittal, Atonement

1. Fifteen months includes date of the double homicide June 12, 1994
2. Wayne Dawkins column, Camden, N.J. Courier-Post, Oct. 6, 1995
3. Both men shared a seat because of a lottery system
4. Richard Prince, Fall 1995 NABJ Journal. Schatzman died July 16, 1997. Source: September/October 1997 NABJ Journal
5. Gannett News Service Oct. 9-13, 1995
6. Wayne Dawkins column, Oct. 20, 1995 Camden, N.J. Courier-Post
7. Glenn Rice, December 1995/January 1996 NABJ Journal
8. Ibid
9. Wayne Dawkins, November 1995 Black Alumni Network
10. Don Williamson, December 1995/January 1996 NABJ Journal
11. Board Bits, December 1995/January 1996 NABJ Journal
12. Don Williamson, December 1995/January 1996 NABJ Journal
13. Ibid
14. Ibid. Also, Roderick Hicks, November/December 1996 NABJ Journal, identifies Ballou for the first time. A District of Columbia Superior Court judge ordered Ballou, 29, to repay over $20,000 and complete 200 hours of community service. Ballou was offered five years probation and a felony charge was reduced to a misdemeanor.
15. Audrey Edwards, June/July 1993 NABJ Journal
16. Tracy Williams, May 1995 NABJ Journal
17. Gregory Bowens, December 1995/January 1996 NABJ Journal
18. Wayne Dawkins column, Camden N.J. Courier-Post, Dec. 1, 1995
19. Pam Newkirk, "Within the Veil," page 194
20. Wayne Dawkins column Courier-Post, Dec.1, 1995. Also Fall 1995 NABJ Journal, "WABJ takes a look at New Republic story"
21. Wayne Dawkins, Black Alumni Network, November 1995 and February 1996 NABJ Journal
22. February 1996 NABJ Journal. The other participants were Betty Winston Baye, Louisville; Gregory Freeman, St. Louis; Derrick Jackson, Boston; Dwight Lewis, Nashville; Charlise Lyles, Norfolk, Va.; Les Payne; Long Island, NY; Peggy Peterman, St. Petersburg, Fla.; Barbara Robinson, Las Vegas; Adrienne Washington, Washington, D.C. and DeWayne Wickham, Gannett News Service
23. Roger Chesley, February 1996 NABJ Journal
24. Ibid
25. NABJ Journal editorial, February 1996
26. Ibid
27. Greg Braxton, February 1996 NABJ Journal

28. Ibid
29. Robert E. Pierre, February 1996 NABJ Journal
30. February 1996 Journal. Also, the association wanted nabj.com, but the domain name was already taken. Barbara Ciara interview, March 7, 2003
31. Garland Thompson, March 1992 NABJ Journal.
32. Robert Pierre, March-April 1996 NABJ Journal
33. Robert Pierre, Ibid

Chapter 10 Online for the Future

1. March/April 1996 NABJ Journal
2. Edwin B. Lake, May/June 1996 NABJ Journal
3. Ibid
4. Gayle Pollard, May/June 1996 NABJ Journal
5. Third president Bob Reid launched the Journal as a newsletter in 1981
6. Herbert Lowe, July/August. 1996 NABJ Journal
7. Ibid
8. Dodson agreed to recuse herself from any matters related to the New York Times while she pursued a lawsuit against the newspaper.
9. E.R. Shipp, September 1996 Black Alumni Network
10. Ibid
11. Ibid. Also, HTML is the markup language used for documents on the World Wide Web.
12. Richard Prince, September/October 1996 NABJ Journal
13. Arthur Fennell, September/October 1996 NABJ Journal column
14. Richard Prince, September/October NABJ Journal
15. Saturday, Aug. 24, 1996 NABJ Monitor
16. Richard Prince, September/October 1996 NABJ Journal. Also, Gore was a last-minute Clinton replacement
17. Ibid
18. Betty Winston Baye, September 1996 Black Alumni Network
19. Richard Prince, September/October 1996 NABJ Journal
20. "Farrakhan sermon," September/October 1996 NABJ Journal
21. Ibid
22. Ibid. Also, Thursday, Aug. 22 NABJ Monitor story explained that sponsors avoided his event.
23. Aug. 22, 1996 NABJ Monitor
24. September/October 1996 NABJ Journal

25. September/October 1996 NABJ Journal editorial
26. Richard Prince, September/October 1996 NABJ Journal
27. Jennifer Cassell, Aug. 23, 1996 NABJ Monitor
28. Jennifer Cassell, Aug. 22, 1996 NABJ Monitor
29. NABJ 1996 Salute to Excellence Awards Program
30. Richard Prince, September/October 1996 NABJ Journal
31. Joel Dreyfuss and Richard Prince, November/December 1996 NABJ Journal
32. Ibid
33. Cheryl Devall, January 1997 Black Alumni Network
34. Ibid
35. Prince, September/October 1996 NABJ Journal

Chapter 11 Chicago

1. February 1997 Black Alumni Network
2. March/April 1997 NABJ Journal
3. February 1997 Black Alumni Network
4. Wayne Dawkins, March 1997 Black Alumni Network
5. Angela Chatman, April 1997 Black Alumni Network
6. and 7. Ibid
8. March 5, 2003 interview with Prince.
9. Wayne Dawkins, May 1997 Black Alumni Network
10. Roderick Hicks, July/August 1997 NABJ Journal
11. Wayne Dawkins, May 1997 Black Alumni Network
12. Roderick Hicks, July/August 1997 NABJ Journal
13. Ibid
14. Barbara Ciara, March 7, 2003 interview
15. Wayne Dawkins, June 1997 Black Alumni Network
16. Wayne Dawkins, July 1997 Black Alumni Network
17. Derrick Z. Jackson, July/August 1997 NABJ Journal
18. July/August 1997 NABJ Journal
19. Ibid
20. Wayne Dawkins, July 1997 Black Alumni Network
21. Ibid
22. Richard Prince, September/October 1996 NABJ Journal
23. Wayne Dawkins, August 1997 Black Alumni Network
24. Ibid

25. Jocelyn Johnson, July 19, 1997 NABJ Monitor
26. Ibid
27. Editorial, September/October 1997 NABJ Journal
28. Wayne Dawkins, August 1997 Black Alumni Network
29. Volume II, "W.E.B. DuBois: The Fight for Equality
and the American Century," was published in 2000
and earned a Pulitzer Prize.
30. Wayne Dawkins, August 1997 Black Alumni Network
31. E.R. Shipp, September 1997 Black Alumni Network
32. Ibid
33. September/October 1997 NABJ Journal
34. Ebony Reed, July 19, 1997 NABJ Monitor

Chapter 12 Strategic Plans

1. Black Alumni Network, October 1997
2. November 1997 NABJ Update
3. Angelia McGowan, Winter 1998 NABJ Journal
4. Ibid
5.. Black Alumni Network, November 1997
6. November 1997 Black Alumni Network
7. Cheryl Devall, January 1998 Black Alumni Network
8., 9. and 10. Ibid
11. February 1998 Black Alumni Network
12. February 1998 Black Alumni Network
Also, Wayne Dawkins, April 1998 NABJ Update
13. April 1998 Black Alumni Network newsletter
14. Winter 1998 NABJ Journal
15. June 1998 Black Alumni Network newsletter
16. Pamela C. Davis, Winter 1998 NABJ Journal
17. Ibid
18. Wayne Dawkins, July 1998 Black Alumni Network
19. Ibid
20. Dawkins, August 1998 Black Alumni Network
21. Toni Randolph, August 1998 Black Alumni Network
22. Wayne Dawkins, August 1998 Black Alumni Network
23. and 24. Ibid
25. Wayne Dawkins, September 1998 Black Alumni Network
26. Donnette Dunbar, August 1998 Black Alumni Network
27. Ibid
28. Wayne Dawkins, September 1998 Black Alumni Network

29. Clarence Thomas was a Pinpoint, Ga. native
30. Wayne Dawkins, September 1998 Black Alumni Network
31. Toni Randolph, August 1998 Black Alumni Network
32. Ibid

Chapter 13 Ethical challenges

1 September 1998 Black Alumni Network
2. Roxanne Jones, December 1998 NABJ Journal
3. Terry Collins, July 1998 NABJ Update
4. Robin Washington, July 1998 NABJ Update
5. Wayne Dawkins, Fall 1998 NABJ Journal
6. Ibid
7. Richard Prince, Fall 1998 NABJ Journal
8. Ibid 9. Ibid
10. Cheryl Devall, August 1998 Black Alumni Network
11. Angela Chatman, November 1998 Black Alumni Network
12. November 1998 Black Alumni Network. Also, September/October 1996 and August/September 1998 NABJ Journal
13. Betty Winston Baye, December 1998 Black Alumni Network; Richard Prince, NABJ Update, December 1998
14. Seattle is in King County, Nov. 8 1998 New York Times
15. Felicity Barringer, Nov. 8, 1998 New York Times
16. February 1999 Black Alumni Network
17. December 1998 NABJ Update
18. Ibid

Chapter 14 Unity '99

1. Board bulletin, February/March 1999 NABJ Update
2. Wayne Dawkins, July 1999 Black Alumni Network
3. Cheryl Devall, July 1999 Black Alumni Network
4. Ibid
5. Kathy Chu, July, 7, 1999 The Unity News
6. Swanston was interim NABJ executive director in the mid-'90s
7. Kathy Chu, July, 7, 1999 The Unity News
8. July 1999 Black Alumni Network
9. Board Bulletin, December 1999 NABJ Update
10. Cheryl Devall, August 1999 Black Alumni Network
11. Dena McClurkin, August 1999 NABJ Update
12. Anu Manchikanti, July 9, 1999 The Unity News
13. Chris Kahn, July 10, 1999 The Unity News

14. Sheila Stainback, Columbia Journalism
Review, September/October 1999.
Also, 400 people hear Bradley, July 9, 1999 The Unity News
15. Wayne Dawkins column, Aug. 29, 1999 Daily Press
(Newport News, Va.)
16. Dena McClurkin, August 1999 NABJ Update
17. Cheryl Devall, August 1999 Black Alumni Network newsletter
18. Sheila Stainback, Columbia Journalism
Review, September/October 1999
19. Wayne Dawkins column, July 19, 1999 Daily Press
20. Dena McClurkin, August 1999 NABJ Update
21. Wayne Dawkins, "Integrity challenged," September 1999
Black Alumni Network
22. "Change the comfort zone," July 6, 1999 Seattle Times
23. Wayne Dawkins, August 1999 Black Alumni Network
24. Megan Scott, August 1999 NABJ Update
25. Ibid
26. Rafiah S. Davis, August 1999 NABJ Update
27. Ibid 28. Wayne Dawkins column, July 25, 1999 Daily Press
29. Rashel Johnson, August 1999 NABJ Update,
30. Mark Johnson, August 1999 NABJ Update
31. Sheila Stainback, CJR, September/October 1999
32. Board Bulletin, December 1999 NABJ Update
33. February 2001 Black Alumni Network

Chapter 15 Recover or perish?

1. Board Bulletin, April/May 2000 NABJ Update
2. December 1999 NABJ UPDATE and April/May 2000 NABJ Update.
3. October 2000 Black Alumni Network
4. Pre-registration was disturbingly low, but there was a surge of
registration on-site and just days before the convention opened
5. Cheryl Devall, September 2000 Black Alumni Network
6. Sheila Stainback, September 2000 Black Alumni Network
7. Wayne Dawkins, February 2001 Black Alumni Network
8. Dan Holly, July 2001 Black Alumni Network 9. Ibid
10. Felicity Barringer, Aug. 13, 2001 New York Times
11. Christopher Boyd, Aug. 24, 2001 Orlando Sentinel
12. Keith Rushing, September 2001 Black Alumni Network
13. Wayne Dawkins, October 2001 Black Alumni Network
14. Sept. 9, 2002 interview with Roy Johnson, New York

Index

Acknowledgments

An effort like this is not possible without the support of many people.

Let's start with Todd Burroughs. He read and critiqued chapters for "Black Journalists: The NABJ Story" (1997) and he read the "Rugged Waters" chapters and provided valuable insights. Todd also persuaded me to write a coda, which is the 15th and final chapter.

Denise Holt Williams was lead editor of this book. She gave me thorough editing and lots of encouragement.

Williams and Pernell Watson proofread the manuscript. C. Gerald Fraser also provided rigorous editing of many of the chapters, plus helpful suggestions.

Thanks to Errin Haines, Tom Morgan, Cheryl Smith and Sheila Stainback, who read various chapters.

Thanks to Yvette Walker, my editor at the NABJ Journal.

Thanks to Rob King, designer of the book cover, his sixth for August Press.

Photographer Darrell Hazelwood has been toting his camera to conventions for years. When I told him in Milwaukee last summer that I had just begun work on the manuscript, Darrell cheerfully volunteered to provide photos, and he delivered.

I received invaluable art production help: Bentley Boyd burned images on CDs. Keith Runyon converted Betty Winston Baye's White House photo of Bill Clinton with the Trotter Group into an electronic image for printing.

Thanks to Bonnie Newman Davis, Sarah Glover and Ernie Suggs for their encouragement and support. Also Gregory Lee, NABJ secretary, for patiently and quickly replying to a flurry of questions about past board decisions.

Thanks to Cheryl Devall and Dan Holly for comprehensive and lively reporting on NABJ during the 1990s for the Black Alumni Network newsletter, our monthly publication produced by Columbia University Journalism Alumni. And thanks to Richard Prince, as always. When I was missing a document, he had a copy. If I needed an answer to a question, "Scoop" usually knew the answer, or knew how to find it.